CCEA
GCSE LEARNING FOR LIFE AND WORK
SECOND EDITION

Amanda McAleer
Michaella McAllister
Joanne McDonnell
Editor:
Dr Alan McMurray

DYNAMIC LEARNING

HODDER EDUCATION
AN HACHETTE UK COMPANY

Whilst the publisher has taken all reasonable care in the preparation of this book CCEA makes no representation, express or implied, with regard to the accuracy of the information contained in this book. CCEA does not accept any legal responsibility or liability for any errors or omissions from the book or the consequences thereof.

Every effort has been made to trace all copyright holders, but if any have been inadvertently overlooked, the Publishers will be pleased to make the necessary arrangements at the first opportunity.

Although every effort has been made to ensure that website addresses are correct at time of going to press, Hodder Education cannot be held responsible for the content of any website mentioned in this book. It is sometimes possible to find a relocated web page by typing in the address of the home page for a website in the URL window of your browser.

Hachette UK's policy is to use papers that are natural, renewable and recyclable products and made from wood grown in sustainable forests. The logging and manufacturing processes are expected to conform to the environmental regulations of the country of origin.

Orders: please contact Bookpoint Ltd, 130 Milton Park, Abingdon, Oxon OX14 4SB. Telephone: +44 (0)1235 827720. Fax: +44 (0)1235 400454. Email education@bookpoint.co.uk Lines are open from 9 a.m. to 5 p.m., Monday to Saturday, with a 24-hour message answering service.

You can also order through our website: www.hoddereducation.co.uk

ISBN: 978 1 5104 0337 6

© Amanda McAleer, Michaella McAllister, Joanne McDonnell 2017

First published in 2017 by

Hodder Education,

An Hachette UK Company

Carmelite House

50 Victoria Embankment

London EC4Y 0DZ

www.hoddereducation.co.uk

Impression number   10   9   8   7   6   5   4   3   2   1

Year   2020   2019   2018   2017

All rights reserved. Apart from any use permitted under UK copyright law, no part of this publication may be reproduced or transmitted in any form or by any means, electronic or mechanical, including photocopying and recording, or held within any information storage and retrieval system, without permission in writing from the publisher or under licence from the Copyright Licensing Agency Limited. Further details of such licences (for reprographic reproduction) may be obtained from the Copyright Licensing Agency Limited, Saffron House, 6–10 Kirby Street, London EC1N 8TS.

Cover artwork by Richard Wendt

Illustrations by Barking Dog Art

Typeset by Hart McLeod Ltd

Printed in Italy

A catalogue record for this title is available from the British Library.

CONTENTS

Introduction ... 4
Skills focus ... 5

UNIT 1: LOCAL AND GLOBAL CITIZENSHIP

Section 1   Diversity and inclusion: challenges and opportunities ... 7
Section 2   Rights and responsibilities: local and global issues ... 34
Section 3   Government and civil society: social equality and human rights ... 43
Section 4   Democratic institutions: promoting inclusion, justice and democracy ... 53
Section 5   Democracy and active participation ... 58
Section 6   The role of NGOs ... 64

UNIT 2: PERSONAL DEVELOPMENT

Section 1   Personal health and well-being ... 69
Section 2   Emotions and reactions to life experiences ... 95
Section 3   Relationships and sexuality ... 100
Section 4   Personal safety and well-being ... 106
Section 5   Responsible parenting ... 118
Section 6   Making informed financial decisions ... 128

UNIT 3: EMPLOYABILITY

Section 1   The impact of globalisation on employment ... 147
Section 2   Preparing for employment: recruitment and selection ... 158
Section 3   Rights and responsibilities of employers and employees ... 174
Section 4   Social responsibility of businesses ... 188
Section 5   Exploring self-employment ... 194
Section 6   Personal career management ... 205

Exam focus ... 212
Glossary ... 215
Index ... 220

INTRODUCTION

About the book

This textbook has been written to support the teaching of CCEA GCSE Learning for Life and Work. It was written by teachers who have considerable experience of teaching and assessing Learning for Life and Work in consultation with CCEA. They have drawn on their knowledge and experience to produce a new edition of CCEA GCSE Learning for Life and Work Student Book to meet the 2017 GCSE Learning for Life and Work specification.

The book has three main units, which cover the content of the units in the CCEA GCSE Learning for Life and Work specification:

▶ Local and Global Citizenship
▶ Personal Development
▶ Employability.

The content for each unit is divided into sections which match the content headings in the specification. Each section provides up-to-date, relevant coverage of key topics and issues. Each section:

▶ starts with the key content you are expected to learn and study
▶ highlights the key words you should know the meaning of; these are defined in the Glossary at the end of the book
▶ contains enquiry-based student activities, which provide opportunities for you to develop skills in addition to knowledge and understanding. You are also encouraged to conduct your own research to deepen your understanding of related issues and topics.

You can also find additional information at the front and back of the book:

▶ **Skills focus** provides information on the skills and personal capabilities that can be developed through the student activities in the book.
▶ **Exam focus** explains the types of examination questions and expected responses, and contains exam practice questions.

About the course

The following is an outline of the structure of the 2017 GCSE Learning for Life and Work specification. For more detailed information visit www.ccea.org.uk.

Units	Type of examination	Weighting	Time
Unit 1: Local and Global Citizenship	External examination	20%	1 hour
Unit 2: Personal Development	External examination	20%	1 hour
Unit 3: Employability	External examination	20%	1 hour
Unit 4: Controlled Assessment Task (investigation)	Internally assessed and externally moderated by CCEA	40%	

The three examination papers each consist of six questions. These include:

▶ short-response questions to assess your knowledge and understanding and application of knowledge and understanding
▶ extended response questions which are intended to assess higher-order thinking skills such as analysis, discussion, making judgements and evaluation (see pages 212–5).

SKILLS FOCUS

Developing skills and personal capabilities

One of the aims of the CCEA GCSE Learning for Life and Work course is to provide students with opportunities to develop skills and personal capabilities. These are an important part of lifelong learning and will support progression to university, college or employment. The importance of these skills and personal capabilities is highlighted throughout the student activities. Each activity suggests an example of one or two skills and/or personal capabilities as a skills focus. Opportunities to develop these are highlighted in the text activities by symbols as shown below:

- (C) Communication
- (SM) Self-Management
- (M) Using Mathematics
- (WO) Working with Others
- (ICT) Using ICT
- (PS) Problem Solving

This section outlines examples of the skills and personal capabilities you will develop. You can use these to evaluate your own learning. Review the skills and personal capabilities on this page and page 6 and record:

1. which skills and personal capabilities you have developed
2. which activities you developed these through
3. which skills and personal capabilities are your strengths and weaknesses, or need further development.

(C) Communication

- ▶ communicate ideas clearly and meaningfully and express feelings and viewpoints in an organised and structured way
- ▶ participate in role plays, group discussions and debates and ask and respond to questions
- ▶ actively listen to and respectfully respond to others' views
- ▶ make oral and written summaries, and presentations that have a clear purpose and suit your audience
- ▶ present information in oral, written and digital formats
- ▶ read, interpret and analyse information to develop your understanding of topics/issues
- ▶ critically examine and respond to sources of information
- ▶ organise and present information in a clear and structured way
- ▶ understand and appropriately use a range of specialist vocabulary and terms related to Learning for Life and Work (see Glossary).

SKILLS FOCUS

(M) Using Mathematics

- interpret and analyse a range of mathematical data
- use appropriate mathematical language when analysing and presenting mathematical information
- use mathematics to solve problems
- assess probability and risk in a range of different situations
- use and present mathematical data in a variety of formats that are meaningful and suitable for your audience.

(ICT) Using ICT

- use ICT in a range of different areas of LLW to access, manage, select and present information
- research information online
- select, evaluate and justify the use of sources.

(SM) Self-Management (Personal Capability)

- plan and organise work
- propose ways of working together
- set personal learning goals and targets to meet deadlines
- work in an organised way to complete a series of activities
- monitor, review and evaluate progress and improve your learning
- effectively manage time.

(WO) Working with Others (Personal Capability)

- learn with and from others through co-operation, share ideas, provide and respond to constructive feedback and participate in peer- and self-assessment activities
- listen actively to others and influence group thinking and decision-making, taking account of others' opinions
- participate in effective teams and accept responsibility for achieving collective goals
- support others and take responsibility for some group actions.

(PS) Problem Solving

- identify and analyse relationships, patterns and themes in information
- reason, form opinions and justify views
- propose justified explanations
- assess and critically analyse information and evidence for bias and agendas
- analyse and evaluate multiple perspectives
- explore unfamiliar views without prejudice
- challenge own and others' assumptions
- weigh up options and justify decisions
- apply and evaluate a range of approaches to solve problems in familiar and unfamiliar situations.

UNIT 1

LOCAL AND GLOBAL CITIZENSHIP

Section 1 Diversity and inclusion: challenges and opportunities

Key content
- benefits and challenges associated with expressions of cultural identity, including influences on a young person's sense of cultural identity
- causes and consequences of prejudice and discrimination in society
- benefits, challenges and impacts of immigration on communities, society and the economy, including reasons for immigration and ways governments can support migrants
- ways to promote inclusion in society through laws, policy, communication and education in schools, communities and the workplace
- causes and consequences of **conflict** at local, national and global levels
- ways to resolve conflict between opposing groups and countries peacefully, including the role of the United Nations

This section explores how an individual's cultural identity is expressed. It explores the causes and consequences of different types of prejudice and discrimination and how this affects society. Furthermore, it examines the changing social landscape of Northern Ireland and in particular focuses on the benefits and challenges of immigration to communities, society and the economy. Northern Ireland has witnessed some population changes in recent years and as a result it is very important that society acts to ensure there is inclusion. This is vital in law-making, policy-making and even in our schools. Finally, this section aims to allow you to understand the causes and consequences of conflict and the various methods that can be used to resolve conflict.

What are the benefits and challenges of expressions of cultural identity?

Our identities as individuals are shaped by our experiences, our backgrounds and other factors such as the homes we live in, the communities we belong to and the schools we attend. Cultural identity forms an important part of a person's image of who they are. It is how they identify with being part of a group culture. They have a shared cultural identity with others in the group. People can gain a sense of belonging to the group by being able to identify with the group's culture. Our cultural identity is formed by the language, beliefs, traditions and customs of the society we live in. Culture relates to your 'way of life' and is learned. Northern Ireland is often perceived as having only two cultures (Catholic and Protestant). This perception tends to ignore the many ethnic minority groups which live in Northern Ireland. These include Chinese, Indian, Polish, Pakistani, Romanian, Filipino and African people and others. Society in Northern Ireland is culturally diverse and multicultural.

UNIT 1 LOCAL AND GLOBAL CITIZENSHIP

Influences on a young person's cultural identity

▲ Today, Northern Ireland is a culturally diverse society

There are a number of factors that can influence the cultural identity of an individual or group, some of which are shown in the table below.

Family	Children learn from watching and imitating their parents and family circle, and are taught family values at home. Family is one of the most important factors that influence a young person's identity.
School	Young people gain knowledge and skills at school where they will also celebrate certain cultural events and learn how to interact with adults and peers. School teaches young people about culture and any particular school values.
Peer group	Friends can be a powerful influence on cultural identity influencing, for example, the way young people dress, the music they listen to, sports teams they support and events they attend.
Religion	Most children learn about religion at home and at school. Religious culture may centre on events and traditions in the calendar which can influence a young person's way of life, such as Lent or Ramadan.
Media	Television programmes, social media, or the way the news is reported can influence a young person's culture. Magazines can influence fashion trends.
Nationality	Your nationality can have a broad range of impacts on your culture including the food you eat, the language you speak, your religion and values.
Heritage (history)	Many cultures will follow historic traditions and hold festivals to celebrate and remember significant events that have occurred. Cultural traditions are passed on from generation to generation.
Sexuality	A person's sexual identity is how a person defines themselves as male, female or both, and their sexual orientation. This can influence their cultural identity by influencing their attitudes, behaviours and the groups they identify with in wider society.
Race	A person of a certain race may self-identify with a racial group which shares a common heritage and culture. This influences their cultural identity and how they perceive themselves in wider society.

▲ Many factors can influence the cultural identity of a young person. These influences on cultural identity are also likely to influence peoples' views and attitudes towards others from a different culture. In some cases they may have negative effect by reinforcing a group's cultural identity leading to the **exclusion** or marginalisation of others. In other cases these influences may be positive and promote respect for other cultures and diversity and inclusion in society.

> **Activity**
>
> **Factors that influence your cultural identity**
>
> 1 Reflect on your own culture. Which of the factors in the table to the left have had the most impact on your culture? Rank the factors from 'most significant impact' to 'least significant impact'. Explain why you have ranked them as you have.
> 2 Explain how each of the factors in the table has influenced your cultural identity.

Expressions of cultural identity

People express their cultural identity in different ways. These include music, dance, art, drama, poetry, sport, language, traditional dress, food, religious beliefs, political views, symbols, flags, parades and marches. People may not always consciously think about expressing their cultural identity but you could probably guess which culture they might identify with from these expressions of identity.

There are occasions when cultural groups want to express their cultural identity more openly. This may be part of a celebration of their culture. There are worldwide religious festivals such as Christmas, Hanukkah, Ramadan and Diwali. Secular cultural celebrations include the National Day of Reason which is held by humanists. Other celebrations include the Chinese New Year, Hogmanay, the Notting Hill Carnival and Gay Pride. Different cultures around the world also express their cultural identity when holding memorial and commemoration events.

UNIT 1 LOCAL AND GLOBAL CITIZENSHIP

Case study: Diwali

Diwali is the Hindu festival of lights and it is celebrated throughout the world by thousands of people from different cultures. It is a festival that celebrates family and friends and it is a time to reflect on the past and look forward to the future with hope for a peaceful world. Diwali also celebrates different historical events and stories are told to symbolise the victory of light over dark, knowledge over ignorance, good over evil and hope over despair.

As Diwali approaches, people clean their homes to remove bad luck in the upcoming year. On Diwali night families gather for a feast and stay up late, celebrating with the help of fireworks and gifts. Hindus believe that the Hindu goddess of good luck visits homes that are brightly lit. Children make small clay lamps called 'diyas' to bring the good luck goddess to their home so they can receive new clothes and toys. One family may have many thousands of these little diyas decorating their home.

Different cultural groups in Northern Ireland also share many of the celebrations, memorials and commemorations that take place across the world. In addition to these, two major communities in Northern Ireland (Catholic/Republican/Nationalist and Protestant/Loyalist/Unionist communities) have their own types of cultural celebrations (hereafter these groups will be simply referred to as Catholic and Protestant communities but it should be noted that they are also associated with these other labels). Many Catholics celebrate their culture with festivals, for example, Feile an Phobail, and Gaelic sporting competitions such as the Ulster championship, or by holding a parade on the feast day of the Irish patron saint, St. Patrick. Many Protestants celebrate their culture by holding Orange Order marches and parades, the main one being on 12th of July each year.

Activity: Cultural celebrations

1. In small groups, discuss and agree one cultural celebration to research. Write down three research questions. Research these questions as individuals, then share and discuss your findings, to create a presentation.
2. In your groups, show your presentation to the class.

Benefits associated with expressions of cultural identity

People like to express their cultural identity as it gives them a sense of belonging to, or solidarity with a group. The need to 'belong' and to be accepted by others is human nature, so is one of many things that are common across cultures.

Activities shared by cultures build relationships between those with a common identity and can therefore be enriching for individuals. This can also create greater harmony and cohesion in society as a whole.

Multicultural societies

Many countries are multicultural, which means that different cultural groups are living together. This is the result of immigration as people move from their country of origin to another country. This has happened in many countries throughout the world, such as America, Canada, Britain and Germany. Each of these countries is now culturally diverse because of the different groups of people living there.

Northern Ireland has also developed into a multicultural society and is enriched by the wide variety of food, language, sport and music that different cultures have brought. Languages spoken in Northern Ireland now include Polish, Russian, Mandarin and Cantonese, and on the high-street there are supermarkets and restaurants from India, Asia, Poland and the Mediterranean.

Understanding cultural differences

Living in a society that contains different cultures can bring many benefits and opportunities. As people learn about one another's cultures they develop mutual understanding, which can help to break down barriers as people grow to trust and tolerate the culture of others. When different cultures participate in society and share cultural experiences it helps to promote inclusion and respect within that society.

Celebration and tourism

The image below shows Culture Night when around 80,000 people visited Belfast city centre in September 2016. This was a celebration of food, music, dancing and festivals from all of the cultures in Northern Ireland. This event was a celebration of diversity and vibrancy in the city.

Cultural events such as Culture Night and Belfast Mela, an annual festival of world cultures, also bring economic benefits to Belfast as they attract tourists who spend money in the city's shops and restaurants during the festivals. Northern Ireland's tourist industry has grown rapidly, and cultural events and festivals are one of the factors boosting tourism and visitor-spend in Northern Ireland.

Challenges associated with expression of cultural identity

As well as benefits, there are many challenges that can be faced when people express their cultural identity. Expressions of cultural identity can create strong bonds amongst people within a group, but this can lead to this group of people being less likely to integrate with the rest of society. People may promote negative values, behaviours and attitudes against others. This can result in intolerance, mistrust, stereotyping, prejudice and discrimination between different groups.

▲ Young people enjoying Belfast Culture Night, September 2016

Activity — Expressions of cultural identity

1 Choose one cultural group in Northern Ireland. Using the internet, carry out research to see how this group have organised events to celebrate their culture. Report back on your findings to the class and explain how the cultural events benefited the people who participated in them.
2 Read through the text and make a list of the benefits associated with expressions of cultural identity.

UNIT 1 LOCAL AND GLOBAL CITIZENSHIP

Global conflicts

While the reasons for global conflict are complex it is likely that cultural differences between groups can reinforce divisions and contribute to tension and conflict. When cultural expressions are viewed negatively this can lead to segregation, division and the marginalisation of groups in society. This has been seen in the Israeli–Palestinian conflict as well as here in Northern Ireland and in other countries.

Prejudice, racism, discrimination, sectarianism, segregation and exclusion can occur when one cultural group perceives themselves as superior to another. Hatred between cultural groups has resulted in major conflicts in the world, including the Rwandan genocide, 1994 and the Bosnian genocide, 1992–95.

Case study: Rwandan genocide, 1994

The genocide that took place in Rwanda was a result of tension and rivalry between two groups: the Hutus (majority) and the Tutsis (minority). Animosity had grown between the two groups since colonial times. The Tutsis were considered to be superior and so they had better educational opportunities, jobs and privileged positions in society for many years during the Belgian control of Rwanda. The Hutus were discriminated against, which caused inequality and resentment between the two communities.

When the Belgians relinquished their control, the Hutus took their place in the independent Rwanda. The Tutsis lost their privileged position and against the backdrop of growing economic problems the decision was made that Rwanda would be better if the Tutsis were wiped out. Racist hate-propaganda was used to incite people to murder. Posters and leaflets were distributed which dehumanised the Tutsis. This led to the genocide of the Tutsi population in 1994 in which 800,000 people were killed. However, some reports put this figure at 2 million.

Case study: Bosnian genocide, 1992–95

The main rivals in the conflict in Bosnia were Serbs (Orthodox Christians), Croats (mostly Roman Catholic), and Bosniak Muslims. As with so many conflicts, there was a complicated set of causes which led to these events. Croats and Muslims wanted independence whereas Serbs wanted to be part of a dominant Serbian state, a 'Greater Serbia'. Political tensions built between the ethnic groups as areas once controlled by Yugoslavia (Slovenia, Croatia and Bosnia–Herzegovina) struggled for independence. Alongside this political tension, differences in religious identity were present in the antagonisms which dominated the Balkan states. Religious identity became intertwined with national identity and so to be Orthodox was to be Serbian.

In April 1992, the government of the Yugoslav republic of Bosnia-Herzegovina declared its independence from Yugoslavia. Over the next several years, Bosnian Serb forces, with the backing of the Serb-dominated Yugoslav army, targeted both Bosniak and Croatian civilians for atrocious crimes. The conflict that erupted came after years of ethnic divisions. The Serbs are accused of carrying out acts of 'ethnic cleansing' against the Croats and Bosniaks during this period.

Conflict in Northern Ireland

Northern Ireland is now multicultural, however, there are two major cultural groups – Catholics and Protestants – that have long-established and separate traditions, based on religious and political views. Many Catholics consider themselves to be Irish and are nationalistic in their political view. Many would like to see a united Ireland which is independent from the United Kingdom. In contrast, many Protestants consider themselves to be British: they are unionist in their political view and want to remain part of the United Kingdom.

Differences between these groups have led to sectarian conflict which has gone on for many years. A segregated education system exists in Northern Ireland, so most Catholics and Protestants attend different schools and live in separate communities. There continues to be disagreement between both groups over flags, versions of the past, symbols, memorials, marching and commemorating the past. An ongoing challenge for successive governments in the UK is to create a shared and more cohesive society in Northern Ireland.

Activity

Challenges associated with expressions of cultural identity

1 Research recent newspaper articles which cover tension created by cultural identity in different countries including Northern Ireland.

2 Analyse the reasons why there had been tension.

3 Describe the actions taken by individuals, society and government to try to resolve the conflict.

What are the causes and consequences of prejudice and discrimination in society?

Prejudice is making judgements about people (pre-judging) based on stereotypes. It is a pre-conceived opinion about someone or something that is not based on reason or experience.

Causes of prejudice

All prejudice can be caused by factors such as fear of change, ignorance, lack of understanding and respect, past experiences, family/community background and learned behaviours.

Cause of prejudice	Explanation
Ignorance, fear, lack of understanding	People fear and feel threatened by what they do not understand and this can lead to unreasoned negative behaviour towards other cultures.
Family members	People can be influenced by family members to 'hate' other cultures and learn that it is acceptable to be narrow-minded.
Peers/friends	Peers might hold negative stereotypical views about people of a different culture. A young person may accept these views to remain part of the group.
Media	The media can portray stereotypes, negative images and views of certain cultures which people might be willing to accept as true.
Religion	Religion is used by people to justify their actions, as people feel very strongly about their religion. Religious views can lead to intolerance and **bigotry**.
Political opinion	Often cultural views are aligned along political views and this can evoke strong emotional responses when there is a difference of political opinion. People may feel that a method of cultural expression is also sending out a political message.
Nationality	Nationality can be a strong cultural identity and where cultures clash problems can arise. This is more apparent now that there are more multicultural societies.
Heritage (history) experiences	Bad experiences or incidents in the past can cause people to hate or distrust other cultures or groups.

▲ Causes of prejudice

Because prejudice frequently involves multiple factors both at the individual and group levels, determining the cause of prejudice in any single person is difficult. Most people do not willingly reveal their prejudices or the reasons for them, if they are even aware of their prejudices at all.

Activity — Prejudice

1. For two causes of prejudice above, carry out research using the internet and find a recent example of prejudice from each cause.
2. For each example, explain the consequences of prejudice for the individual experiencing the prejudice.
3. Analyse the examples of prejudice and the similarities in the consequences of each type of prejudice. Explain your answer.

UNIT 1 LOCAL AND GLOBAL CITIZENSHIP

Causes of discrimination

Discrimination is when a person is treated differently – unfairly or fairly – as a result of the group or category to which they belong. Discrimination arises when people act on their prejudices and it is caused by the same factors which lead to prejudice.

Discrimination takes many forms, such as sectarianism, racism and sexism. Other forms of discrimination are related to the groups listed under Section 75 of the Northern Ireland Act (see page 24). These forms of discrimination result in the existence of inequalities in society.

Consequences of prejudice and discrimination

The effects of prejudice and discrimination on an individual and on society are varied.

Effects on an individual

Discrimination can have a direct effect on a person's psychological well-being. It can result in feelings of anxiety, stress, sadness, guilt and emptiness. This in turn can translate into depression, loss of interest, eating disorders and stress-related illnesses. It may result in a person not achieving their potential and may make it difficult for them to trust others and build relationships.

A victim of discrimination may take to alcohol or drugs or may form their own negative opinions of others or withdraw from people, due to decreased self-esteem and self-confidence. As a result of this the individual may lose their job, refuse to go to school or perform poorly at school. This could further lead to social injustice issues such as homelessness and poverty.

Effects on society

- ▶ Effects on businesses
    - ▶ Businesses that fail to take strong action on discrimination tend to be lower in productivity. People who are discriminated against within an organisation are disgruntled, have low morale, and are less motivated to work.
- ▶ Effects on democracy
    - ▶ If people are judged, not on their abilities, but on the prejudices of others, then society will ultimately lose out as not everyone will have an equal opportunity to do well for themselves. Discrimination is a threat to democracy and so a society which has discrimination may face social inequality and injustice issues.
- ▶ Effects on politics
    - ▶ Where there is discrimination in a society, the political system is likely to be affected. People may be less likely to vote because they are disaffected by government policy, different political parties may emerge and more pressure groups may work to put pressure on the government to introduce change.
- ▶ Effects on justice
    - ▶ In a society based on discrimination this will also be evident in the media and the justice system, which will lead to further inequality and marginalisation of targeted minority groups.

Section 1 Diversity and inclusion: challenges and opportunities

> **Activity** — **Acts of discrimination** — PS
>
> For each of the following **scenarios** analyse:
> - the causes of the discrimination displayed
> - the consequences of the discrimination for the person or people discriminated against.

Scenario A

Peter suffers from Tourette syndrome – a condition which can result in tics, including vocal tics. Peter attends an interview for a retail position, but is turned away because of his swearing.

Scenario B

A Japanese family has recently immigrated to America. The son, Hiroki, is attending a local school and has been bullied because he is from Japan. He is called racist names, pushed around in the hallway, and told to 'go home'. The parents have complained to the teacher and the principal but the school has not taken any action against the racial harassment, and the bullying has continued. Hiroki does not wish to attend school and his school marks have fallen.

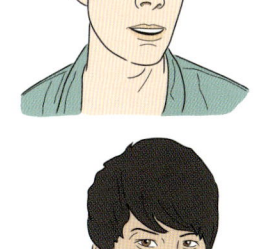

Scenario C

Due to a worsening disability, Jane will soon need to rely on a wheelchair. She tells her landlord that she will need a ramp in order to access her apartment. Her landlord tells her that he does not have the money to install a ramp and that she should just move.

Scenario D

Sally is a lesbian and she goes to view an apartment for rent with her partner, Rebecca. The landlord asks Sally if she has boyfriends who will visit. She says no and explains that she and Rebecca are partners. The landlord tells Sally that he runs a 'family building' and will not rent to her and her partner.

Sectarianism

Sectarianism describes excessive attachment to a particular religion or sect. It involves having a strong, narrow-minded dislike towards another religion and rejecting those who do not share the same beliefs. This strong intolerance towards another religion can lead to prejudice, discrimination and even violence.

Sectarianism has been, and continues to be a major problem in Northern Ireland and around the world. According to the Department of Justice crime statistics, in 2014–15, 1,043 crimes were reported as having sectarian motivation, the highest since 2009–10 when sectarian crimes were recorded. Sectarianism is also a significant issue in other countries and can contribute to conflict between different groups with different religious beliefs. In the Central African Republic in 2014, over 1,000 Christians and Muslims were killed as a result of sectarian violence and nearly 1 million people were displaced.

UNIT 1 LOCAL AND GLOBAL CITIZENSHIP

> **Activity** — **Pakistan: Shia and Sunni Muslims** (PS)
>
> Research the sectarianism in Pakistan by watching the clip: '101 East – Sectarian divide' on www.youtube.com.
>
> 1 Can you explain the main reasons for the divide between Sunni and Shia Muslims?
> 2 Analyse the consequences of sectarianism on Pakistan's individuals and society.
> 3 For each consequence or effect, suggest a solution that the government could put in place to reduce sectarian crime in Pakistan.
> 4 Analyse Source A. What do you notice about the violence in Pakistan?
> 5 Explain one reason why an individual may be sectarian.

SOURCE A A graph to show the number killed or injured in sectarian attacks in Pakistan between 1989 and 2014. The red line shows the median number.

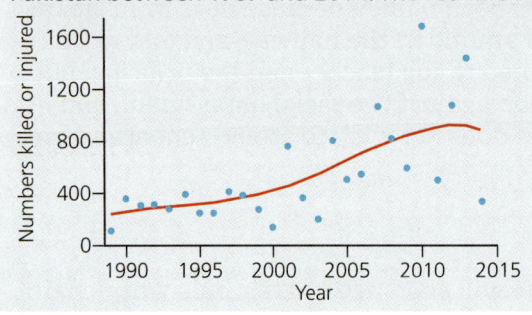

> **Activity** — **Racism in football** (C)
>
> Read Source B and watch a clip showing the events in Paris described: search YouTube for 'Chelsea fans prevent black man boarding Paris metro train'.
>
> 1 Explain how these events would have made the person feel.
> 2 Analyse the reasons for the racism shown in the clip.
> 3 Explain the consequences of the racism highlighted in the clip.
> 4 Analyse three ways that the government could attempt to stop racism in Northern Ireland.

Racism

Racism is a form of discrimination which can occur when different groups consider themselves to be superior to other groups because of their skin colour or ethnic origin. Racism is an issue in multicultural societies.

SOURCE B An article on racism published on the *Daily Mail* website, 24 March 2015

Racism is rife in English football with over 350 incidents from the Premier League to grassroots since 2012, investigation reveals.

- An investigation has revealed a widespread racism problem in England.
- Information from 24 police forces – only around half of the number in the country – reported over 350 incidents since 2012.
- Chelsea supporters have been involved in the highest number of incidents.

Racism is widespread in English football with police having to deal with hundreds of incidents from the top of the game right down to grassroots level, an investigation has revealed.

It also revealed that Chelsea supporters have been involved in the highest number of reported racist incidents as they travelled to and from matches on trains.

It follows the high-profile case of a black man who was prevented from boarding a train in Paris by Chelsea fans as they sang a racist song, with five of them due in court this week.

The information, gathered from 24 police forces across the country, shows there have been over 350 incidents since 2012. But as that only accounts for around half the police forces in the country, the actual figure is likely to be much higher.

Press Association

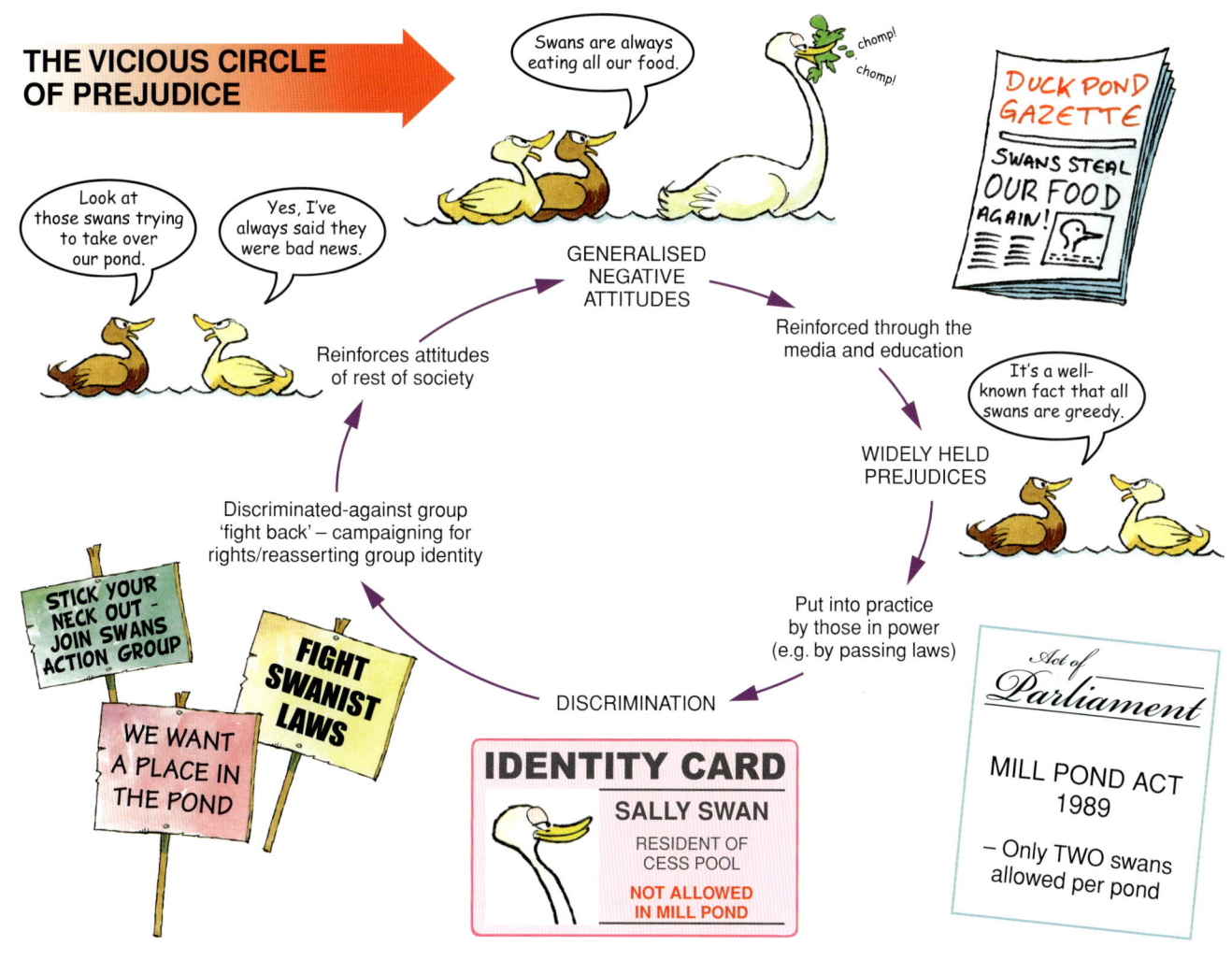

Section 1 Diversity and inclusion: challenges and op...

▲ The vicious cycle of prejudice and discrimination

What are the benefits, challenges and impacts of immigration on communities, society and the economy?

Currently immigration and issues related to immigration are at the centre of political and public debate and media coverage in many countries throughout the world. In simple terms, there are those who argue against free movement of people and want tighter controls on immigration in host countries, and those who argue for immigration.

Those representing opposing sides of the argument present a range of evidence including public opinions to support their perspective. These arguments for and against usually include reference to the social and economic impact of immigration on the host countries.

When considering evidence concerning immigration the reader should consider the following:
- Is the information biased?
- Is the information based on facts, opinions or both?
- Is the information cherry-picked to suit an agenda?

D GLOBAL CITIZENSHIP

Large-scale global immigration has taken place over a short period of time and, although it presents specific challenges for each country, there are also common challenges. However, immigration figures for Northern Ireland are relatively low at around 4 per cent (2014). This means that the impact of immigration on Northern Irish society and economy is likely to be negligible or less than in other countries.

The following sections are intended to provide you with the facts about the benefits and challenges of immigration to host countries. However, if you are interested in finding out more about immigration you should conduct your own research and critically examine evidence from a range of sources.

Immigration levels

SOURCE A The number of immigrants in 2013, according to the UN

Key
140
46, 000, 000

SOURCE B A bar chart showing the number of babies born in Northern Ireland to UK- and non-UK born mothers

Key
- Babies born to mothers who were born in the UK
- Babies born to mothers who were born outside the UK

Year	UK-born mothers	Non-UK born mothers
2005	20,500	1,800
2010	22,100	3,200
2015	21,100	3,100

Activity

Immigration levels

1 Study Source A.
   a Name three countries with the highest level of immigration and three with the lowest.
   b Can you explain these differences in global levels of immigration?

2 Study Source B.
   a What is the percentage increase in babies born in Northern Ireland to mothers born outside the UK:
      i between 2005 and 2010
      ii between 2010 and 2015?
   b Can you explain these increases?

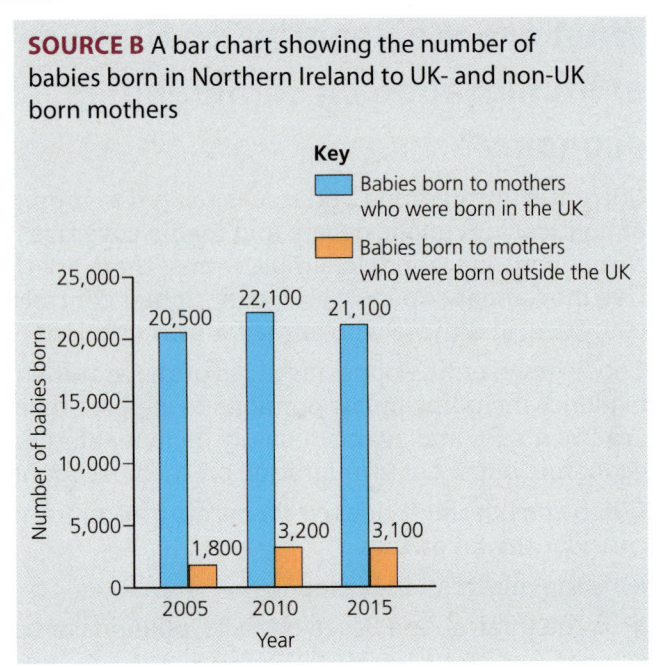

Reasons for immigration

Immigration and emigration are very much a feature of the globalised world we now live in. Some people choose to migrate for career opportunities, for example, and some people are forced to migrate because of war or famine.

A refugee is someone who is forced to leave their home country without having a new place to live.

Some of the reasons people immigrate are given below.

Economic

▶ The majority of people identify work as their main reason for migrating to another country. Financial stability and better future prospects will entice a person to move, especially if another country offers higher wages, more job opportunities and a higher standard of living.

Social

▶ Some countries have a higher standard of living in terms of housing, education and healthcare. The lifestyle choices may be more varied in another country, and the climate and culture can be more appealing.

▶ Many people immigrate due to educational opportunities. Some countries are renowned for the standard of their education – be it top-class universities, high schools, colleges or professional institutes.

▶ Often families and friends will follow loved ones who have emigrated, especially if news from the new country is very positive.

Political

▶ Sometimes immigrants leave their home because they may face persecution there for their political beliefs.

▶ Some people leave because they want more political freedom or a different political direction.

Conflict/War

▶ Some people flee to escape war or violence.

Environmental

▶ People may move to escape natural disasters. Their home country may be prone to flooding, hurricanes or earthquakes.

Activity — Reasons for immigration

1 The reasons why people immigrate can often be classified into 'push' and 'pull' factors. Push factors are factors that force someone out of their old country and pull factors are factors that encourage people to a new country. Classify each of the reasons for immigration, given on the left, into push and pull factors.

2 Carry out a 'hot seat' activity. Choose one person to take on the role of an immigrant and design three questions to ask them about their motivations for moving countries.

Benefits of immigration to the community/society

People who emigrate to another country bring with them expressions of their own culture such as music, dance, language, traditional dress, cuisine and art. If they integrate within the new society they will contribute to the cultural diversity there. Engaging with others from different ethnic minority groups can also enhance understanding and tolerance as people learn about different cultures. In turn, this can also reduce prejudice and enable people to build relationships and a more cohesive community.

Benefits to the economy

People coming to other countries contribute to the economy by bringing skills and labour to areas where there is a shortage (see page 154). In many different sectors in Northern Ireland, such as the food, agriculture, hospitality and construction industries, there are many immigrant workers from different ethnic groups. Most migrants are young, highly productive workers, meeting shortfalls in different industries and providing the labour and skills that Northern Ireland needs. Other immigrants have set up their own businesses, helping to generate more income and provide much-needed jobs for local communities. Furthermore, anyone who works in Northern Ireland has to pay taxes to fund public services and therefore contributes to the economy in this way.

Immigration figures

A report published in 2014 by Queen's University Belfast outlined that immigration brings substantial economic and social benefits to Northern Ireland. The report cited immigration as contributing to sustaining economic growth, filling labour shortages, bringing much-needed skills and enriching society through cultural diversity. The report's main findings stated that:

- migrant workers contributed about £1.2bn to the economy from 2004 to 2008
- 4 per cent of the Northern Ireland workforce is made up of migrant workers
- 3 per cent of the total number of students attending school in Northern Ireland are from ethnic minorities
- 81.5 per cent of migrants in the UK are employed
- less than 5 per cent of European Union (EU) migrants claim Jobseeker's Allowance.

From a global perspective migration plays a key role in the economy of many countries. A report published by the OECD in 2014 found that:

- migrants accounted for 47 per cent of the increase in the workforce in the United States and 70 per cent in Europe over the past ten years
- migrants fill important niches both in fast-growing and declining sectors of the economy
- migrants contribute more in taxes and social contributions than they receive in benefits.

> **Activity** — **The benefits of immigration to society**
>
> After reading about the benefits of immigration to society, turn to your partner and 'think, pair, share'. This means thinking about the issue individually, discussing it in a pair to draw conclusions and make notes, and sharing your findings with the class.

Challenges of immigration for the community/society

Increasing numbers of immigrants create challenges that communities and societies must address.

Social challenges

One of the main social challenges for countries with increasing numbers of migrants is ensuring social stability and building social cohesion. A large increase in numbers of migrants into local communities within countries in a relatively short time can lead to tension and conflict between them and local people. Many migrants live in areas of affordable accommodation. As this tends to be in working-class communities it is local people who are most affected. In some cases, groups of migrants may live in areas which become segregated communities or, even worse, ghettos, leading to them becoming marginalised from wider society. This can reinforce differences in cultural identity and divisions between them and local people. It can also negatively influence people's attitudes and result in prejudice and discrimination.

Economic challenges

Immigration figures for the UK from 1996 to 2016 have increased each year. In 1996 the total number of immigrants entering the UK was 318,000 and in June 2016 the annual number of immigrants peaked at 650,000. Taking into account emigration figures for 2016, there was an increase in population due to immigration of 350,000.

This increased population places pressure on schools to provide school places for children. Schools also have to overcome cultural differences and language barriers. They have to provide additional classes and teachers to support students to learn the language of the host country. Other countries such as Germany face similar challenges. In Germany, between 2014 and 2015, its schools had to make educational provision for 325,000 refugee children. It is estimated that Germany will require 20,000 additional teachers at a cost of around €2.3 billion each year. In Northern Ireland there are now 12,900 newcomer students, 3.8 per cent of the school population.

Increased immigration may place an additional burden on healthcare provision in many countries. This includes primary care services, GPs and hospitals, dentists, pharmacies and interpreter services for migrants who may not speak the language of the host country. For example, in 2013/2014 there were 600,000 new migrant GP registrations in England, Wales and Northern Ireland.

Many countries will have to provide adequate social housing to accommodate the increasing numbers of migrants and ensure that they have an opportunity to feel part of society rather than living in segregated communities. The government also have to ensure that unscrupulous private landlords do not take advantage of migrants or the housing benefit system. Governments may also have to provide welfare and housing benefits to unemployed migrants.

Section 1 Diversity and inclusion: challenges and opportunities

Security/law enforcement and the justice system

The governments in democratic countries also view immigration as a potential threat to their national security associated with the threat of global terrorism. There is additionally the problem of illegal immigrants and those with criminal records entering the host country. These include sex offenders, people traffickers and terrorists. Ensuring national security involves the costs of policing, border control and intelligence gathering.

Immigration and security also impacts on society. In cases where immigrants are associated with criminal activity this can negatively influence public perceptions and lead to stereotyping, prejudice and discrimination.

People's perceptions of immigration

People's views about immigration are usually captured in surveys. These often make headline stories in the media. While it is important that people's views are acknowledged, they may not agree with research evidence. However, they do provide an indication of what people view as the main issues in society. When examining information from these types of surveys it is important to consider:

- who funded and published the research
- when the survey was carried out
- the size of the sample
- how representative the sample is of the whole population
- whether there is bias in the questions
- whether there is factual evidence to support people's views
- that people's views can change.

Sources C and D on this page, and Source E on page 22, are some examples of people's views compiled from survey data.

Activity

The challenges of immigration

1. Work in a group. Agree on *one* immigration issue raised in the text to research. Research the issue for two countries.
2. Use the research data you have gathered to write your own report on the issue. Your report should include a comparison of the impact of the issues in the two countries.
3. Review your work with a partner and make suggestions for improvement.

Germany

SOURCE C Attitudes to immigration in Germany, measured in November 2015 and January 2016 (from www.yougov.co.uk)

In general, do you think that Germany could welcome more asylum seekers or do you think that the number is already too high? %

Men (Nov / Jan): 55 / 60 — too high; 18 / 16 — about right; 22 / 22 — welcome more
Women (Nov / Jan): 51 / 63 — too high; 25 / 16 — about right; 19 / 14 — welcome more

Key:
- The number of asylum seekers is already too high
- The number of asylum seekers is about right
- Germany could welcome more asylum seekers
- Don't know

UK

SOURCE D Perceived consequences of lower immigration in a UK survey, 2015 (from www.yougov.co.uk)

Below are some arguments that people have made against limits on immigration. Generally speaking, do you think these arguments are true or false?

Argument	Probably true ✗	Probably false ✓
Lower immigration would damage the growth and success of British business.	21%	57%
Lower immigration would mean Britain would need to have higher taxes to pay for our ageing population.	30%	48%
Lower immigration would mean difficulty filling jobs in the NHS.	39%	46%
Lower immigration would mean a lack of people to do low-paid work, like cleaning or fruit picking.	40%	44%

21

UNIT 1 LOCAL AND GLOBAL CITIZENSHIP

Northern Ireland

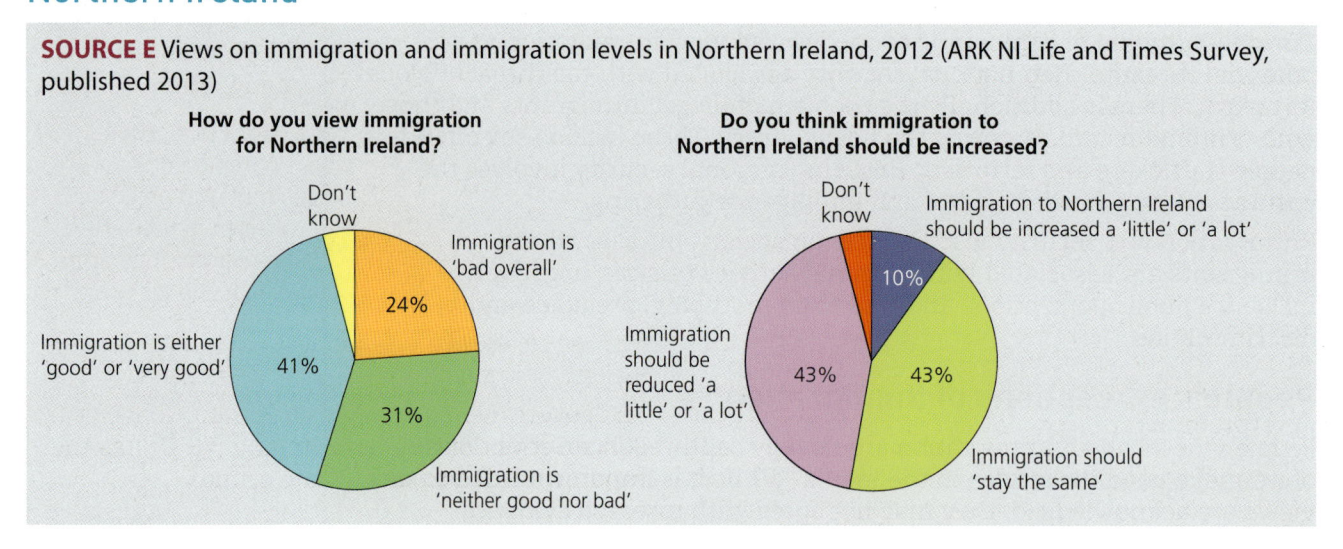

SOURCE E Views on immigration and immigration levels in Northern Ireland, 2012 (ARK NI Life and Times Survey, published 2013)

How do you view immigration for Northern Ireland?
- Don't know
- Immigration is 'bad overall' 24%
- Immigration is either 'good' or 'very good' 41%
- Immigration is 'neither good nor bad' 31%

Do you think immigration to Northern Ireland should be increased?
- Don't know
- Immigration to Northern Ireland should be increased a 'little' or 'a lot' 10%
- Immigration should be reduced 'a little' or 'a lot' 43%
- Immigration should 'stay the same' 43%

Activity — Perceptions of immigration

1. Analyse the information in the three surveys shown in Sources C–E. Explain the main findings for each.
2. What is the likely impact of these findings on government immigration policy?
3. Select one source, and suggest how people's attitudes might impact on society. Justify your answer.

Government support for immigrants

- Access to healthcare
- Accommodation/housing
- Access to education
- Protection from discrimination
- Assistance with learning a new language
- Support in the community

▲ The needs of an immigrant family arriving in a new country

When an immigrant family arrive in a new country, such as Northern Ireland, there are a number of needs that must be addressed before they can successfully integrate into society. Many of these needs can be met by government action. The government gives funding to different organisations to support the integration of immigrants into Northern Ireland.

Accommodation/housing

Housing is one of the first priorities of any immigrant family. Organisations funded by the government such as NI Direct will provide information on a range of issues relating to property and housing, including buying and renting a home, social housing and where to find advice if you are homeless. The Northern Ireland Housing Executive (NIHE) will support immigrants with applications for social housing, organise payment of benefit for those who are unemployed or on a low income and support people who are homeless. The NIHE will also provide an interpreter if required.

Access to healthcare

The government will ensure that immigrants are provided with information on how to access health and social care services in Northern Ireland. This information is given through organisations such as NI Direct. The information is given in easy-to-understand language and includes advice and information on registering with a GP/dentist. The government also offers an interpreting service which is free of charge to the patient, professional and confidential.

Access to education

In the education system, the government must ensure schools are given financial support to enable schools to support the integration of newcomer students. NI Direct provide information on education, training and skills and advice on choosing a school for children, options available for young people, adult education and children's welfare at school. The information is accessible for those who do not have English as a first language. The government also funds an organisation called the 'Inclusion and Diversity Service'. This organisation provides advice and assistance to schools regarding provision for students who require additional English language support. It also arranges phone or face-to-face interpreting when required.

Protection from discrimination

The government of Northern Ireland passed the Northern Ireland Act in 1998 (see page 24). Section 75 of this Act ensures that all public bodies must promote good relations between groups of people of different race, religion or politics. Passing legislation helps to ensure migrants' rights are protected in society and in the workplace.

The government also needs to ensure that the Police Service of Northern Ireland (PSNI) has the funding needed to tackle hate crime.

Assistance with learning a new language

The government have the power to introduce strategies to ensure the integration of migrants into society. One action could be to expand opportunities for English language learning. The ability to speak English is possibly one of the most important factors which will help immigrants integrate, open up job opportunities for them, allow them access to education and healthcare and create for them an overall sense of belonging.

Support in the community

If a new family moved into your community, think of the challenges they would be facing. There are many ways that individuals can help. Simply being friendly, offering advice and showing people around the area can help ease many of the challenges which may be faced by a new family. Similarly, the community can help by being welcoming and ensuring that any discriminatory attitudes or behaviour are not accepted.

Activity — Government support for immigrants

1. Analyse the ways that the government can support immigrants.
2. Read the following article: www.bbc.co.uk/news/uk-34139960. 'Migrant crisis: What is the UK doing to help?' 28 January 2016. Describe the ways that governments are helping migrants.
3. Class discussion: Do you think that governments are doing enough to help migrants? Can you suggest any other action which could be taken to help?

How can inclusion be promoted in society?

In a multicultural society, it is important that everyone is included and that differences between cultures are respected. This is necessary in order to build a cohesive society, that is, one where there is harmony, mutual understanding and equality for all.

One of the most effective and successful ways of making sure that everyone is included and that everyone receives their basic human rights is to pass laws to make discrimination on the grounds of colour, ethnic origin, gender, disability, political opinion, sexual orientation or religion illegal.

Role of government: laws

Promoting a fair and inclusive society means having laws in place which are just, which can promote equality and which can help to reduce discrimination. The government must ensure laws uphold human rights. One of the most important laws in Northern Ireland is the Race Relations Order (1997) which protects people from being discriminated against on the grounds of race. This law is important because it also made it illegal to encourage others to become racist or act in a racist way (inciting racial hatred).

The Northern Ireland Act

After the Good Friday Agreement was signed in 1998 the government made a promise to its citizens that it would be committed to promoting equality of opportunity for all. As a result, Section 75 of the Northern Ireland Act (1998) was passed. This law means that it is compulsory for government departments such as Education, Health and Justice and other public bodies such as the Housing Executive and the PSNI to promote equality actively. Section 75 states that government bodies and public bodies must promote equality between people of different:

- religious groups
- ages
- racial groups
- marital status
- sexual orientation
- gender
- political opinion.

And between persons:

- with or without a disability
- with or without dependants (children or older people they look after).

Giving people their rights helps ensure that they have protection from discrimination. The government must ensure policy and practice actively promote equality and provide citizens with a sense of security and a guarantee that their rights will be protected.

Role of government: policy

The government can support legislation by ensuring that all public bodies have an inclusion policy. This means that organisations must set out the rights and **responsibilities** of their members to promote inclusion. Organisations must be expected to outline action that will be taken if any incidents occur which lead to the exclusion of individuals or groups.

Role of government: communication

The government can communicate to society the importance of inclusion and the effects of exclusion. They can do this by creating media campaigns which highlight the importance of inclusion. For example, in 2014 the Northern Ireland government gave funding for the Media Initiative for Children Respecting Difference Programme. You can find out more about the Media Initiative for Children Respecting Difference Programme online at: www.early-years.org/mifc/characters.php. This aimed to foster acceptance and respect and encourage the inclusion of children who have a disability or physical difference. This initiative gave funding for the production of a series of short animations, accompanying story books and resources provided to schools.

Role of government: education

The government can ensure inclusion is part of the curriculum. This is done in Northern Ireland through subjects such as Learning for Life and Work. Schools are also expected to have an inclusion policy and their admissions must be inclusive. Funding can also be given to youth groups and community organisations to educate people in society on the importance of inclusion and the consequences when people or groups are excluded.

> **Activity**
>
> **Government and inclusion**
>
> 1 Analyse the ways that the government can support immigrants.
> 2 Evaluate the role of government in promoting inclusion.

Ways to promote inclusion: schools

In schools there are lots of different students with different needs and backgrounds. Some have specific learning difficulties or physical disabilities, some speak English as an additional language and some have different religions and cultural backgrounds. It is important that all students feel included in school life and are respected.

Schools provide opportunities for students to learn the importance of accepting others who are different. Students can be encouraged to respect difference in each other and to promote the importance of human rights. Schools have inclusion, Special Educational Needs (SEN) and anti-bullying policies in place to try to avoid students feeling excluded and discriminated against.

In addition to formal policies and the curriculum there are other activities that schools can do to promote diversity and inclusion such as:

- holding a 'celebration of culture' day
- organising special assemblies
- providing food in the canteen catering for different dietary needs
- ensuring after-school clubs include all students.

Ways to promote inclusion: community

Local communities play a vital role in helping to shape society. There are a range of local community groups across Northern Ireland aimed at challenging issues such as racism and sectarianism in the local community and helping to build a more inclusive society.

Ways to promote inclusion: workplace

There are laws in place to protect people from discrimination and to promote inclusion in the workplace. For example, the Equal Pay Act (1970) means that it is illegal to discriminate on the grounds of gender regarding pay and conditions. Other laws (see employability section, pages 147–211) make it illegal to discriminate on the grounds of religion, sexual orientation, race, age, ethnicity and against those with a disability. Employers have a legal responsibility to provide a safe and healthy working environment for their employees.

To ensure inclusion is promoted the workplace will have policies and guidelines for staff so that they know the strategies that are in place. These guidelines will outline the roles and responsibilities of all members of staff. Training will also be given to staff and activities conducted which promote good working relationships and ensure respect for diversity.

Activity

Inclusion in schools

1. What activities does your school carry out to promote diversity and inclusion? Research the different strategies that are already in place at your school to make sure all students are treated fairly and are included.

2. Individually, or in pairs, look at the following groups of students who may not feel included in school life and try to think of ways that they could be fully integrated:
   a. students with physical disabilities
   b. students with learning difficulties
   c. students with English as an additional language
   d. students from different religions.

3. Describe why it is important that all students are given the same opportunities.

4. Analyse the consequence for students and the school if inclusion policies or strategies are not used to make sure all students are included.

Activity

Inclusion in the local community

5. Carry out research to find out if there are any community groups working to promote inclusion in your local community. You could work in a group with the people in your class who are from the same local area.

   You will need to present your research using information and communication technology (ICT). In your findings you should include:
   - where the community group got funding from to carry out the inclusion project
   - the aims of the project
   - the activities the project is engaged in
   - an evaluation of the impact of the project.

UNIT 1 LOCAL AND GLOBAL CITIZENSHIP

> **Activity** — **Workplace inclusion**
>
> 1 Do you think this article is an example of discrimination? Explain your answer.

SOURCE A Discrimination in the workplace as reported on 7 March 2017 in the *Telegraph*

Maternity leave discrimination: A working mother's story of losing her job – and how she got over it

One working mother of two reveals how she battled maternity discrimination and being pushed out of her former job to get her career back on track, as figures show 50,000 women each year are unable to get their jobs back after maternity leave.

One minute you're playing peekaboo with your beautiful, chubby baby and meeting up with the other mummies in the park for tea and babyccinos, the next you realise that nine months have flown by and it's time to get back to reality. Work.

But for 50,000 women each year, going back to work after maternity leave is neither straightforward nor a pleasant experience. New research published this week found that 14 per cent of the 340,000 women who take maternity leave are unable to return to the job that they had left because of discrimination by employers, with many finding their positions under threat when they try to return to them.

They are denied the right to work part-time, or flexible hours, to enable them to factor in childcare pickups and drop-offs. Others are shoehorned into more junior posts, or return to virtually no job description at all, while others still are effectively constructively dismissed. Pay rises and promotions are also harder to come by for those that do go back.

It happened to me

It makes grim reading. To be on the receiving end is even more depressing. I know because it happened to me. When I had my first child, I made the mistake of informally arranging with my boss to come back to work part-time, but later that offer was rescinded. I was told I couldn't go back at all due to "cutbacks", and eventually that I could return on the exact terms of my previous employment (five long days) or nothing at all.

It was messy, maddening and incredibly stressful, especially as I had no paperwork to back anything up, at a time when I felt financially vulnerable, knackered, and lacking in confidence after many months away from the office.

Had I gone back full-time I would have seen my baby, awake, for less than 23 hours a week. That's if I could even have found childcare to meet my working hours (which I couldn't). It didn't add up. With a heavy heart, I walked away.

I'm not alone. This kind of experience is very common, and fighting it is harder than ever. New government rules mean that mothers seeking to challenge maternity discrimination will have to pay £1,200 to bring their case to an employment tribunal.

http://www.telegraph.co.uk/women/mother-tongue/10270357/Maternity-leave-discrimination-A-working-mothers-story-of-losing-her-job-and-how-she-got-over-it.html

What are the causes and consequences of conflict at local, national and global levels?

Conflict can occur at all levels of society for a huge number of reasons. These include:
- land disputes
- differences in political opinion
- religious differences
- cultural differences
- the distribution and use of resources.

Most conflicts are caused by a combination of factors and it is very difficult, in most cases, to highlight dominant and less dominant causes.

Section 1 Diversity and inclusion: challenges and opportunities

Case study: Local conflict: Northern Ireland

Northern Ireland has witnessed conflict as a result of religious, political and cultural differences. As a result of this local conflict, segregated housing and schooling exists where Catholics and Protestants live in separate areas and attend separate schools. Some argue there has been a lack of government willingness and policy to promote integrated social housing and schooling, and as a result the separation has led to fewer opportunities for the two sides to mix. A more integrated approach in terms of education and housing could in turn break down barriers and encourage people to move away from learned stereotypes and prejudices.

As the overall level of political violence in Northern Ireland has subsided, so conflict has shifted to other arenas of tension. 'Interface' areas – where Protestant communities live directly alongside Catholic communities, often separated by so-called 'peace-lines' – are one such physical manifestation of new areas of tension and intercommunal violence.

Causes of conflict in interface areas in Belfast

The causes of conflict in interface areas are multifaceted and complicated. They include:

- tensions as a result of people's past experiences through the period of conflict
- loss of socio-economic status with the decline of heavy industries in the region
- the perception by some communities that the peace process and all its parts are threatening and eroding their identity, thereby fuelling a defensive territorial attitude
- the perception that parading, marching and the use of flags to mark different groups' and communities' territory are threats to the identity of the opposing sides
- political beliefs, which in turn threaten the status and identity of the opposing group.

Consequences of conflict in interface areas in Belfast

The consequences are wide-reaching and include:

- a culture of violence due to the tensions
- an increase in anti-social behaviour and so-called 'recreational rioting'
- sectarianism and division due to past experiences and lack of integration
- bigotry and prejudice, which will emerge if there is a lack of understanding and tolerance
- a rise in racially motivated harassment and attacks as communities become inward-looking and tend to view anyone from outside of the community as a threat.

▲ Peace walls and interface areas in Belfast

Case study: National conflict: Syria

A national conflict is when one part of a nation turns against another part of the same nation. The conflict in Syria is the deadliest the twenty-first century has witnessed thus far. The conflict began in 2011 and since then more than 450,000 Syrians have been killed in the fighting, more than a million injured and over 12 million – half the country's pre-war population – displaced from their homes.

Causes of the conflict in Syria

- This war began as part of the Arab Spring against an **autocratic** leader. The Arab Spring was a series of anti-government protests, uprisings and armed rebellions that spread across the Middle East in early 2011. The movement originated in Tunisia in December 2010 and quickly took hold in Egypt, Libya, Syria, Yemen, Bahrain, Saudi Arabia, and Jordan.
- In 2011 pro-democracy protests took place. The protestors were demanding democratic reform due to state oppression, human rights abuses and sectarianism between the Sunni majority and Shia Alawite sect.
- In response to the protests, President Assad's security forces opened fire on the protestors. This action led to increased anger and a further wave of protests took place.
- Thousands took to the streets in protest at the regime's oppressive rule. Protestors hardened their resolve and took up arms, in order to protect themselves from government forces.
- As a result, violence escalated and the country descended into civil war as rebel brigades formed to battle against government forces to gain control of towns and cities.
- A further dimension was the rise of the jihadist group, Islamic State (IS), who wanted to take control of the country.

Consequences of conflict in Syria

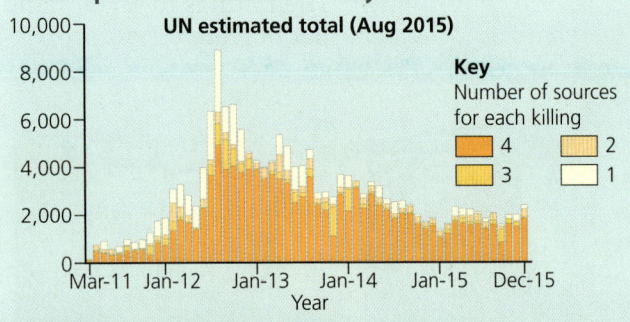

The documented number of killings in Syria per month from March 2011 to December 2015 (from Violations Documentation Center, Syrian Shuhada, Syrian Network for Human Rights, Syrian Center for Statistics and Research)

Consequences for the individual

- Civilians are being denied their basic needs as the UN has found that food, water and health services are being blocked as a method of war.
- Civilians are witnessing and enduring death, mass killing, torture, rape, hostage-taking and people going missing. IS has carried out public executions and amputations.
- People have been forced to leave Syria and millions of Syrians are now displaced (1.2 million Syrians were forced to leave their home in 2015).
- In 2015 the UN reported that 70 per cent of the population is without access to adequate drinking water, one in three people are unable to meet their basic food needs and four out of five people live in poverty.

Consequences for society

- Neighbourhoods have been turned into war zones, hugely reducing the quality of life of Syrians.
- The impact of living in a conflict zone for society is immeasurable; for example, the education system has collapsed and it was reported in 2014 that 3 million children were out of school. This is due to the destruction of school buildings but also discrimination and lack of funding for education in Syria. These children have lost the protective benefits of education and the possibilities for their future are impacted. This will have a severe impact on Syria's economy in years to come.
- The death toll of the conflict will have a huge impact on the future of the country.
- Infrastructure has been destroyed and will take decades to rebuild.

Consequences for the economy

In Syria almost every economic sector has experienced a negative effect:

- The economy has slumped and economic ties with other trading nations have been broken.
- The loss of life has resulted in a decline in the size of the Syrian labour force.
- Infrastructure destruction and the trade embargo on Syria has led to a rapid downturn in the economy – as a result the cost of doing business increases, and a decline in productivity results.

Global conflict: causes and consequences

A global conflict refers to a very serious disagreement that takes place on a worldwide stage. Many of the factors that can cause global conflict are the same as those that can lead to local and national conflict. They include:

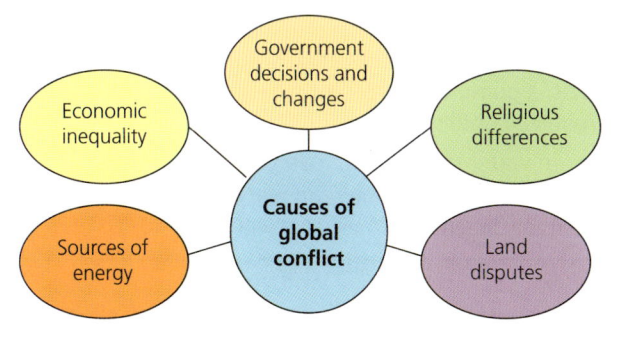

▲ Factors that can lead to global conflict

National conflicts can also have global consequences. In Syria, forces from Russia and the USA have become involved, and as the refugee crisis has developed countries such as Greece, Italy and Germany have become embroiled in the consequences of the conflict.

> **Activity** — **Global conflict** PS
>
> 1 Carry out some research about a global conflict. The following are possible examples: Syria, Iraq, South Sudan, Afghanistan and Yemen.
> 2 Select an image to represent this conflict. Around the image on one side identify the causes and on the other side identify the consequences.
> 3 Compare the causes and consequences of the global conflict you have chosen with the causes and consequences of the local conflict in Northern Ireland and the national conflict in Syria detailed here.
> 4 Explain the similarities and differences between the causes and consequences of global and the causes and consequences of local conflicts.

How can conflict be peacefully resolved?

Conflict can be resolved in different ways. This section explores a variety of methods used to resolve conflict at local, national and international levels.

Local methods of conflict resolution

Local initiatives play a key role in dealing with the underlying causes of conflict and moving communities towards reconciliation. For example, in many parts of Africa, community elders act as locally respected independent mediators and help to resolve issues which cause conflict. Women with family ties to several different clans have a unique ability to build bridges between warring communities and pressure elders to mediate peaceful resolutions.

Northern Ireland today

There are many communities and groups working hard to resolve conflict across Northern Ireland after years of unrest which have had a negative impact on society. Communities have been pulled apart and completely segregated, with many still divided in terms of housing and schools.

For many people in Northern Ireland, differences in identity or background have been seen as a threat, rather than something to be celebrated or valued. Even today, despite the peace process, many young people continue to experience the reality of sectarianism and racism.

Belfast Conflict Resolution Consortium

During the conflict in NI, one of the worst-affected areas was Belfast, which still experiences difficulties today in terms of rioting in 'interface' areas (see page 27). Organisations such as the Belfast Conflict Resolution Consortium (BCRC) are involved in dealing with conflict resolution in the city and trying to promote inclusion and peace. Their main focus of work is on local interface interventions, community safety initiatives and community development activities on an ongoing basis, and this local work is tied into the city-wide approach of BCRC to address issues impacting on interface communities. Their aim is to understand why barriers still exist that prevent different communities from coming together.

The BCRC provides opportunities for the two main communities to build positive relationships and work together in the interests of one another. This group plays a valuable part in helping Northern Ireland to move forwards from conflict and the legacy of a violent past, to a future of peace and prosperity.

UNIT 1 LOCAL AND GLOBAL CITIZENSHIP

> **Activity** — **The BCRC**
>
> 1 Go to the BBC news website www.bbc.co.uk/news, click 'Search' and then type in 'Belfast Conflict Resolution Consortium'.
> 2 Choose two articles, read them and explain the actions taken by the group and the impact the group may have had in trying to promote peace between the two main communities.
> 3 Share your findings with a partner.

National methods of conflict resolution: Non-Governmental Organisations

Across the globe there are a wide range of Non-Governmental Organisations (NGOs) that work in countries where there is conflict. These groups work to resolve difficulties which have arisen between different groups.

Community Relations Council

This organisation was set up to promote good relations between the two main communities in Northern Ireland as well as advocating inclusion for ethnic minorities. Its main aim is to promote peace, reconciliation and mutual trust by:

- providing support (financial, training, advice) for local groups and community organisations
- providing opportunities for cross-community projects to build trust and understanding.

It also works with other organisations to help them to develop good community relations and encourage greater acceptance of and respect for cultural diversity. Many of the groups that they support work within local communities trying to find peaceful ways of resolving disputes.

▲ People from both communities working together on a council tree planting project

> **Activity**
>
> **The Community Relations Council**
>
> Go to www.youtube.com and search for: 'Lessons from the Peace Lines'. There are five clips which were part of the work of the Community Relations Council. These clips will develop your understanding of projects which run across Belfast to attempt to resolve conflict and promote peace.
>
> 1 Watch one of the clips and evaluate the work that is going on in communities to try to resolve conflict.
> 2 From watching the clip, can you explain two ways that an individual can work to resolve conflict peacefully?

Carter Center

Founded in 1982 by US president Jimmy Carter, this NGO works to advance peace and has helped to improve people's lives in more than 80 countries by resolving conflicts.

The Carter Center in Syria

This organisation works to promote peace and reconciliation in Syria. Since July 2013, the Carter Center has held workshops and individual consultations with Syrians and government representatives in the USA, Europe and the Middle East, and has worked to broker a transition to peace and future governance in Syria. The Center has established a unique and diverse network of Syrians across political divides working together on how to move towards peace. Syrians engaged to date include lawyers, judges, senior political officials, representatives of paramilitary groups, academics, activists, civil society representatives, as well as international experts. Workshops have provided an opportunity to overcome prejudice and find common ground on issues surrounding the war in Syria. Following each workshop, the Center updates and refines a working paper that encompasses participants' contributions and stances regarding options for peace in Syria.

Truth and reconciliation

Some countries have established truth and reconciliation commissions to reveal past wrongdoing by a government or important figures, in a bid to help resolve conflict. One notable example is South Africa's commission, established after apartheid, which invited both victims and perpetrators of violence and gross human rights violations to give their testimonies. The perpetrators who gave their testimonies could request amnesty from both civil and criminal prosecution.

Ways to resolve conflict between countries peacefully

A number of different methods of trying to restrain or stop conflict internationally also exist.

International mediation

International mediation can take place over trade and commerce issues or be an attempt to prevent or halt armed conflict. Many countries use international mediation to settle disputes on a variety of issues.

Mediation involves negotiation using an independent and impartial third party (the mediator) who helps to solve disputes or disagreements between two or more groups of people. A sovereign nation with a strong interest in international or regional stability will often serve as a mediator in international disputes.

In mediation, each person or group is given the opportunity to explain their views and how they relate to the conflict, so both sides listen to each other's point of view. The ultimate goal is for each side or group to understand or empathise with the other. This helps to build trust and is an essential part of the mediation process.

In the area of trade and commerce conflicts, the World Trade Organization (WTO) has developed its own dispute resolution system. The WTO is actively involved in settling many trade disputes. The United Nations (UN) has created the Model Law on International Commercial Conciliation. The EU has designated methods of alternative dispute resolution, like mediation, a top political priority for EU countries in all conflict situations.

Mediation challenges

However, there are many challenges facing international mediation. It can be complicated by cultural and language barriers. There are also situations where the parties have a strong sense of national identity and a willingness to use force to maintain or overthrow the current balance of power. Mediation of seemingly intractable conflicts requires a deep understanding of the parties' grievances and a commitment to resolving the conflict. Furthermore, some groups may not trust the mediator or accept that they are impartial.

International courts

Peace negotiations often bring together people and groups who have committed atrocities and are eager to absolve themselves of responsibility. If they do not receive an amnesty from justice, there is the threat that they will restart the conflict and commit further crimes.

Cases can be tried by national or international courts. The International Criminal Court (ICC), based in The Hague, tries people accused of the most serious crimes – genocide, crimes against humanity and war crimes. It will act only if a case is not being investigated by a national court. The independent court was established in 2002, but its effective functioning is weakened by the United States' refusal to recognise the court's jurisdiction.

Sanctions, boycotts and embargoes

These are often used by governments that are trying to change the behaviour of another government without using violence. Instead the offending party is punished economically, socially or politically. If a country is considered guilty of committing human rights abuses, the governments of other countries might:

- ban exports from that country, which means they will refuse to buy any products or goods from that country (boycott)
- withhold aid or loans (sanctions).

Activity

Methods of international conflict resolution

1. Make a list of all the ways to resolve conflict between countries peacefully.
2. Rank each method, from most effective to least effective. You must be able to explain and justify your choices.
3. Create a persuasive piece of writing to convince a Member of Parliament in the UK to introduce a certain method of conflict resolution. You must provide examples of where this method has worked in the past.

UNIT 1 LOCAL AND GLOBAL CITIZENSHIP

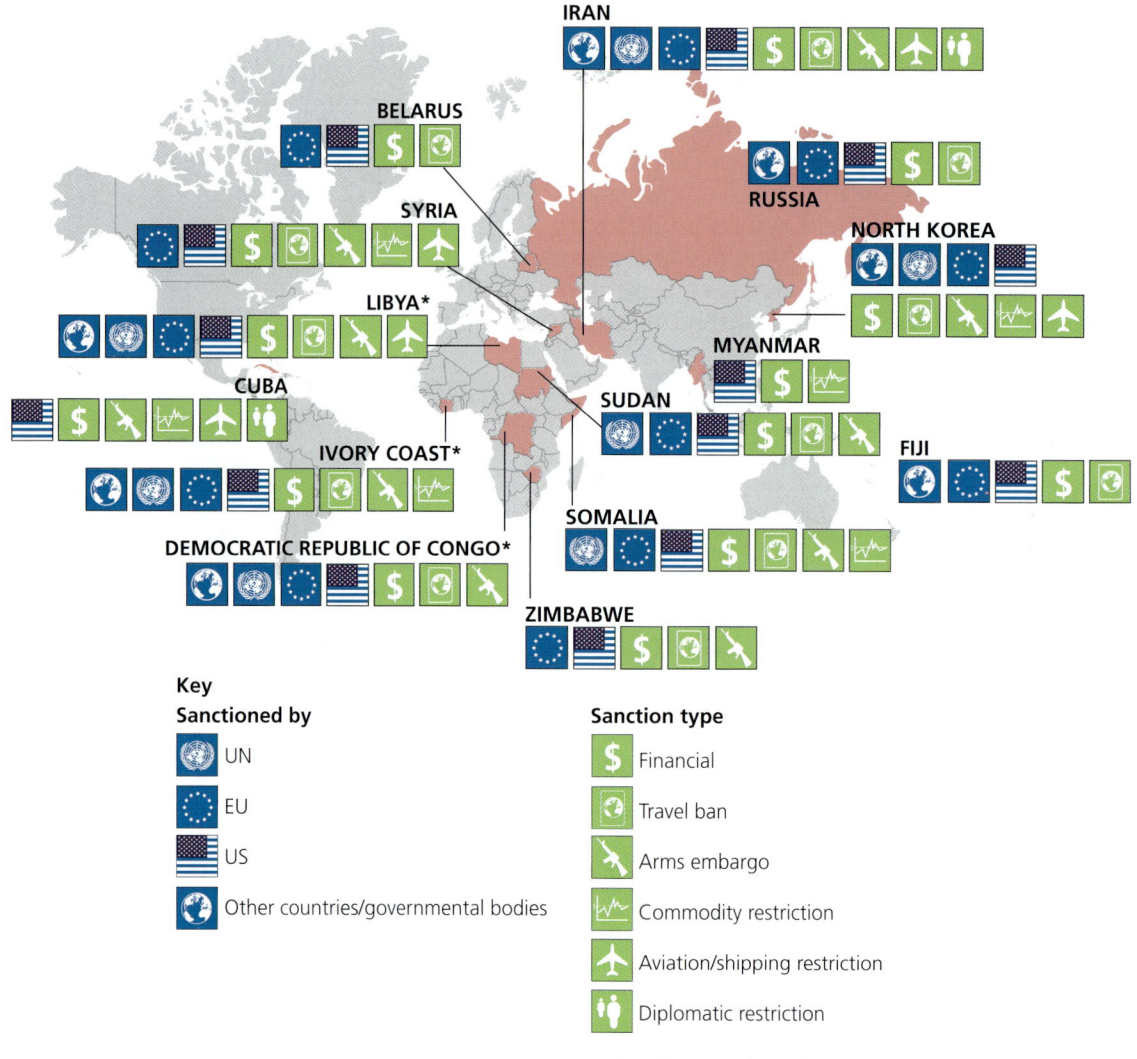

▲ Major UN/Western sanctions in place worldwide (from Targeted Sanctions Consortium, Peterson Institute for International Economics, US Treasury, Office of Foreign Assets Control, UN, EU)

The role of the UN in resolving conflict

The UN consists of 193 member states. One of its key roles is resolving conflict and peacekeeping in countries throughout the world. Its main strategies include the following:

▶ **Conflict prevention and mediation:** this involves using diplomatic measures to stop tensions and disputes from escalating into violent conflict. Diplomatic measures can involve mediation and talks to reach agreements.

▶ **Peacemaking:** this involves bringing together hostile groups to reach a negotiated agreement. Peacemakers may be **envoys**, governments or groups of states.

▶ **Peace enforcement:** this can involve the use of military force to restore international peace and security in areas where there is a threat to peace or an act of aggression has taken place.

Section 1 Diversity and inclusion: challenges and opportunities

▶ **Peace building:** this process aims to work in areas after conflict has been resolved in order to maintain peace. It addresses the core issues affecting that area so that the conditions for a sustainable peace can be created.
▶ **Peacekeeping:** the UN has sent peacekeeping forces to many countries around the world to try to resolve conflict through peaceful means. The peacekeeping force will remain in the country once a peace has been agreed to ensure the peace continues. In solving a conflict or disagreement in a particular country, the use of peacekeeping forces is not always the best solution and other methods of conflict resolution such as mediation, international law, sanctions and boycotts are often used.

▲ UN peacekeepers at work in South Sudan in 2016

Activity — UN peacekeeping

1 Watch the following clip on www.youtube.com: 'UN Peacekeeping is': www.youtube.com/watch?v=jAXVbtdBu10.
2 Describe the ways that the UN tries to resolve conflict.
3 Using the internet to help you, research the work of the UN. Analyse the challenges facing UN peacekeeping forces which are trying to promote peace in many areas around the world.
4 Evaluate the role of the UN in trying to resolve conflict.

UNIT 1

LOCAL AND GLOBAL CITIZENSHIP

Section 2 Rights and responsibilities: local and global issues

Key content
- The importance of human rights in society, including participation rights, protection rights, and survival and development rights, in relation to:
  - the Universal Declaration of Human Rights (UDHR)
  - the United Nations Convention on the Rights of the Child (UNCRC)
- The following types of human rights abuse:
  - child and slave labour
  - child soldiers
  - sexual **exploitation**
- Balancing protecting the human rights of the individual with those of society

In this section you will gain a greater understanding of the importance of human rights in society and you will examine different articles from the UDHR and the UNCRC. This section will increase your knowledge and understanding of human rights abuses and you will also gain a better understanding of what it means to balance protecting the human rights of the individual with that of society.

Why are human rights important in society?

Human rights are the basic rights and freedoms that belong to every person in the world, from birth until death. They apply regardless of where you are from, what you believe in or how you choose to live your life. Human rights are meant to enable humans to survive, develop, be protected and ensure their participation in society. These basic rights are based on values such as dignity, fairness, equality, respect and independence. Human rights are protected by law.

There are many challenges in society such as racism, sexual abuse, exploitation and discrimination. Human rights are a means of protecting people against these challenges. They aim to allow human beings to flourish as individuals safely and with freedom.

Human rights are:
- universal: they belong to all of us, to everybody in the world
- inalienable: they cannot be taken away from us
- indivisible and interdependent: governments should not be able to pick and choose which are respected.

The Universal Declaration of Human Rights

The notion of human rights was born from the feeling, following the Second World War, that the atrocities seen there should never occur again. The formation of the UN in 1945 paved the way for more than 50 member states to contribute to the final draft of the UDHR, adopted in 1948. This was the first attempt to set out at a global level the fundamental rights and freedoms shared by all human beings and was signed as a pledge made by governments around the world to safeguard these rights.

The UDHR consists of 30 articles (promises) describing the basic rights of every person. It is important to remember that these rights are only 'promises' and are not legally binding. Only when they are made law can they be considered legal rights. Although many countries have signed up to the UDHR, human rights abuses still continue in some countries.

The Human Rights Act is a UK law passed in 1998. It means that you can defend your rights in the UK courts and that public organisations (including the government, the police and local councils) must treat everyone equally, with fairness, dignity and respect.

The 30 articles of the Universal Declaration of Human Rights

Everyone:
1. Is born free.
2. Is equal.
3. Has the right to life.
4. Should be free from slavery.
5. Should be free from torture.
6. Has rights no matter where they go.
7. Is equal before the law.
8. Should have their human rights protected by law.
9. Has the right not to be unfairly imprisoned.
10. Has the right to a fair trial.
11. Has the right to be innocent until proven guilty.
12. Has the right to privacy.
13. Should have freedom of movement.
14. Has the right to seek a safe place to live.
15. Has the right to a nationality.
16. Has the right to marriage and family.
17. Has the right to your own things.
18. Has the right to freedom of thought.
19. Has the right to freedom of expression.
20. Has the right to public assembly.
21. Has the right to democracy.
22. Has the right to housing, education and child care and help if you are old or ill.
23. Has the right to a job, a fair wage and membership of a trade union.
24. Has the right to rest from work and to relax.
25. Has the right to an adequate standard of living.
26. Has the right to education.
27. Has the right to copyright protection of ideas and inventions.
28. Has the right to a fair and free world.
29. Has a responsibility: we have a duty to other people, and we should protect their rights and freedoms.
30. Finally, no one can take away your human rights.

▲ The 30 articles of the UDHR

Activity: UDHR articles

1. Read the articles of the UDHR shown here and work together in groups to classify the articles under the following headings:
   - Participation rights
   - Protection rights
   - Survival rights
   - Development rights.
2. Choose nine articles from the UDHR and carry out a diamond-ranking exercise in a group to identify which you believe are the most important.
3. For each human rights article you have chosen as most important, explain why you feel this human right is important.
4. Use evidence to justify your answer. Carry out research on the internet to find examples of how these human rights articles are being abused around the world. In particular, analyse the reasons why the human right was abused and describe the consequences on the individuals and society affected.

UNIT 1 LOCAL AND GLOBAL CITIZENSHIP

> **Activity**
>
> **Human rights in Iraq**
>
> 1. Read the case study about human rights in Iraq.
> 2. Explain which human rights have been abused in Iraq since 2014.
> 3. Analyse the impact this has had on the people of Iraq.

Case study: Human rights in Iraq

Human rights conditions in Iraq have deteriorated since 2014. Suicide attacks, car bombs and assassinations have become more frequent and lethal. Government security forces and pro-government militias have carried out attacks on civilians in Sunni and mixed Sunni–Shia areas, including kidnapping and summary executions, and are responsible for arbitrary arrests, disappearances and torture. As a result, close to 500,000 people have become displaced.

The IS group continues to carry out numerous atrocities in Iraq, including: car bombings and suicide attacks in civilian areas; summary executions; torture in detention; discrimination against women; forced marriage; sexual assault and slavery of some women and girls; destruction of religious property; and killings and kidnappings of members of religious and ethnic minorities – the Shia and Yezidis.

In April 2016, in the lead-up to parliamentary elections, authorities closed media stations critical of the government and journalists were prohibited from broadcasting unfavourable coverage of government military and security operations.

Elections on 30 April were largely peaceful, but there was evidence of harassment and bribing of voters.

The United Nations Convention on the Rights of the Child

A summary of the United Nations Convention on the Rights of the Child

The Convention places a duty on governments in the following areas for children:

- the right to life
- the right to their own name, identity, own language and the practice of their own culture
- the right to be kept safe and not suffer from abuse or exploitation
- the right to education
- the right to have their privacy protected
- the right to be raised by, or have a relationship with, their parents and family or those who will care for them best
- the right to express their opinions and have these listened to and, where appropriate, acted upon
- the right to play.

▲ A summary of the UNCRC

The UNCRC is an international human rights treaty that grants all children and young people (aged 17 and under) a comprehensive set of rights on a global scale. It is a promise, made by any government that signs it, that they will work to make sure children are protected and that their human rights are upheld. The UNCRC is the most rapidly and widely ratified human rights treaty in history (194 countries have signed it). The only country that has not ratified the treaty is the United States (correct in January 2017). The UK signed the convention in 1990 and it came into force in the UK in 1992. The UNCRC is a very important document because it is specially written for children to ensure their survival, protection and development.

Section 2 Rights and responsibilities: local and global issues

Countries that sign the treaty pledge to protect children from economic and sexual exploitation, violence and other forms of abuse, and to advance the rights of children to education, healthcare and a decent standard of living. The convention also addresses children's rights to a name and nationality, to be heard, to be fairly treated when accused of offences or deprived of parental care, and other rights.

> **Activity**
>
> **The UNCRC**
>
> Analyse how the UNCRC has had a positive impact on children's lives.

What human rights abuses are taking place in the world?

Although the UDHR was adopted around 70 years ago, there still exist around the world many incidents of human rights abuses.

Child labour

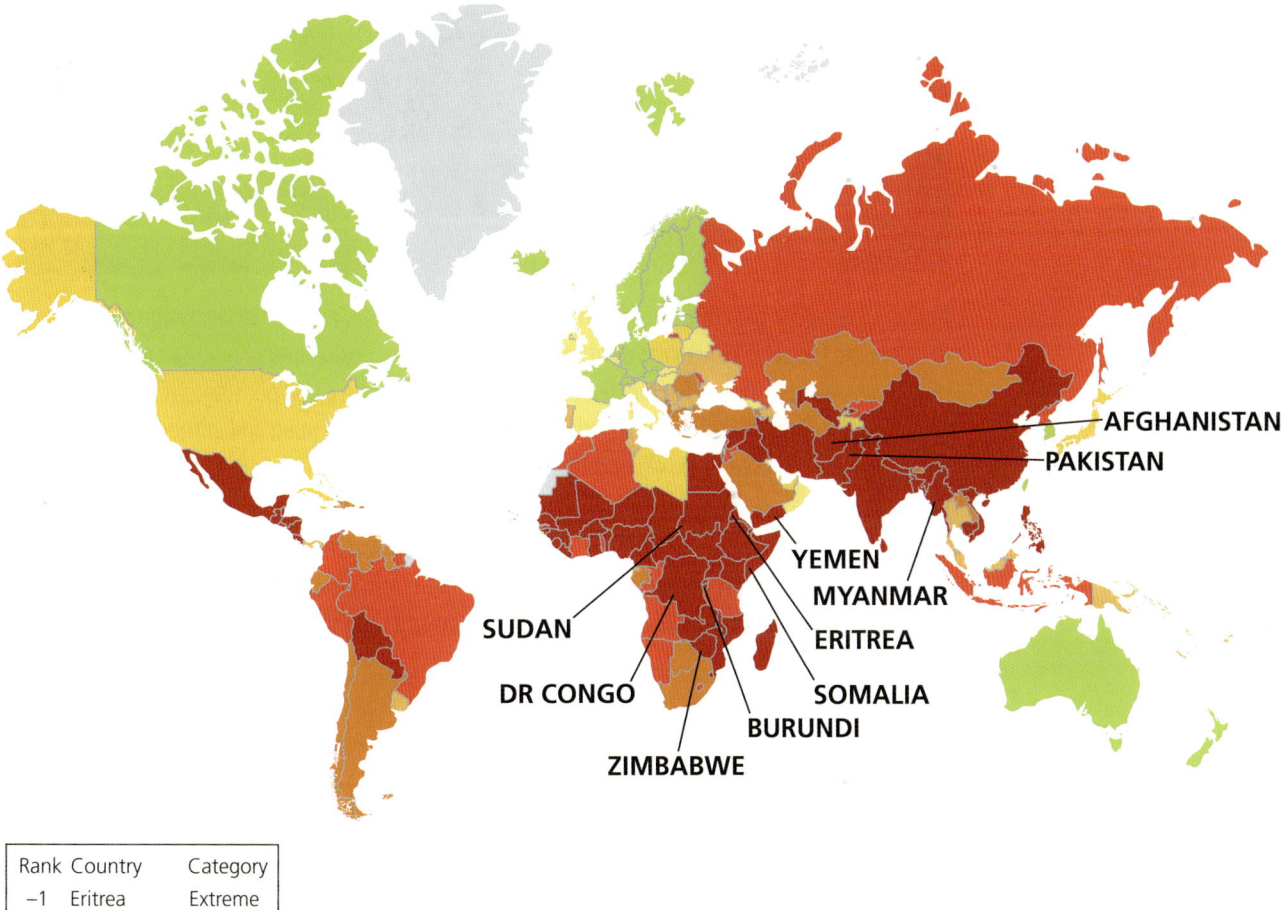

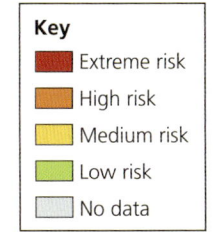

Rank	Country	Category
−1	Eritrea	Extreme
−1	Somalia	Extreme
−3	DR Congo	Extreme
−3	Myanmar	Extreme
−3	Sudan	Extreme
−8	Afghanistan	Extreme
−8	Pakistan	Extreme
−8	Zimbabwe	Extreme
9	Yemen	Extreme
10	Burundi	Extreme

Key
- Extreme risk
- High risk
- Medium risk
- Low risk
- No data

▲ The child labour index, showing the countries in which children are at risk of being used as child labour, 2014 (from Maplecroft)

37

UNIT 1 LOCAL AND GLOBAL CITIZENSHIP

The following case study is just one story of a child denied their basic human rights. Children are used as slave labour in many developing countries around the world.

Case study

A story of chocolate and child labour, July 2016

At 6 a.m., ten-year-old Emmanuel wakes and readies himself for a day of labour in the cocoa fields. Along the way, he watches as other kids walk in the opposite direction — towards school. He reaches the fields at sunrise and uses his machete to slice ripe cocoa pods from the tree. Later, he carries the cocoa pods he's harvested from the field, hacks them open and gathers the beans, which will later be used to make chocolate.

We expect to see ten-year-olds going to school in the morning carrying backpacks, not machetes. We expect to see them playing sports, painting or making music, opening their minds. Every child deserves the opportunity to learn, to grow and to benefit from his or her childhood. Emmanuel's work in the cocoa fields deprives him of that childhood and the chance to develop to his fullest potential.

Emmanuel's experience should give pause to everyone who consumes chocolate. Well over half of the chocolate the world consumes is harvested in two West African countries: Côte d'Ivoire and Ghana. As consumers, we need to ask ourselves if we are doing all we can to empower the children and families whose futures depend on farming the cocoa that we enjoy.

(www.huffingtonpost.com/eric-r-biel/a-story-of-chocolate-and_b_7899998.html)

Activity — Children and chocolate

Read the case study on chocolate and child labour.
1. Describe the reasons why Emmanuel goes out to work instead of going to school.
2. Emmanuel works to harvest cocoa pods for chocolate. Can you name other products which might use child labour?
3. Explain which human rights (see page 35) are being abused when children are used as child labour.
4. Analyse the effects and consequences of being a child used for child labour.

Child soldiers

A child soldier is any person under 18 years of age who is part of an armed force.

- There are an estimated 250,000 child soldiers in the world today.
- Children are often abducted from their homes and forced to become soldiers.
- It is estimated that 40 per cent of all child soldiers are girls. They are often used as non-combatant 'wives' (sex slaves) of the male combatants.
- Child soldiers are recruited by government forces as well as rebel groups.
- Not all children take part in active combat; some are porters, cooks or spies.
- Children are sometimes forced to kill or maim a family member, breaking the bonds with their community and making it difficult for them to return.
- A village may be forced to provide a certain number of children as soldiers in exchange for them staying safe.
- In some cases children volunteer, perhaps to avenge the death of a family member.

▲ A child soldier in Yemen, 2016

> I thought I was the only one. The only one in the world.

Activity — Child soldiers

1 Look back to the articles of the UDHR on page 35. Explain which human rights are being abused by using children as soldiers.
2 Carry out research on child soldiers. Find a recent story of a child soldier. Share your findings with the class through a presentation using your chosen media, for example a collage, poster, interview, presentation, film.
   a Try to empathise with the child; compare their life to your own.
   b What organisation helped the child soldier? How did they help?

Sexual exploitation

Child sexual exploitation (CSE) is a type of sexual abuse. Children in exploitative situations and relationships receive things such as gifts, money or affection as a result of performing sexual activities or others performing sexual activities on them. Sexual exploitation can happen to young people in gangs; others can be groomed online.

CSE is a hidden crime. Young people often trust their abuser and are tricked into believing they are in a loving, consensual relationship. They do not understand that they are being abused. They may depend on their abuser or be too scared to tell anyone what is happening.

Some children and young people are trafficked into or within the UK for the purpose of sexual exploitation. The following facts were published by the National Society for the Prevention of Cruelty to Children (NSPCC):

- Over 230 children in the UK were trafficked for sexual exploitation in 2014.
- The most common reasons for children to be trafficked are sexual exploitation and criminal exploitation.
- One in five indecent images of children shared online were taken by the child themselves.

CSE is child abuse. If you suspect that a young person is a victim or is at risk of CSE you must get professional help. You can call:

- Barnardo's on 0121 359 5333
- ChildLine on 0800 1111
- NSPCC Helpline on 0808 800 5000.

UNIT 1 LOCAL AND GLOBAL CITIZENSHIP

How can a balance be achieved between protecting the human rights of the individual with those of society?

Human rights can never be taken away and most governments in democratic countries support and uphold human rights. However, human rights are not absolute. They may be limited by governments on the grounds of:

- public interest
- national security interests
- preserving public order
- preserving public health
- respecting the rights of others.

The terrorist threat

National security is becoming more problematic for governments because of the rise of international terrorism and the mass movement of people. Countries have reacted to terrorist attacks by introducing new anti-terrorism laws which impact on human rights. For example, following the 9/11 attacks in America, some countries froze the bank accounts of individuals that they suspected of working with Al-Qaeda (Al-Qaeda is a terrorist group founded by Osama bin Laden in the late 1980s).

The challenge for governments is to strike the right balance between security and liberty. Governments must act to prevent terrorism, but their actions should still respect an individual's privacy. Some individuals and human rights groups believe that the threat of terrorism means that there must be a review of human rights and that these rights need to be accompanied by declarations of duty. Currently, there is a conflict between maintaining the rights of citizens and government efforts to keep society safe.

The right to privacy

The transformation in communications technology and the use of social media has, in turn, seen an increase in the capability of governments, agencies of the state and private businesses to keep tabs on individuals. This is an infringement of a person's right to privacy.

However, it is also the case that this same transformation in communication has made it easier for terrorists to plan and co-ordinate their campaigns. The fight against terrorism sometimes involves the state taking on new powers of surveillance and enforcement to protect society, and this can sometimes be viewed as being at odds with the rights of an individual to privacy.

The right to freedom of expression

Peaceful protest is a vital and healthy part of democratic society. Within a democracy citizens have a right to peaceful protest. Governments need to balance the rights of those protesting with the rights of others to go about their business without fear of intimidation or serious disruption to the community. Rights to peaceful protest do not include violent or threatening behaviour and police are given powers to deal with this. This can include the banning of protests, marches or parades. However, banning these may be perceived as a breach of a person's right to meet with others.

▲ Junior doctors protest over contracts, London, October 2015

The right to travel freely

Human rights law means governments have a duty to promote and protect human rights, such as the right to privacy, the right to be free from inhuman or degrading treatment, and the right to freedom of movement. This can result in a tension between collective interests and individual rights, particularly with regard to public health measures and actions taken that could potentially lead to a perceived or real violation of basic human rights. To balance public health concerns and human rights protection, international law provides that public health may be invoked as a grounds for limiting certain rights. One such example may be the spread of an infectious disease whereby people are quarantined to ensure the disease is confined.

However, regardless of these changing circumstances, it is vital that governments do all they can to maintain people's human rights and civil liberties, not least because a free society is, in the long term, one of the best protections against terrorism and crime.

> **Activity — Balancing the rights of individuals and society** (PS)
>
> 1 Explain one challenge for governments in trying to balance the rights of the individual with those of society.
> 2 Suggest and justify reasons why a government may need to restrict human rights on the grounds of preserving public order.

The case study below and Source A on page 42 are examples of balancing the human rights of the individual with those of society.

> **Case study — Asher's Bakery**
>
> In Belfast, Gareth Lee tried to buy a cake from Asher's Bakery depicting the *Sesame Street* characters Bert and Ernie below the motto 'Support gay marriage' for an event to mark International Day Against Homophobia in 2014. The bakery refused on the grounds that they would be endorsing gay marriage. Mr Lee reported the incident to the Equality Commission who took the case to court. The bakery was found guilty of discrimination for refusing to bake a cake supporting gay marriage.
>
> The bakery appealed the verdict but the judgement was upheld by the Court of Appeal. Lord Chief Justice Declan Morgan stated that, 'The fact that a baker provides a cake for a particular team or portrays witches on a Halloween cake does not indicate any support for either.' Following the judgement, Daniel McArthur, owner of the bakery, said: 'This ruling undermines democratic freedom, religious freedom and freedom of speech.' Mr McArthur argued that it would have been sinful for him to make the cake.

> **Activity — The rights of the individual and of society** (C)
>
> Read each of the examples given.
> 1 Write a speech either for or against one of the following two propositions. Research will need to be carried out to ensure arguments are substantiated. Then use your speeches to carry out a class debate.
>
> - **Proposition 1:** 'Businesses should have the right to refuse service to customers on the grounds of their religious beliefs.'
> - **Proposition 2:** 'A person should be able to wear the burka, niqab or hijab if this is part of their religious beliefs.'

UNIT 1 LOCAL AND GLOBAL CITIZENSHIP

SOURCE A An extract from an article from the *Telegraph* news website, 8 July 2016

Burka bans: the countries where Muslim women can't wear veils

Key
- Partial ban
- National ban

A map showing the countries where the veil is banned

For the first time in Switzerland's history, the country has enforced a ban on the full-face veil – which means women wearing a burka (full body covering with mesh over the eyes) or niqab (full body covering with a slit for the eyes) could face fines of almost 10,000 euros.

But it is not the only country to introduce such a controversial law. Here's where Muslim women stand on wearing the veil across the world …

France

France was the first European country to ban the burka in public. It started in 2004, with a clampdown on students in state-run schools displaying any form of religious symbol. But in April 2011, the government went further by bringing in a total public ban on full-face veils. President Nicolas Sarkozy saying they were 'not welcome' in France.

Women can be subjected to 150 euro fines and instructions in citizenship for breaking the ban. Anyone who forces a woman to cover her face risks a 30,000 euro fine.

Belgium

Belgium followed closely in France's footsteps by introducing its own ban on full-face veils in 2011. It outlaws any clothing that obscures people's faces in public places. A woman caught wearing a veil can be jailed for up to seven days or forced to pay a 1,378 euro fine. The government passed the law almost unanimously.

Chad

Women have been banned from wearing a full veil in Chad since two suicide bomb attacks in June 2015. The government banned it two days later. The prime minister Kalzeube Pahimi Deubet called it 'camouflage' and said all burkas seen on sale would be burnt. People could be arrested and sentenced to jail time for wearing them.

Congo-Brazzaville

The veil has been banned here since 2015 in public places to 'prevent any attack of terrorism'.

(www.telegraph.co.uk/women/life/burka-bans-the-countries-where-muslim-women-cant-wear-veils)

LOCAL AND GLOBAL CITIZENSHIP

Section 3 Government and civil society: social equality and human rights

Key content
- **Social responsibility** of the following in supporting democracy, social justice, social equality and human rights:
  - government, politicians, Members of the Legislative Assembly (MLAs) and public representatives
  - media companies
  - young people
- Causes and consequences of social inequality and social injustice
- The role of the government in promoting social equality, social justice and human rights through the following:
  - legislation
  - policies
  - communication
  - education
- The importance of Section 75 of the Northern Ireland Act 1998 in promoting equality of opportunity, promoting good relations and protecting people from discrimination
- The role of the Equality Commission for Northern Ireland in promoting equality, promoting good relations and preventing discrimination
- The role of the Northern Ireland Human Rights Commission in safeguarding and protecting human rights
- The role of civil society, including NGOs, in promoting social equality and safeguarding human rights

This section explores how an individual can become more aware and active in local, national and global issues. This is known as 'social responsibility'. This section examines issues of social inequality as well as the causes and consequences of social injustice. It goes on to explore the role of government in promoting social equality, social justice and human rights. The government have a key role to play through the use of policy, education, communication and laws such as Section 75. This section will develop understanding of the role of key organisations such as the Equality Commission for Northern Ireland and the Human Rights Commission for Northern Ireland. Finally, you will analyse how society, as well as the government and the individual, has a part to play in promoting social equality and social justice and safeguarding human rights.

What is social responsibility?

The campaigner, the activist and the volunteer are all examples of individuals acting in a socially responsible way. Social responsibility is when individuals, groups, media and governments within society commit themselves to making a difference to the lives of others and have a genuine concern for the welfare of others. People who are socially responsible want to contribute to society, change society for the better and make a difference – they care about the rights of others. They make a stand and speak out for those who are discriminated against or treated unfairly. When people choose to be socially responsible, they are helping to try to bring about justice and equality for all.

> **Activity — Social responsibility** (ICT) (PS)
>
> 1. Carry out research to find a young person who has acted in a socially responsible way. You could try the following websites: www.millionminutes.org, www.prideofbritain.com. Or research 'Spirit of Northern Ireland'.
> 2. Suggest and justify the reasons why the individual could be described as socially responsible.
> 3. Describe the types of people that have been helped or supported by the work of the individual.
> 4. Choose a person you know of (local, national or global) who has acted in a socially responsible way and inspires you. Explain why they are an inspiration to you. Share your findings with the class.
> 5. Do you notice anything in common about people who act in a socially responsible way? Explain your answer.

The social responsibility of the government

A democratically elected government has a social responsibility to its citizens. It is elected by the people and so has a duty to act in the interests of the people. The government has a responsibility to:

- ensure people's human rights are safeguarded and protected
- ensure laws are upheld
- ensure the health and well-being of citizens – in the UK this is provided through the National Health Service
- ensure the education of its citizens – in the UK there is free education provided for all children and young people
- support democratic processes
- ensure that society is inclusive and minority rights are upheld
- protect the environment
- support the economy.

The social responsibility of politicians and MLAs

In democratic countries elected politicians have a social responsibility to ensure that they make decisions in the interest of the common good of the public. They are also accountable to the public for the decisions they make and their actions. Politicians are expected to uphold the law and not to use their position for personal gain. They are usually expected to adhere to standards and principles defined by a code of conduct. You can find an example of this for MLAs in Northern Ireland on page 57.

The social responsibility of public representatives

Public representatives include people in various leadership positions in government agencies or bodies. Many of these may be appointed rather than elected. They commonly work with a government department and provide a service to the public. These services are paid for by the taxpayer.

Examples of public bodies in Northern Ireland include the Education Authority and the Council for the Curriculum Assessment and Examinations (CCEA). Public agencies include the Northern Ireland Prison Service and the Social Security Agencies.

Public representatives in these types of organisations have a social responsibility, in the same way as politicians, and are accountable to the public for ensuring the services they provide are value for money and meet the needs of the public.

The social responsibility of the media

The growth in technology in recent years has created new forms of media, including online and social media networks which connect people throughout the world. The ways in which the media presents information and educates the public about certain social and human rights issues can influence people's thinking, attitudes and behaviour. That is why the media's role in ensuring that it acts in ways which demonstrate a sense of social responsibility is so important.

The media has a social responsibility:

- to ensure it follows a code of practice: this sets out the rules that newspapers and magazines must follow and ensures that the media balances both the rights of the individual and the public's right to know
- to provide accurate unbiased information to the public: the media must not interpret news in a way that could be viewed as narrow or that fails to respect the rights of the individual
- to inform, raise awareness and educate the public: this can involve reporting on social injustices, inequality, human rights abuses or acts against democracy
- to challenge and hold the government/politicians to account on policies and practices: by highlighting areas where the government need to act, this can in turn ensure that politicians are following their code of conduct and acting in the best interests of the people
- to be pluralist and reflect the diversity of the society, giving access to various points of view and rights of reply: this stems from the right to freedom of expression and the media must not infringe this right
- to avoid the use of inflammatory language or content that will cause offence or civil unrest or public disorder
- to ensure media professionals work to high standards: this involves editors and publishers maintaining in-house procedures to ensure all work meets the code of practice
- to be accountable to society.

Media ownership

The media is owned by different people and therefore reflects different political perspectives in its broadcasts and publications. In the UK, terrestrial television is mainly controlled by ITV plc; digital, satellite and cable television is generally controlled by two companies: News Corp (owned by Rupert Murdoch) and Virgin Media (owned by Richard Branson). A small number of individuals own British newspaper companies. This gives a lot of power to a small number of individuals as these people control what we see, hear and read.

The media can influence political agendas in parliament, in the workplace and in the home. An example of how the media is controlled was highlighted in the Leveson Inquiry, when Rupert Murdoch commented that if someone wanted to know his opinion on a subject they should just read the Sun newspaper.

> **Activity**
>
> **Government social responsibility**
>
> 1 Research ways governments can demonstrate social responsibility at a global level.
> 2 Describe the actions that governments can take to act in a socially responsible way.
> 3 Analyse the ways that the government can act in a socially responsible way to support human rights and social justice.

SOURCE A Extract from an article from the *Express* website on benefits, 13 March 2016

UK welfare fiasco: the 100,000 addicts and obese who get benefit bonanza

NEARLY 100,000 people are receiving benefits because they are too fat or drug- or alcohol-dependent to work.

New figures show nearly 100,000 drug-dependent or obese people are receiving unemployment benefits. Figures released by the Department for Work and Pensions (DWP) under the Freedom of Information Act show that 92,000 people have been receiving disability benefits after being assessed as unable to work because of obesity, alcohol or drug misuse.

They are claiming Employment Support Allowance (ESA), which is awarded to those who have an illness or disability that affects their ability to work. The benefit replaced incapacity benefit, income support and severe disablement allowance with an annual cost to the taxpayer of £700 million a year.

According to the figures for May 2015, the most up to date available, 57,940 people with alcohol problems receive ESA, while 32,310 drug addicts are also claimants. In addition 47,000 people with stress and 1,750 who are obese receive the handout, worth up to £103 a week. David Cameron launched a review to work out the cost of preventable conditions to the welfare state.

'The current system needs reform because it fails to provide incentives to work, and traps people on welfare.' (The Department for Work and Pensions)

Birmingham has the most claiming disability benefits due to obesity (60), while Edinburgh has the most drug addicts (1,040) and Glasgow the most alcoholics (2,390) receiving the handouts.

In July the Prime Minister launched a review to work out the cost to the taxpayer of preventable conditions such as obesity and drug and alcohol abuse. At the time he suggested that those who refused treatment could be stripped of their benefits.

(www.express.co.uk/news/uk/652082/welfare-state-thousands-claimants-benefits-drug-addicts-obese-employment-support-figures)

Activity

The media and social responsibility

Read Source A.

1. Carry out a class discussion on the following question: 'Is this article an example of the media fulfilling its role to be socially responsible?'
2. Choose a social justice issue and search the internet for a newspaper article which reports on the issue. Analyse how the article is an example of the media acting in a socially responsible way.

The social responsibility of young people

Being a socially responsible citizen, ungrudgingly helping to improve the quality of someone's life in some small way, should be something we aim to undertake on a daily basis. Examples of ways a young person could act in a socially responsible way include:

- volunteering
- helping vulnerable people
- participating in a social campaign
- participating in marches/demonstrations
- contacting/lobbying politicians about an issue
- raising awareness about issues using social media
- fundraising
- starting/signing a petition about an issue
- behaving responsibly towards others.

Activity

Social responsibility

1. Explain the ways a young person can act in a socially responsible way. Give an example.
2. Analyse the reasons why a young person may act in a socially responsible way.
3. Describe the challenges a young person could face in attempting to be socially responsible.
4. Explain the benefits to society of young people acting in a socially responsible way.

Section 3 Government and civil society: social equality and human rights

What are the causes and consequences of social inequality and social injustice?

Social inequality occurs when resources in a society are unevenly distributed. This means that some people in society have fewer advantages than others because of the situation into which they are born. This inequality exists within countries and between countries globally.

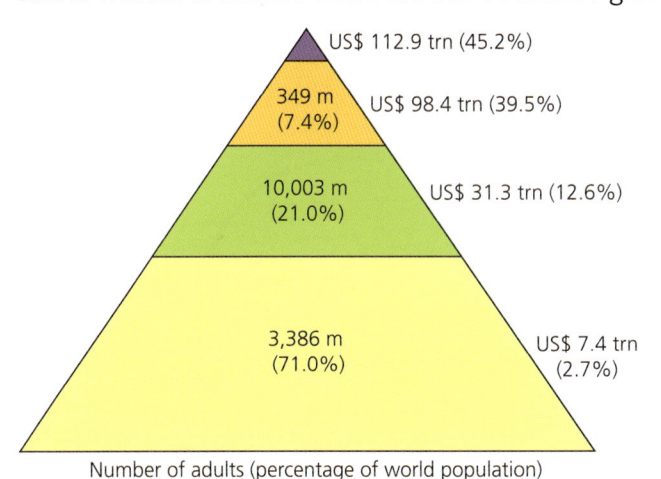

US$ 112.9 trn (45.2%)

349 m (7.4%) — US$ 98.4 trn (39.5%)

10,003 m (21.0%) — US$ 31.3 trn (12.6%)

3,386 m (71.0%) — US$ 7.4 trn (2.7%)

Number of adults (percentage of world population)

▲ Global wealth pyramid (from Credit Suisse Global Wealth Databook, 2015)

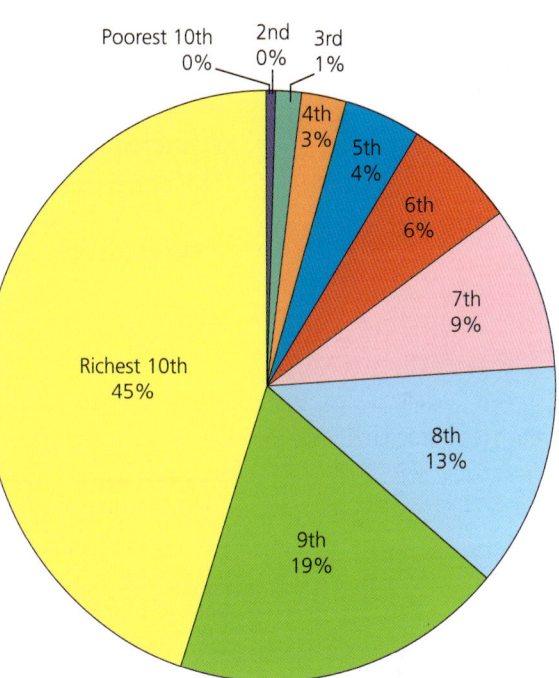

Poorest 10th 0%
2nd 0%
3rd 1%
4th 3%
5th 4%
6th 6%
7th 9%
8th 13%
9th 19%
Richest 10th 45%

▲ Pie chart showing wealth distribution in the UK (from www.equalitytrust.org.uk)

Causes of social inequality

Social inequality is caused by many economic and social factors. The diagram below summarises the main causes.

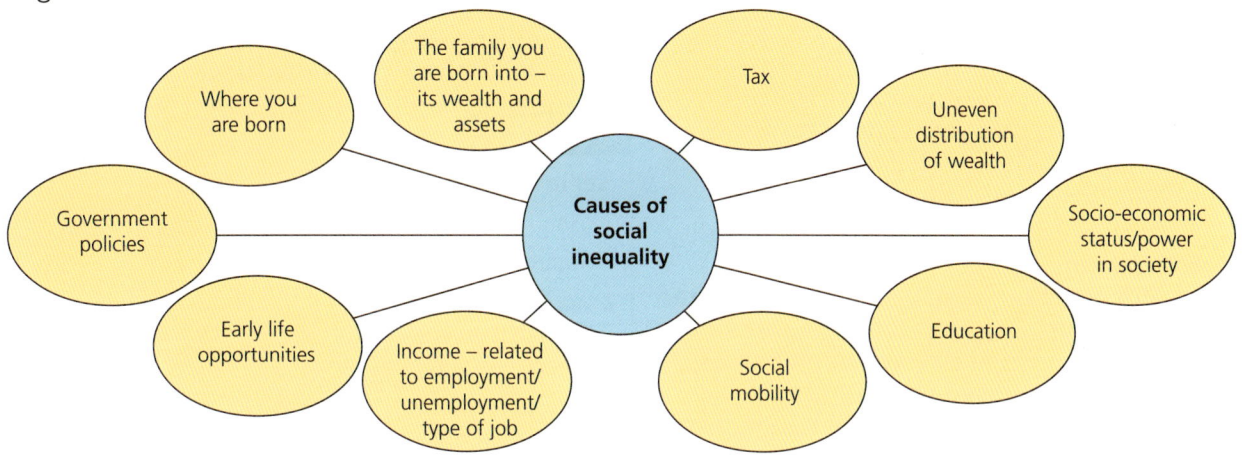

Causes of social inequality:
- Where you are born
- The family you are born into – its wealth and assets
- Tax
- Uneven distribution of wealth
- Socio-economic status/power in society
- Education
- Social mobility
- Income – related to employment/unemployment/type of job
- Early life opportunities
- Government policies

▲ Some of the causes of social inequality

Consequences of social inequality

These social inequalities can have the following consequences for the individual and for society. Consequences of social inequality for the individual include:

- poverty
- homelessness
- poor health
- lack of education
- marginalisation
- discrimination
- mistrust/lack of willingness to participate in society.

47

UNIT 1 LOCAL AND GLOBAL CITIZENSHIP

Consequences of social inequality for society include:
- economic impact due to the increased strains on the health service
- economic impact of people on benefits
- reduced number of skilled workers
- lack of participation of all members in society
- increases in crime.

The consequences of social inequality often feed back into the causes and make it very difficult for people to change their position in society, as the diagram below shows.

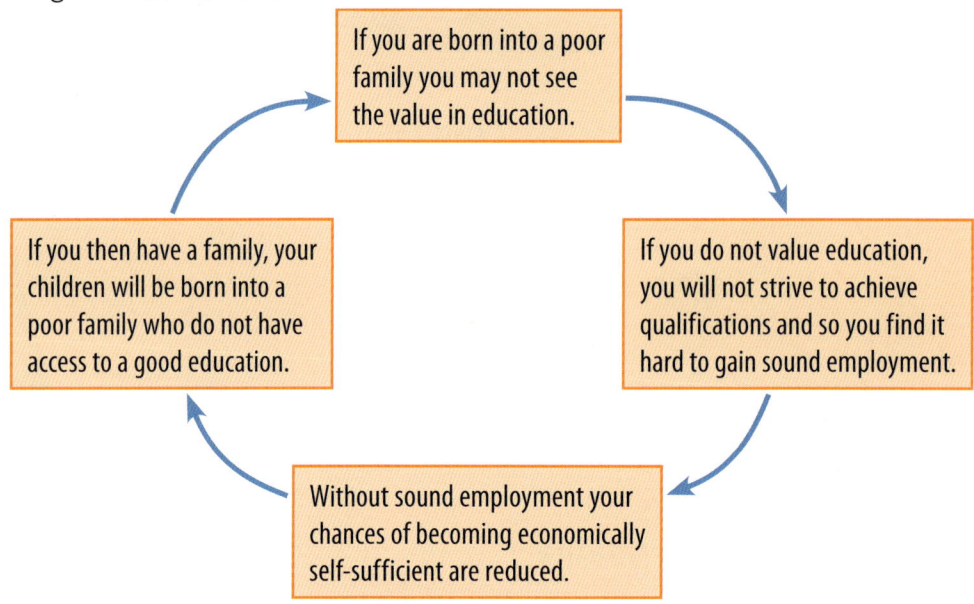

```
If you are born into a poor family you may not see the value in education.
    ↓
If you do not value education, you will not strive to achieve qualifications and so you find it hard to gain sound employment.
    ↓
Without sound employment your chances of becoming economically self-sufficient are reduced.
    ↓
If you then have a family, your children will be born into a poor family who do not have access to a good education.
    ↑ (loops back)
```

▲ The circularity of social inequality

Causes of social injustice

Social justice refers to the principle of the fair distribution of a society's goods, resources and benefits among its citizens. These include people's human rights, healthcare and education.

Social injustice occurs when there is an inequality in the distribution or access to society's goods, resources and benefits. Some people benefit more than others and certain groups of people are not treated fairly. Examples of this are when groups of people are **disadvantaged** because of their race, religion, age, gender, sexual orientation, or because they have a disability.

The level of social justice in a society is indicated by, for example, levels of poverty, educational provision and outcomes, access to employment, health and life expectancy. These provide a measure of the well-being of society. Governments can use this information to address social injustice issues. Civil society groups including NGOs also use this evidence to inform their work.

Social injustice leads to social inequalities and these lead to the same consequences.

Activity

Social justice

1. What would you use to measure levels of social justice in a country?
2. You have been asked to conduct research about social justice in Northern Ireland. Write down ten questions you might ask.
3. Discuss and share your questions with a partner. Comment on:
   a. how useful the questions are
   b. where you would find the information to answer the questions
   c. what answers you would expect if you used the same research questions in, for example, England, Ireland and India.

Section 3 Government and civil society: social equality and human rights

SOURCE A Social Injustice as reported by David Conn in the *Guardian* on 1 February 2017

Premier League clubs face legal threat unless disabled access is improved

- EHRC chair David Isaacs says the time for excuses from the clubs is over
- Thirteen of 20 top-flight teams do not have required wheelchair spaces.

Premier League clubs' failure to provide minimum levels of access for disabled supporters has been described as "disappointing" by the Equality and Human Rights Commission (EHRC), which has again threatened legal action if they do not comply.

The warning followed a Premier League report which revealed that 13 of its 20 clubs' grounds do not incorporate the minimum number of wheelchair spaces set out in the accessible stadia guide (ASG) and that nine of the clubs will not make the necessary improvements in time for the league's own self-imposed deadline of this August.

https://www.theguardian.com/football/2017/feb/01/premier-league-clubs-threatened-legal-action-failure-disabled-supporters

Activity — Wheelchair access in football stadiums

Read Source A.

1. Explain how this is an example of social injustice.
2. Analyse the impact these experiences could have on football fans with a disability.
3. Describe actions that the FA and the government could take to ensure this does not continue.

What is the role of the government in promoting social equality, social justice and human rights?

One of the main responsibilities of a democratically elected government is to promote social equality, social justice and human rights. This can be done through legislation, policy, communication and education.

Legislation

The government must ensure that all laws promote and protect social equality, social justice and human rights. Examples of laws which do this are Section 75 of the Northern Ireland Act 1998 and the Disability Discrimination Act 1995. The government must work with key agencies to ensure laws promote good relations between all sections of society.

Furthermore, the justice system can support legislation by ensuring that people are prosecuted and punished for breaking the law. Punishments must be robust for crimes relating to equality and human rights to ensure the message is understood that inequality and injustice will not be tolerated.

Policy

Government policy should ensure targets are met and actions are carried out and should monitor them to measure their effectiveness. Policy can include actions to build good community relations, investigating areas where there might not be equality of opportunity and taking action to change this.

The Northern Ireland Assembly has a key role to work with all the departments in the Executive to ensure the promotion and protection of equality and human rights. They develop a programme of government which works to improve the lives of the people. Policy which is derived from this programme then enables action to take place.

▲ Members of the Northern Ireland Assembly discuss policy matters

UNIT 1 LOCAL AND GLOBAL CITIZENSHIP

Communication

Using the media, the government can communicate the reasons why it is important that society has equality, good relations, social justice and human rights. It can inform people about how to behave responsibly and what policies the government has introduced to help.

The government can use websites to help inform and educate, for example the Northern Ireland Assembly Education Service (http://education.niassembly.gov.uk/). The police can highlight crimes using the media and thus seek support from the public; local government can raise awareness of activities taking place which foster good relations in the community.

Education

In school the government can ensure these issues are covered in the curriculum through subjects such as Learning for Life and Work. The government can ensure that groups who work to promote social equality, social justice and human rights are given funding to produce educational resources and have an education programme as part of the work that they do. Some of these groups include the Northern Ireland Human Rights Commission and the Community Relations Council (see pages 51 and 30). The government will work with a range of NGOs to support this work.

> **Activity** — PS
>
> **Government and social equality** — C
>
> Evaluate the impact of the Northern Ireland government in promoting social equality.

What is the importance of Section 75 of the Northern Ireland Act 1998?

This law means that designated public authorities must ensure that all groups in Northern Ireland have access to the same opportunities. The purpose of this law, introduced in 1998, was to transform society and improve the quality of life for people in Northern Ireland. Its aim was to change the practices of government and public authorities so that equality of opportunity and good relations are central to policy making, policy implementation, policy review and service delivery. There are two statutory duties which public bodies must comply with.

Section 75: promoting equality of opportunity

This is the first duty. It requires public authorities in carrying out their functions relating to Northern Ireland to have due regard for the need to promote equality of opportunity between the nine equality categories: persons of different religious belief, political opinion, racial group, age, marital status or sexual orientation; men and women generally; persons with a disability and persons without; and persons with or without dependants.

Section 75: promoting good relations

This second duty requires that public authorities in carrying out their functions relating to Northern Ireland have regard for the desirability of promoting good relations between persons of different religious belief, political opinion and racial group.

Section 75: protecting people from discrimination

In carrying out the above duties the hope is that public bodies will identify which groups of people experience inequality or disadvantage and take steps to address this in their work.

> **Activity** — PS
>
> **Section 75** — C
>
> Analyse the significance of Section 75 and the impact it has had on society in Northern Ireland.

Section 3 Government and civil society: social equality and human rights

What is the role of the Equality Commission?

The Equality Commission is an independent public body which was set up to promote equality and tackle discrimination in Northern Ireland. The Commission gives free advice to individuals, businesses and public bodies on equality issues. It works to ensure fair treatment for individuals in Northern Ireland.

▲ The logo of the Equality Commission NI

Activity: The Equality Commission

Search www.youtube.com for 'Your Equality Commission – who we are' and watch the clip. Also visit the Equality Commission's website: www.equalityni.org.

1 Name four roles of the Equality Commission.
2 Explain how the Equality Commission carries out these roles.
3 Name the categories of cases that feature most in the work of the Equality Commission.
4 As a class, design your own Equality Survey based on the questions in the video clip. Carry out the survey in your class or year group. Make sure it is completed anonymously. Present your findings.
5 Describe the actions students and the school could take to address these equality issues.
6 Search www.youtube.com for: 'Your Equality Commission – what we do'. Analyse the work of the Equality Commission to prevent inequality in Northern Ireland.

What is the role of the Northern Ireland Human Rights Commission?

The Northern Ireland Human Rights Commission (NIHRC) was established as part of the Good Friday Agreement, 1998. The role of the Commission is to support society as it rebuilds following conflict and grows to respect and uphold human rights standards and responsibilities. The NIHRC describes itself as the centre of excellence on human rights. It ensures government and other public bodies protect the human rights of everyone in Northern Ireland. It also helps people understand what their human rights are and what they can do if their rights are abused. Its work includes:

▶ advising the Westminster government, the Northern Ireland Executive and Assembly, and key agencies on legislation and ensuring that laws comply with human rights
▶ promoting awareness of human rights through education, training and research
▶ **monitoring** international treaties to ensure they promote and protect human rights
▶ providing legal advice work including taking strategic legal cases
▶ engaging with other national human rights institutions in the UK
▶ working as part of the Joint Committee with the Irish Human Rights and Equality Commission (IHREC).

Activity: The NIHRC

Go to: www.youtube.com and search for: 'Northern Ireland Human Rights Commission – what we do'.

1 Explain the actions taken to support, promote and protect human rights in Northern Ireland.

UNIT 1 LOCAL AND GLOBAL CITIZENSHIP

What is the role of civil society (including NGOs) in promoting social equality and safeguarding human rights?

Public sector	Private sector	Civil sector
Government	Business	Organisations that act in the public's interests but are not motivated by profit or government, for example NGOs

▲ The sectors of society

'Civil society is the conscience of our communities.'
(Barack Obama)

There is no agreed definition of civil society but for our purposes we can describe it as a public space between the state, the market and the ordinary household, in which people can debate and take action. It is when groups work in the interests of citizens. A civil society demands from each of us **goodwill** and respect, fair dealing and forgiveness. We are all part of civil society and we all have to work towards it. Civil society is about the ability of groups of people to come together to make a difference in society and the world, to co-operate and break down barriers.

The UN once dealt only with governments. However, peace and prosperity cannot be achieved without partnerships involving governments, international organisations, the business community and civil society. In today's world, all of these groups are dependent on each other.

Civil society can include any voluntary collective activity in which people combine to achieve change on a particular issue, but not political parties, even though civil society has a political dimension. By this definition, civil society includes: charities; neighbourhood **self-help** schemes; international bodies like the UN or the Red Cross; pressure groups; human rights campaigns in repressive societies; and NGOs improving health, education and living standards in both developed and developing nations.

Examples of civil society in action worldwide can be seen at the street, community, national and international level, and on a host of different issues. Civil society is an essential feature of a free society. Civil society can bring about change, monitor governments and put pressure on governments when they are not safeguarding human rights.

Activity — The actions of civil society

1. Think about and discuss examples of groups (local, national, global) which work to make the world a better place. Try to think specifically of groups which promote social equality and safeguard human rights.
2. Investigate the work that they do and name the ways the organisations promote social equality or safeguard human rights.
3. Analyse the role of civil society in promoting social equality and safeguarding human rights.
4. Write down six groups/organisations which are part of Northern Ireland civil society.

UNIT 1

LOCAL AND GLOBAL CITIZENSHIP

Section 4 Democratic institutions: promoting inclusion, justice and democracy

Key content
- The significance and the key features of the 1998 Good Friday (Belfast) Agreement
- The structure of the Northern Ireland Assembly
- The main roles of the Northern Ireland Assembly
- The structure of the Northern Ireland Executive
- The main roles of the Northern Ireland Executive
- The role and responsibilities of MLAs, including the Code of Conduct of the Northern Ireland Assembly
- The role of the Police Ombudsman's Office in investigating complaints about the PSNI

This section examines the main institutions that were set up under the Good Friday (Belfast) Agreement (hereafter referred to as the Good Friday Agreement) signed in 1998. It explores the main features of the Agreement which have impacted on the citizens of Northern Ireland. It examines the role of the Northern Ireland Assembly and the Northern Ireland Executive. Furthermore, it explores the role of MLAs and the function of the Northern Ireland Police Ombudsman in investigating complaints about the PSNI.

What are the significance and main features of the Good Friday Agreement 1998?

The Good Friday Agreement brought to an end the 30 years of conflict in Northern Ireland. It was the result of a series of multi-party talks held from 1996 which led to an agreement between most political parties in Northern Ireland and also the British and Irish governments about how Northern Ireland should be governed. The Agreement was signed on Good Friday 10 April 1998 and ratified in a referendum in May 1998.

The agreement outlined proposals for a Northern Ireland Assembly with a power-sharing executive, new cross-border institutions with the Republic of Ireland and a body linking devolved assemblies across the UK with Westminster and Dublin. The Republic of Ireland also agreed to drop its constitutional claim to the six counties which formed Northern Ireland. There were also proposals on the decommissioning of paramilitary weapons, the future of policing in Northern Ireland and the early release of paramilitary prisoners.

▲ The signing of the Good Friday Agreement, 1998

Devolved government

Devolution is the statutory delegation of powers from the central government of a state to a regional or local level. Devolution in the UK essentially means the transfer of powers from the UK parliament in London to assemblies in Cardiff, Belfast and the Scottish parliament in Edinburgh. This process of devolution allows regions to have self-government. The devolved governments have power to make legislation on certain areas, which are known as 'transferred matters'. In Northern Ireland, the devolved government is the Northern Ireland Assembly at Stormont.

Scotland	Wales	Northern Ireland
Agriculture, forestry and fishing	Agriculture, forestry and fishing	Agriculture
Education	Education	Education
Environment	Environment	Environment
Health	Health and social welfare	Health
Housing	Housing	Enterprise, trade and investment
Justice, policing and courts	Local government	Social services
Local government	Fire and rescue services	Justice and policing
Fire service	Highways and transport	
Economic development	Economic development	
Some transport		

▲ Examples of the major devolved powers in Scotland, Wales and Northern Ireland

Power-sharing government

The Good Friday Agreement set up a power-sharing assembly to govern Northern Ireland by cross-community consent. This means that the government must be made up of unionists and nationalists. Members of the Assembly must register themselves as nationalist, unionist or other. Power sharing means there must be shared responsibility and cross-community support/parallel consent for key decisions made. This model of democracy means:

▶ the offices of First and Deputy First Minister must be represented by a unionist and a nationalist, with equal powers
▶ there must be a multi-party executive made up of nationalist and unionist parties
▶ there must be proportional representation
▶ there is a Petition of Concern which gives veto rights to the minority. This is a measure to safeguard minority rights.

The principle of consent

The principle of consent is one of the key points of the Good Friday Agreement. It acknowledges the aspiration of a United Ireland and acknowledges that the majority of the people of Northern Ireland wish to remain part of the United Kingdom. The principle underlines the right of self-determination for the people of Northern Ireland and the Republic of Ireland.

> **SOURCE A** An excerpt from the Good Friday Agreement explaining the principle of consent
>
> Article 1 [The British and Irish Governments will:]
>
> (ii) recognise that it is for the people of the island of Ireland alone, by agreement between the two parts respectively and without external impediment, to exercise their right of self-determination on the basis of consent, freely and concurrently given, North and South, to bring about a united Ireland, if that is their wish, accepting that this right must be achieved and exercised with and subject to the agreement and consent of a majority of the people of Northern Ireland.

The right to hold British and Irish citizenship

The Agreement also upheld the right for the people of Northern Ireland to hold both British and Irish citizenship – see Source B.

> **SOURCE B** An excerpt from the Good Friday Agreement explaining the right of the people of Northern Ireland to identify themselves as Irish or British or both
>
> [The British and Irish governments will:]
>
> (vi) recognise the birthright of all the people of Northern Ireland to identify themselves and be accepted as Irish or British, or both, as they may so choose, and accordingly confirm that their right to hold both British and Irish citizenship is accepted by both Governments and would not be affected by any future change in the status of Northern Ireland.

Safeguards for human rights and equality

Part of the Good Friday Agreement contains safeguards. These are in place to ensure that all sections of the community can participate and work together successfully and that all sections of the community are protected. This means that all laws and key decisions have to adhere to the European Convention on Human Rights, which now also includes the Human Rights Act UK (1998). To ensure this happens the Assembly can set up a committee to examine and report on whether a piece of legislation conforms to equality requirements.

On assuming their position, each minister must take a Pledge of Office. Part of this pledge is that ministers will serve all people of Northern Ireland equally and in turn promote equality. Furthermore, to ensure the protection and promotion of equality, the Equality Commission was established. The Agreement also established the NIHRC to protect and promote human rights. You can read more about the role of the Equality Commission and the NIHRC on page 50.

Recognition of linguistic diversity

The Good Friday Agreement recognises the importance of linguistic diversity as a method to promote respect, understanding and tolerance. The languages referred to are the Irish language, Ulster-Scots and the languages of the various ethnic communities in Northern Ireland. There must be action taken in order to promote these languages, encourage the use of these languages and make arrangements for liaising with the Irish language community. Therefore, there is a statutory duty on the Department of Education to encourage and allow Irish-medium education similarly to integrated education.

> **Activity** PS
>
> **Key features of the Good Friday Agreement**
>
> 1. Suggest and justify the reasons why the following elements were included in the Good Friday Agreement:
>   - devolved government
>   - power sharing.
> 2. Explain one reason why the following elements were included in the Good Friday Agreement:
>   - principle of consent
>   - dual citizenship
>   - recognition of linguistic diversity.
> 3. Describe how the Good Friday Agreement safeguards human rights and equality.

What is the structure of the Northern Ireland Assembly?

▲ The Stormont buildings

The Northern Ireland Assembly is led by the First Minister and the Deputy First Minister, and is composed of 90 elected members, known as Members of the Legislative Assembly (MLAs). The Assembly sits at Parliament Buildings, Stormont Estate, in Belfast. It is chaired by a Speaker and three deputy Speakers. The Assembly involves cross-community power sharing between unionists and nationalists.

The Assembly has a number of Statutory Committees. These Committees advise and help each of the Northern Ireland ministers to develop policy in different areas.

Northern Ireland Assembly

▲ The logo of the Northern Ireland Assembly

55

LOCAL AND GLOBAL CITIZENSHIP
Section 5 Democracy and active participation

UNIT 1

Key content
- Ways in which young people can participate in democratic processes (for example, in school, the community and the wider world) and influence change for the benefit of society
- Benefits of the participation to the young person and to society

This section explores the term 'democracy' and the features of a democratic state. Participation is a key part of democracy and so this section explores how a young person can participate in democratic processes through school, in the community and on a global scale. Active participation enables young people to demonstrate their capacity to make a difference and develop the soft skills sought by employers. Young people have a lot to offer and learn as active members of communities. This section will outline the ways that young people can influence change for the benefit of society. Furthermore, it will discuss the benefits for society if people are participants in decision making.

What is democracy?

Democracy by definition means 'government by the people'. A democratic country or organisation is one in which ordinary people have the power to influence how things are run. They can participate in decisions. Democracy is associated with notions of liberty, equality and human rights. There are different types of democracy:

- Direct democracy means each person in a group directly casts their own vote – this is established in some parts of Switzerland.
- Representative democracy is when a person is elected to take decisions on the behalf of the people (electorate) – this is practised in the UK.

Not all societies are democratic and even among those that claim they are democratic, questions could be asked of the status of human rights, freedoms and equality.

The illustration to the right outlines some of the features of a democratic state.

Regular free and fair elections — Co-operation and compromise — **Multi-party system** — **LEGISLATIVE ASSEMBLIES** — Rights for minorities — Majority rule — Freedom of association — Head of State — **JUDICIARY AND RESPECT FOR THE LAW** — Citizen participation — Human rights — Freedom of speech

▲ Features of democracy

58

Active citizenship

The strength of a democracy depends on people's participation in the democratic process which supports it. Democracy is based on the principles of inclusion and equality. Everyone has equal rights and a social responsibility to participate in public life and decision-making processes to bring about change for the benefit of society. This is active citizenship.

Democracies uphold human rights, which include citizens' rights to participate in public life.

Democratic processes include:
- voting in elections
- participating in informed debate, public discussion forums and consultations
- supporting petitions
- lobbying
- campaigning, peaceful marches and protests
- volunteering
- engaging with politics and political activities.

Democratic processes are important ways of:
- challenging and holding the government to account
- raising public awareness of social injustice, social inequality and human rights issues that need to be addressed
- ensuring citizens' views are voiced
- influencing decision and policy makers
- influencing change in society.

SOURCE A An article from the *EU Observer*, 27 January 2016

Bulgaria seen as most corrupt in EU

Perception of corruption in Bulgaria is the highest in the EU, with Denmark viewed as the most transparent, according to a report by activist group Transparency International (TI). The report, published on Wednesday (27 January), is based on polls of experts from around the world on topics including free press, access to budget information, integrity and independent judiciaries. Out of the 168 countries probed, Denmark is seen as the least corrupt with Somalia and North Korea as the most. Amongst the 28 EU states, Bulgaria is at the bottom, ranked at 69.

The European Commission, for its part, is set to publish its annual monitoring report on Bulgaria and Romania on Wednesday. Last year, it found Bulgaria had done little to curb corruption and organised crime despite having joined the EU in 2007. As the EU's poorest nation, Bulgaria has grappled with political instability and a compromised judiciary.

In the TI index, Italy is not far ahead of Bulgaria in 61st place, behind Romania and Greece both at 46. Trends in Europe also suggested Hungary, Spain, Macedonia and Turkey were becoming more corrupt. Anne Koch, TI's director for Europe and Central Asia, said they were 'seeing corruption grow, while civil society space and democracy shrink' in all four nations.

The biggest drop in Europe, compared to the past four years, is Spain. Anger at Spanish corruption cases has helped give rise to new political parties like Podemos and Ciudadanos. Some of the most improved countries include Austria, the Czech Republic, Greece, Slovakia and the UK.

(https://euobserver.com/justice/132012)

Activity — Democracy and corruption

Read Source A and answer the following questions:

1. Explain the challenges that democratic states face in trying to ensure they uphold democracy.
2. Research one of the countries named in Source A which has high levels of corruption and one which has low levels. Present your findings on why each country has a different level of corruption.
3. Analyse Source A and explain why it is important that people should participate in democratic processes.

UNIT 1 LOCAL AND GLOBAL CITIZENSHIP

How can young people participate in democratic processes?

An effective democracy depends on young people's participation in democratic processes. The view of youth should be represented, especially on decisions that will affect them and their future. Young people have unique experiences of the challenges they face in society and are best placed to contribute to possible solutions. They may have a different perspective on society and how it should be governed.

A democratic school encourages young people's involvement in its decision-making processes, especially on decisions that affect them. Democratic schools promote the idea of the student voice. They listen to and value student views and will consider them when making decisions.

Active citizenship in schools

One of the ways schools can help young people to learn about democracy and democratic processes is by providing them with opportunities to express their views and to participate in decision-making processes, especially in decisions which affect them. The idea of young people having a say in school is often referred to as the 'pupil voice'. This is a way of upholding Article 12 of the United Nations Convention on the Rights of the Child (see page 36). This gives children the right to express their views and to be involved in decisions which affect them. The pupil voice is inclusive and is about schools giving all children and young people a voice, listening to them, respecting and responding to their views. This can lead to improvements which benefit the school and young people's schooling experience. Schools may provide a range of opportunities for young people to express their views and to contribute to school decision-making processes. Some of these are given below.

School councils

Many schools operate a school council. A school council is set up with an agreed constitution. The constitution states the aims and objectives of the council, the rules for elections, processes for sharing information and members' roles and responsibilities. The school council consists of an agreed number of teachers and students. Students who are interested in becoming a member of the council have to be nominated for election under agreed rules. Students vote for whom they want to represent them and the successful candidates are those with the majority of votes.

▲ Students participating in a school council discussion

School council meetings are held throughout the year. Students put forward issues they want to raise to their council representative and these are placed on a meeting agenda and discussed. The outcomes are shared with students and staff.

By participating in the school council young people can learn about working together, election processes, consultation and conducting meetings, framing proposals for discussion, setting agendas and taking minutes. They also learn debating and discussion skills.

> **Activity** — **School councils**
>
> 1. In pairs discuss the benefits of a school council. Write down your ideas and share them with the class.
> 2. Explain how you could find out if a school council is effective.
> 3. Explain why participating in public discussion and debates is important in society.

Mock elections

Some schools may hold mock elections. Groups of young people set up school political parties. They decide on what their party represents and run an election campaign. Candidates participate in debates on their key issues. Young people then have a chance to vote in an election. This helps young people to learn about the democratic process of voting.

Section 5 Democracy and active participation

Student evaluation

Some schools may use student surveys, questionnaires or one-to-one interviews or focus groups to obtain students' views about their learning experiences and other issues that affect them.

Class discussion and debates

In their day-to-day learning young people may have the opportunity to participate in structured discussions or debates, for example on social, democratic and human rights issues. These activities help young people to gain confidence when speaking in front of others, to think critically, to present reasoned arguments and to listen and respond to others. These are important skills required for democratic participation.

Volunteering

Pupils may have opportunities to participate in school or community projects. They can gain experience of school or local community issues. They could be involved in making decisions about how to deal with them. They could plan and organise activities or events to support the school or community.

▲ Students working together on a planting project in their community

Active citizenship in the community

Democracy is present in the community in many forms.
- Local newspapers allow communities freedom of expression, a forum in which they can have their voice heard and through which they can challenge injustices in the community.
- A community centre and its workers are vital to ensure freedom of association.
- Community meetings allow people to influence change and take part in democratic processes.

There are a range of ways that young people can also participate in the democratic processes to influence positive change in the community. Youth and community groups such as the Northern Ireland Youth Forum, which set up the Youth Congress as a pilot for a Youth Assembly, allow young people to let their voice be heard. The purpose of the Forum is to provide a mechanism whereby young people can raise and discuss issues of importance to them and bring these issues directly to the attention of elected decision makers at a regional, national and European level. It also provides a means by which government departments can seek the views of young people.

Youth clubs are also a great asset to a community. The government supports initiatives in youth clubs which encourage young people to participate actively in their communities. The government believes that giving young people direct influence in decision making and enabling them to lead change helps to engage them in a positive relationship with their communities and ensures that services meet their needs.

Active citizenship in the wider world

Young people also have a role to play as global citizens. There are many global issues which affect people in many countries. These include poverty, homelessness, hunger, lack of clean water, inadequate healthcare and education, conflict, human rights abuses and environmental sustainability.

As active global citizens, young people can take action to help address these and other global issues. Young people can use some of the methods discussed on this page and on page 60, such as volunteering with a global NGO, campaigning and organising fundraising activities and events to support a cause they are passionate about. For example, young people can raise awareness among their peers and adults of issues such as ethical consumerism and fair trade. They can research companies, their products, where and how they were produced and workers' pay and conditions, and highlight companies which exploit their workers. Raising awareness can impact on a company's reputation and sales, which may make the business improve its employees' working conditions. In this regard young people can help influence people's consumer choices and ultimately the actions of businesses.

UNIT 1 LOCAL AND GLOBAL CITIZENSHIP

Young people as decision makers

The UN Youth Delegate Programme makes it possible for young people from all over the world to be included in decision making and to have real influence in making sure that the decisions made in important forums of the UN reach out to the young population of the world.

Many people believe that the decision-making processes at local, national, regional and international level need to be opened up to allow young people to have real influence throughout all parts of the process. Providing young people with the necessary information and then letting them take part in the decisions would make the process, the decision and the result more relevant, effective and legitimate. Young people are active participants, leaders, initiators and actors for change. They are already changing the world.

Influencing change for the benefit of society

'Young people should be at the forefront of global change and innovation. **Empowered**, they can be key agents for development and peace. If, however, they are left on society's margins, all of us will be impoverished. Let us ensure that all young people have every opportunity to participate fully in the lives of their societies.'

(Kofi Annan, Former Secretary-General of the United Nations)

You have already looked at the different ways young people can be part of the decision-making processes at a school, community and wider world level. Some of the ways that they can influence change to bring about benefits to society are listed below:

- Buy ethical products like chocolate and coffee. Book travel with companies that protect children from exploitation.
- Get more involved in the fight against child slavery by becoming an advocate. Donate, fundraise, lobby your local MLA or MP and raise awareness.
- Report abuses to the police.
- Do not allow people to laugh or make fun of those who are subjected to human rights abuses.
- Use social media to interconnect, highlight and raise awareness of issues, for example the 'ice bucket challenge'.
- Become a youth delegate in the UN.
- Join a Youth Council.
- Become a Member of the UK Youth Parliament.
- Become part of the UK Youth Media Council.

Activity — Youth action

1. Look at the different ways suggested in which youth can bring about change in society. Choose one of the methods.
   a. Do some research on this method and find out why it is effective.
   b. Write a short report about this method, detailing its strengths and weaknesses.

What are the benefits of youth participation in democratic processes, for young people and for society?

Participation empowers children and young people as members of civil society and active citizens. It has benefits both for the young people and for society.

Benefits for young people

The benefits of participating in democratic processes for young people themselves include:

- developing their knowledge and understanding of democracy, policy making and social issues
- developing their knowledge and understanding of global issues
- enhancing self-esteem, self-confidence and motivation
- developing skills such as communication, working with others, self-management and problem solving, all of which are skills sought after by employers
- becoming familiar with group and democratic processes
- encouraging a sense of individual and social responsibility
- enhancing civic consciousness and political maturity
- enhancing personal development, as it provides young people with the opportunity to make a difference
- encouraging young people to be active citizens and more engaged in their communities
- gaining experience that can be put to use in future employment and social life.

Benefits for society

The practice of participation strengthens children's ability to hold organisations, institutions and government to account. It enables children to play an active part in civil society and to compensate for their exclusion from formal political processes. It increases the visibility of children and children's issues, ensuring that they are given greater weight in economic, social and political agendas.

Therefore, by increasing accountability to children, the democratic space is enlarged and good governance is encouraged. Allowing young people to participate could change the perception of young people and their needs. Listening to young people will ensure policy is created which allows change where change is needed and this should in turn benefit all of society.

> **Activity**
>
> **The benefits of youth participation**
>
> 1. Analyse the benefits of participation for young people.
> 2. Explain the importance for the community and the wider world of young people participating in democratic processes.

LOCAL AND GLOBAL CITIZENSHIP
Section 6 The role of NGOs

UNIT 1

- The role of NGOs in promoting social equality, social justice, human rights and democracy by tackling local, national and global issues such as:
  - health
  - relief in natural disasters
  - poverty
  - welfare or social security
  - animal rights
  - the environment
  - war and conflict
  - human rights abuses
  - homelessness
- Factors that limit the impact of NGOs' work

This section examines the role of a range of NGOs in promoting social equality and justice, human rights and democracy. It will explore the impact that NGOs are making and how they work to improve the lives of people around the globe who are suffering.

What are NGOs?

NGOs are an important part of civil society. There are a wide range of NGOs which focus on a variety of social and human rights issues. Some operate at a local level, while others work at national or global levels. NGOs are independent from the state and government. They are not-for-profit organisations and usually depend on public donations to fund their work, although some may also be funded by or receive grants from the government. They mainly rely on volunteers who believe in the actions of the NGO.

One of their main aims is to improve people's quality of life by effecting changes in wider society. They try to influence the attitudes and behaviour of individuals, groups and businesses to be more socially responsible. They also aim to influence decision makers, those people who are in positions to address issues, and bring about change. This includes local councillors, politicians and government policy makers. The main ways NGOs achieve this are through education programmes, campaigns, peaceful protests, demonstrations, marches and lobbying. This can lead to the government taking action to deal with issues, for example, by developing and implementing policies, and by passing and enforcing laws. NGOs also take direct action to tackle issues. They provide a range of services to support people, usually the most vulnerable groups in society.

What is the role of NGOs?

The following is a list of the main ways that NGOs work to tackle issues:

- NGOs campaign to raise awareness and gain public support about social equality, social justice and human rights. NGOs organise media and marketing campaigns to raise awareness of their issues and aims. Although campaigns are costly, their message reaches a wide audience.
- NGOs rely on fundraising to finance their work and the resources and services they provide. Fundraising events and activities also help to raise awareness of issues.

- NGOs conduct research to investigate issues and provide reliable evidence which they use to prioritise their work, make policy decisions and inform the public.
- NGOs hold peaceful protests, demonstrations and marches to highlight areas of social inequality in society.
- NGOs lobby politicians, business leaders and other decision makers to influence change. They may lobby government to create or amend laws or to address a particular issue or cause.
- NGOs have an advocacy role. They represent the most vulnerable groups in society and ensure their voices are heard on issues that are important to them. They also defend and protect their rights.
- NGOs work in partnership with local communities. They can support people in local communities to deal with local issues such as poverty, homelessness and healthcare. They can provide advice, training, facilities and resources.
- NGOs play a vital role in education and training. In some places such as Africa and India they provide, develop and implement education programmes and work in schools and community groups to educate people about the importance of social equality.
- NGOs provide emergency or short-term aid by supplying food, water, shelter and healthcare to people who might not have access to these goods and services because of the effects of a natural disaster.
- NGOs provide support and offer counselling to people who have suffered. For example, people might need help with coming to terms with losing a loved one or with losing their home and possessions.

Issues addressed by NGOs

NGOs promote social equality, social justice, human rights and democracy by tackling issues at a local, national and global level. These issues include the following.

Health

People around the globe suffer from a variety of health issues from physical to mental ailments. They and their families require support to accept a diagnosis or help to lead an active and fulfilling life or to share experiences with like-minded people. For example, if a person is diagnosed with cancer there are NGOs that will support the family by giving advice or respite care. When natural disasters or poverty occur there can be higher rates of mortality due to health risks such as disease. NGOs can work on the ground to try to save lives through offering medical assistance or training local people in methods to prevent disease or illness.

Natural disasters

Natural disasters are natural events, such as a flood, earthquake, tsunami, volcanic eruption or hurricane, that cause great damage or loss of life:

▲ The images above show the damage caused by natural disasters in Haiti

- According to a 2014 report by the UN, since 1994, 4.4 billion people have been affected by disasters which have claimed 1.3 million lives.
- Furthermore, in 2015 the UN published a report that stated that weather-related disasters have increased in the past 20 years and 90 per cent of major disasters are recorded as floods, storms, heatwaves and droughts.
- Indonesia, India and the Philippines are among the five countries hit by the highest number of disasters.
- The 2015 UN report outlines that women and children in developing countries are the most vulnerable after a natural disaster occurs.

Natural disasters are calamitous and can wreak havoc on communities, causing death and health risks such as the spread of disease, destruction, food scarcity and emotional aftershock. In a natural disaster, NGOs can assist with rescue efforts and provide emergency aid in the form of clean water and sanitation in temporary camps and shelters. They can provide essential items such as hygiene kits and send experienced staff to help communities where there are shortages of food.

> Go to www.bbc.co.uk/science/earth/natural_disasters for a better understanding of the impact of natural disasters.

Poverty

Poverty is not having enough money for your basic needs such as food, shelter and clothing. However, poverty is also about not being able to take part in leisure activities, not being able to send children on a day trip with their schoolmates or to a birthday party, not being able to pay for medications for an illness. These are all the costs of being poor. Malnutrition is one of the biggest effects of poverty.

- A total of 14.3 per cent of people in developing countries face hunger. In July 2014, poor nutrition caused 45 per cent of deaths in children under the age of five.
- Poverty also damages childhoods and life chances. Life expectancy and child mortality are affected by poverty, as statistics show that life expectancy in poor nations is up to 30 years below that of wealthy nations.
- Poverty also affects a person's education, as many people living in poverty are unable to attend school. It is argued in the Borgen Report, published in 2014, that if 171 million people obtained a basic education this could bring people out of poverty.

There is no single cause of poverty and it is a very complex issue, which is why NGOs are continually working to combat poverty. NGOs can tackle poverty at ground level by providing food such as Plumpy'Nut® which can save people from severe malnutrition. They can also provide education and training to local communities to empower them with the tools they may need to break the cycle of poverty.

Welfare or social security

The welfare state was established after the Second World War to protect the health and well-being of people in the UK. It allowed access to social security, a national health service, free education and council housing. NGOs can offer advice and help to people struggling to lead an active life by providing them with information on the help available.

Animal rights

Animal rights is the idea that most animals are entitled to life and that their most basic interests – such as the need to avoid suffering – should be afforded the same consideration as similar interests of human beings. Many people believe that it is morally wrong to inflict suffering on an animal, such as in animal testing, using animals for clothing or medicine, hunting or using animals for entertainment. There are NGOs that work to prevent suffering to animals and to raise awareness of incidents of animal cruelty and in turn put pressure on governments to take action against offenders.

The environment

'There are no passengers on spaceship Earth. We are all crew.'

(Marshall McLuhan)

Human activity has an impact on the environment. NGOs work to reduce this impact for the benefit of the natural environment and humans. Issues relating to the environment can include over-population, global warming, pollution, intensive farming, deforestation, flooding, natural disasters, nuclear power and waste management. All these issues have varying effects, including climate change, habitat destruction, birth defects, pollution and deforestation. NGOs can carry out research on these issues, inform people and advise governments on how to limit the consequences of these issues.

The graph below demonstrates the rapid growth in world population, which will in turn have an effect on the environment and the planet's available resources.

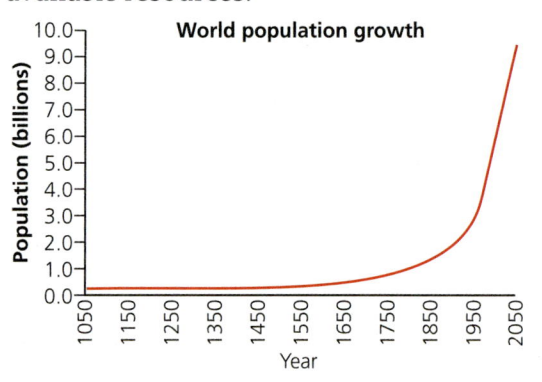

War and conflict

War and conflict can leave immediate and lasting effects, even after peace has been agreed. Conflict causes loss of life, injury and destruction of the infrastructure of society such as buildings, roads and access to services. People in conflict zones need support to get access to basic needs. Also, even years after conflict has ended, there are still the bitter experiences for those who endured the violence and death of war. These communities need support to rebuild their lives after conflict.

Imagine a war zone in your mind. What challenges can you envisage for people living in the war zone? What help will they need? This is where the NGO can support people to rebuild homes, schools and hospitals. This can be done through providing labour and materials. NGOs can also help local communities to work towards reconciliation between warring factions.

▲ An image showing the devastation of Aleppo during the conflict in Syria, 2016

Human rights abuse

Over 60 years after the creation of the UDHR, violations still exist in every part of the world. Human rights abuse includes child abuse, child labour, torture, unfair trials and ethnic cleansing. It causes a loss of dignity and life. People who do not know their rights are more vulnerable. NGOs get active to fight for universal human rights, particularly through lobbying and raising the profile of issues.

UNIT 1 LOCAL AND GLOBAL CITIZENSHIP

Homelessness

Homelessness does not just describe people sleeping on the streets; it also applies to people who do not have a suitable permanent home. It can happen to anyone, for any number of reasons. Even if you have a roof over your head, you may still be homeless if you are:

- sleeping on the streets
- staying with friends or family
- staying in a hostel
- staying in a bed and breakfast
- living in very overcrowded conditions
- at risk of violence if you stay in your home
- living in poor conditions that are damaging your health
- living in a house that is unsuitable for you.

It was reported in 2014 that homelessness was higher in Northern Ireland than anywhere else in the UK. Therefore, it is important that people facing this issue are given support and suitable accommodation, which is where the work of NGOs is focused.

Activity — Researching NGOs

1. Use the internet to research NGOs that deal with the above issues. For each issue write down two NGOs which deal with the issue.
2. Select one NGO from your list. Write a report for a newspaper article to inform people about its work. The report should include:
   - what the issue is
   - what the NGO does to deal with the issue
   - what the outcome of the work is.
3. Select one of the issues that an NGO deals with.
   - Plan a campaign about the issue to raise public awareness.
   - Give reasons to justify your choice of issue.

What factors exist which limit the work of NGOs?

NGOs carry out a huge amount of beneficial work at the local, national and global level. However, there are factors which limit the extent of the work they can undertake:

- **Lack of funds:** money is needed to carry out the work of an NGO and so it must fundraise and rely on donations to continue its work.
- **Lack of people/volunteers:** work for NGOs is unpaid and so it can be difficult to find people willing to give up their time to support its work.
- **Lack of supplies/resources:** depending on the NGO, work could include providing medicine, clothing, food or water. NGOs often face challenges getting support to the people most in need. This can be because of violence in the area or because of transport or infrastructure issues. At times some governments refuse to allow aid into the country to help certain groups of people.
- **Facilities:** building and office space and the overheads of running them can be costly, but to carry out their work NGOs need a central space from which to work.
- **Communication network:** it can be frustrating and challenging when no one is listening to or taking action as a result of your message. It takes persistence and tenacity on the part of volunteer workers to keep pressuring governments to make changes.

UNIT 2

PERSONAL DEVELOPMENT

Section 1 Personal health and well-being

Key content

- Living a healthy lifestyle – the impact of diet, exercise and attitudes to health and well-being
- The causes, consequences and impact on health and well-being associated with unhealthy lifestyle choices: drinking alcohol, smoking, using drugs (misuse of legal prescription drugs and illegal substances)
- The causes, consequences and impact of lifestyle factors on people's physical and mental health: hygiene, stress, **work/life balance** and low income
- Developing a healthy mind – dealing with the causes and consequences of anxiety, stress and depression
- Supporting young people with **addictions** and mental health issues, and sources of support

This section examines the various pressures that can sometimes be experienced by young people to pursue lifestyle choices which will have negative effects on their health and well-being. It looks at why people choose seemingly negative actions, and the varying impacts they can have on both the individual and those around them. It also looks at issues such as stress and depression. Many of these choices can have serious repercussions and can leave people feeling isolated, so advice is given on where to receive help for those experiencing any of the situations examined.

Living a healthy lifestyle: what are the impacts on health and well-being of diet, exercise and attitudes to social, emotional and physical health?

When we think of the term 'health', we tend to associate it with our physical well-being and whether or not we are physically ill. However, as shown in the diagram below, health and well-being encompass a lot more.

Physical health
Physical health is anything that has to do with the physical state of the body. Good physical health can help you lead a satisfying and successful life.

Emotional health
Emotional health (also known as mental health) is how you think, feel, act and how you are able to cope with life in general. To be emotionally healthy you should talk about feelings, ask for help when you need it, keep in touch with friends and do something you enjoy regularly.

Social health
Social health is concerned with how you interact with other people in various situations and how well you can make and maintain relationships. To be socially healthy you should be able to hold and contribute to conversations, have friends and to feel a sense of belonging to such groups as family, class and peers.

▲ Health and well-being can be broken down into three parts

UNIT 2 PERSONAL DEVELOPMENT

Overall well-being can be influenced by many factors. This section looks at diet, exercise and attitudes and how they affect social, emotional and physical health.

A balanced diet

Eating the right foods and consuming the correct nutrients in the right quantities is an important step towards good health. Studies have shown that the more balanced and nutritious a person's diet, the healthier they will be. What we eat affects our mood, growth and ability to concentrate. The National Health Service (NHS) recommends that people should eat from the five main food groups. These are:

- bread, cereal (including breakfast cereals) and potatoes (starchy foods)
- fruit (including fresh fruit juice) and vegetables
- meat and fish
- milk and dairy foods
- fat and sugar.

From looking at Source A, below, it is clear that to have a **balanced diet** we should eat plenty of fruit and vegetables and starchy foods but limit foods which are high in fat and sugar. A balanced diet also includes eating at regular times. It is recommended that we eat three main meals per day – breakfast, lunch and dinner.

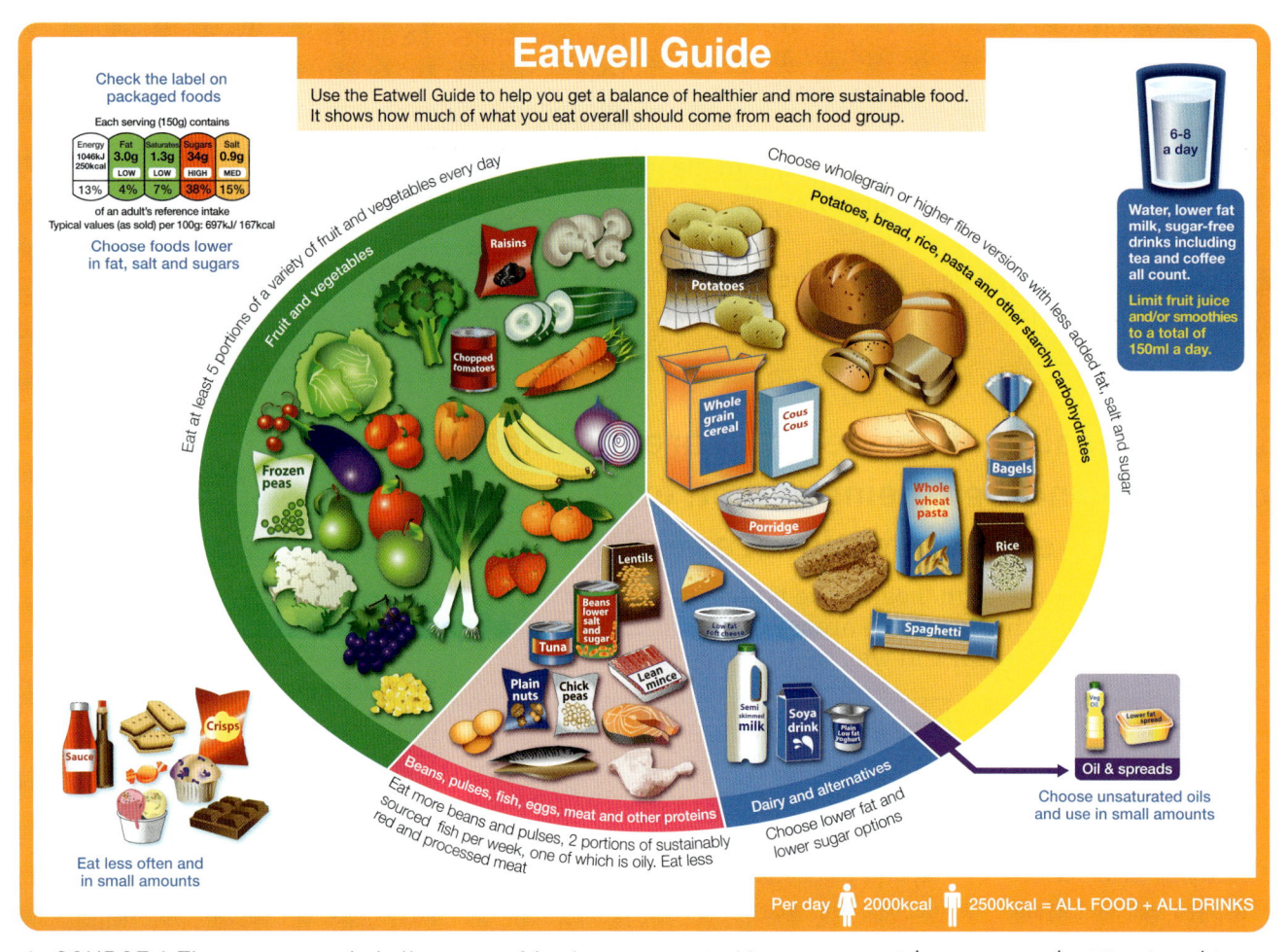

▲ SOURCE A The recommended allowance of foods as suggested by www.gov.uk/government/publications/the-eatwell-guide

Section 1 Personal health and well-being

Sticking to a balanced diet

People can often find it difficult to stick to a balanced diet and instead adopt a non-healthy diet. They tend to lead busy lives and so find it difficult to prepare fresh meals and some cannot help giving in to the temptation of unhealthy foods.

The availability of junk food, convenience food and fast food makes it easy for people to disregard the benefits of a balanced diet. There are many reasons why people choose to eat these unhealthy foods and many reasons why they should not, as illustrated in the diagram below.

Why people choose to eat fast food/ junk food/convenience food	Why people should not eat fast food/junk food/convenience food
<ul><li>taste</li><li>low cost</li><li>readily available</li><li>extensive advertising</li><li>quick or no preparation time</li><li>can be part of a social event.</li></ul>	<ul><li>low nutritional value</li><li>can be addictive</li><li>unknown nutritional content</li><li>desire to lose weight</li><li>desire to eat a balanced diet</li><li>desire to learn how to cook.</li></ul>

▲ Reasons for buying fast food, and reasons to avoid it

The physical, emotional and social effects of diet

Diet affects our overall well-being and as such having a healthy or non-healthy diet will inevitably affect physical, social and emotional health. The three different types of health are inter-related and are dependent upon each other.

The table below summarises the effect a healthy (balanced) diet could have on the three inter-related types of health.

Effects of a healthy diet on:				
Physical health	**... which can have knock-on effects on ...**	**Emotional health**	**... which can have knock-on effects on ...**	**Social health**
A healthy diet gives your body the nutrients it needs to perform physically, maintain wellness, and fight disease.	⟷	Being free from illness means the body is functioning properly. You are more likely to feel upbeat and have an improved state of emotional health.	⟷	Being physically and emotionally well could result in increased opportunities for social occasions, where friendships could be developed and formed.
Increased energy levels.	⟷	Having more energy could allow for regular exercise, result in better moods and decrease the chances of a sedentary lifestyle.	⟷	Being more active and energetic could allow you to become social with like-minded individuals, for example, at an exercise class.
Eating certain healthy foods calms your nervous system and triggers a sleep-inducing hormonal response.	⟷	If the brain is well rested a person will be much more able to cope with their **emotions** and deal with daily stresses, resulting in improved emotional health.	⟷	Being well rested, emotionally well and able to cope with stressors more easily could result in a more relaxed and tolerant persona. This could result in a person being able to make and retain friendships, increasing social health.
Eating healthily could allow a person to maintain an adequate weight.	⟷	Maintaining an adequate weight will improve self-confidence and self-esteem, which could improve emotional well-being.	⟷	Being positive, having self-confidence and self-esteem may allow a person to actively seek out ways to socialise with others, limiting the feelings of inadequacy.
Having a balanced diet can help aid recovery when ill.	⟷	Getting physically better quicker could result in less time being spent at home recovering, decreasing the chances of feeling sad, isolated or depressed.	⟷	Chances are that recovering quicker from illness and being emotionally healthy will decrease the chances of missing social events.

▲ The effects of a healthy diet on physical, social and emotional health

Section 1 Personal health and well-being

> **Activity** (ICT) (PS)
>
> **The physical, emotional and social effects of diet**
>
> 1 Using the table on page 72 as a guide, copy and complete the table below showing the negative results of an unhealthy diet on physical, emotional and social health.
> 2 The table below focuses on how physical health affects emotional health and how this then affects social health. Reversing the trend in the table, fully explain the emotional health of a person who is socially unhealthy. Give one example to illustrate your point.

Effects of an unhealthy diet on:				
Physical health	**… which can have knock-on effects on …**	**Emotional health**	**… which can have knock-on effects on …**	**Social health**
Having a **deficiency** such as a lack of iron can cause physical health problems such as anaemia.	←→		←→	
Eating too much fat can result in **obesity**.	←→		←→	
Too much sugar can result in tooth decay.	←→		←→	
An unhealthy diet can lengthen recovery time from illness.	←→		←→	
Not eating healthily can lower immunity and increase frequency of illness bouts.	←→		←→	
Eating unhealthily can increase the likelihood of developing a chronic illness such as coronary heart disease.	←→		←→	
An unbalanced diet can result in interrupted sleep patterns.	←→		←→	

UNIT 2 PERSONAL DEVELOPMENT

Health risks of an unhealthy diet

There are many health risks of an unbalanced diet. If the body lacks a particular vitamin or mineral it can lead to a deficiency-related disease. For example, a lack of vitamin C can cause scurvy, a lack of calcium can result in brittle bones and a lack of iron can result in anaemia. Similarly, if the body receives too much of certain vitamins and minerals it may not function to the best of its ability.

Perhaps the biggest food-related health risk to people in Northern Ireland is an unbalanced diet where people take in too much salt, sugar and fat. The table below shows the main health risks which can occur as a result of excess amounts of each of these food types:

Nutrient	Excess amounts can cause:
Salt	High blood pressure; coronary heart disease; a stroke
Sugar	Tooth decay; weight gain or obesity; an aggravation of asthma; mood swings
Fat	High blood **cholesterol** which can cause heart disease, weight gain or obesity

Activity — Unhealthy foods (ICT) (PS)

1 Do you think that packaging on junk food encourages young people to buy it? Identify and explain two reasons for your answer.

2 a Research the nutritional value of the following foods:
- BIG MAC®
- Large portion of French fries
- Medium-sized pizza
- MARS®
- Packet of crisps
- Tub of Pringles®
- A Pot Noodle

For each food, write down the amount of a) salt, b) fats (saturated) and c) calories. This can be done by looking at the packaging or using a company's website for nutritional information.

b Does any of the information you gathered surprise you?

The impact of exercise on physical health

Exercise has many proven physical, emotional and social health benefits and can be defined as an activity or an effort whereby people aim to improve physical fitness and overall health.

Keeping physically active can prevent major illnesses and is the basis for a healthier lifestyle. The UK government recommends that adults aim to do at least 30 minutes of moderate-intensity activity on five or more days per week and that children and young people do around 60 minutes every day.

BUPA states that the signs that you are doing moderate-intensity activity are:

▶ an increase in your breathing rate

▶ an increase in your heart rate to a point where you can feel your pulse

▶ feeling warm.

Physical activity does not necessarily mean everyone should take time out to go to the gym for long periods of time, but instead it can be incorporated into everyday life – for example, walking to and from school, cycling, taking the stairs instead of a lift.

Section 1 Personal health and well-being

There are many physical health benefits of doing exercise; some are short term, others are more likely to benefit you in the long term. See the table below.

GYM

Short-term benefits:	Long-term benefits:
• burns excess calories which could turn into fat if the body does not use them • improves sleep • increases flexibility • increases energy levels • increases blood flow to the brain, which improves concentration • increases body temperature which, stimulates glands, nerves, joints and the circulatory system.	• improves body shape, muscle tone and posture • stronger bones and muscles • increases stamina, endurance and balance and can lead to faster reactions • stronger immune system, which helps fight against infections • reduces the risk of certain illnesses including type 2 diabetes, coronary heart disease and certain cancers • reduces blood pressure • increases 'good' cholesterol and decreases 'bad' cholesterol • helps control weight • prevents premature ageing • promotes healthy growth and development in children.

▲ The short-term and long-term benefits of doing exercise

The impact of exercise on social and emotional health

Apart from the many physical benefits exercise can bring, exercise has been shown to help improve emotional and social health. Physical activity helps get rid of stress and aggression in a harmless way. Success in physical activity or sport can improve self-confidence and self-esteem. It can give you something to aim for, provide a challenge and increase motivation. Studies have shown that people who exercise tend to be more optimistic and happy compared to those who do not and therefore emotional health can increase. Additionally if you are physically healthy and illness-free due to exercise, you are much more likely to be energised, upbeat and generally in a better mood.

Social health can also be improved by leading an active life. Being physically and emotionally healthy can firstly allow a person to participate in exercise activities. As a result, exercising helps you meet new people and make friends, especially if you join a sports team, gym or exercise class, which can help you learn and develop new skills – for example, teamwork and co-operation – as well as giving you a sense of belonging. All these factors can help contribute to a more socially healthy person.

Activity — Physical activity (PS) (SM)

1 Explain *two* ways you could become more physically active by changing certain elements of your daily routine.

2 Having clear goals can help motivate you and keep you focused. Identify your top *three* fitness goals for the next month.

3 What do you think the key message in Source B is? Is this the best way to deliver the message?

4 Do you think the poster in Source B and its message could affect young people's exercising habits? Identify and explain *three* reasons for your answer.

5 Look at Source C. Do you think over-exercising can be a negative thing? Identify and explain *two* reasons for your answer.

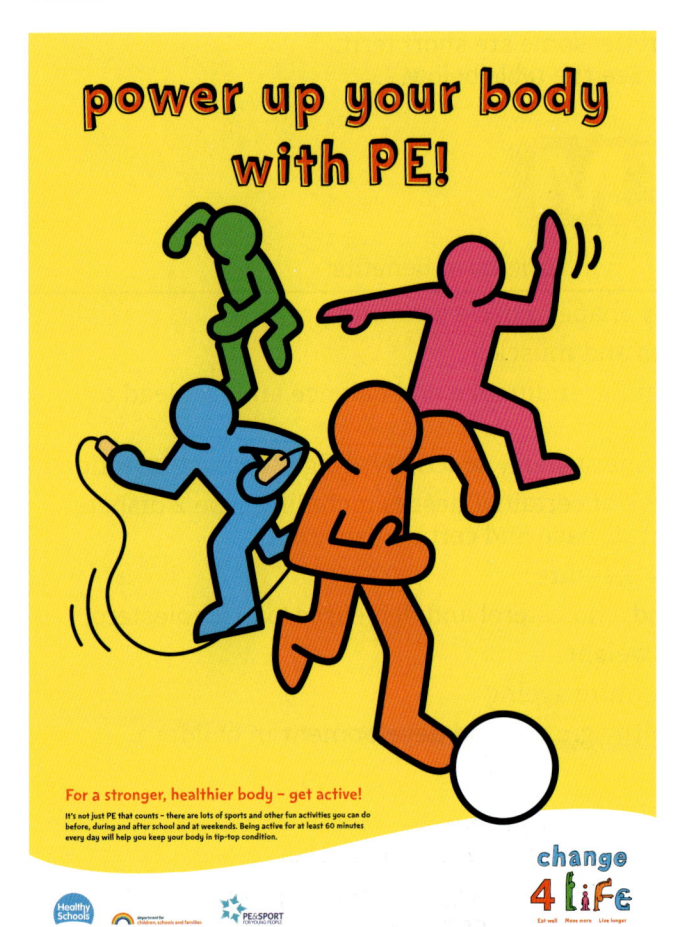

UNIT 2 PERSONAL DEVELOPMENT

The impact of positive attitudes on health and well-being

A person's diet and exercise habits are influenced by their knowledge of and attitudes towards these behaviours. Through educational programmes in schools and prolonged media campaigns in society, the majority of people are well aware that diet and exercise improves well-being. Most people could even make an attempt at citing the recommended exercise guidelines and many have a good knowledge of the 'Eatwell Plate', as seen on page 70.

Below are extracts of the government factsheets for exercise which aim to highlight the recommended physical activity guidelines in the promotion of well-being. These can be found at: www.nhs.uk/Livewell/fitness/Pages/physical-activity-guidelines-for-adults.aspx

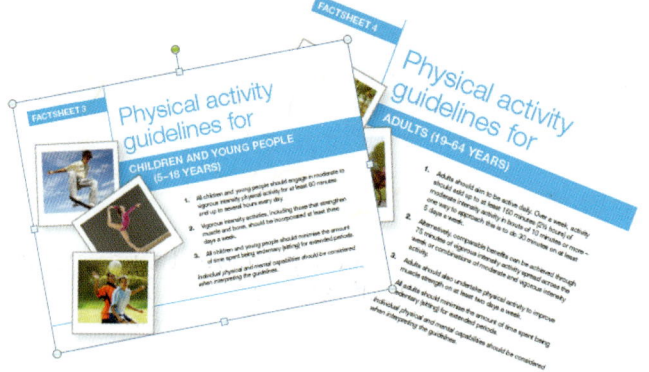

▲ SOURCE B Change4Life poster

▲ SOURCE D Government factsheets recommending how long a person should exercise

With many people being well aware of the importance of eating well and exercising often to promote well-being, why are there still those who ignore the recommendations? This partially comes down to the attitudes people hold regarding a healthy diet and exercise. Some negative attitudes to diet and exercise are summarised below, which inevitably negatively impact on well-being. Some people:

▶ feel that they cannot be bothered to put the effort into eating healthily as it involves more planning and preparation
▶ make excuses, such as they are too busy to exercise/plan meals
▶ use short-term measures to achieve a quick goal, such as losing weight quickly by **crash dieting**, but end up putting it back on just as quickly
▶ follow fad diets but then relent very quickly into old habits

▲ SOURCE C Female bodybuilder

Section 1 Personal health and well-being

- continuously put it off – 'I will start on Monday', but Monday never comes
- start healthy eating, do well, but then give up at the first temptation.

Developing positive attitudes

Some people fail to recognise that a balanced diet and exercise regime should be a way of life. Developing this positive attitude and being committed to this way of life can start at any time as long as the person is in the correct mindset. Attending slimming classes or fitness classes or working with a personal trainer or nutritionist can help a person to commit to positive attitudes towards fitness and diet which will result in sustained health and well-being.

Evidence suggests that if a positive attitude starts early in life and is instilled at a young age then these attitudes are more likely to be held into adulthood.

There are many ways that adults can help children and teens develop a healthy approach to food and exercise. Examples include the following:

- ✓ Avoid punishing or rewarding children with food.
- ✓ Be a good role model for healthy eating and exercising.
- ✓ Be a good role model by having a positive self-image, regardless of body shape and size.
- ✓ Avoid judging other people's weight and size in front of a child or teens.
- ✓ Not teasing or criticising a child about his or her weight or shape.
- ✓ Avoid encouraging a young person to lose weight.
- ✓ Make children healthy food and snacks.
- ✓ Make exercise fun by playing outdoors and playing energetic games.
- ✓ Be positive about their own exercise regimes and talking about their benefits.
- ✓ Being interested in school work or homework that promotes a healthy lifestyle.
- ✓ Highlighting and chatting about media campaigns that promote a healthy lifestyle.
- ✓ Be the gatekeeper to computer games and TV, which encourage a sedentary lifestyle.

Activity

Physical activity for youth

1 Design a pamphlet to be delivered to the parents of a local primary school. It should:
   a outline the benefits of developing positive attitudes to exercise and diet early in life
   b provide tips to parents to help develop and promote positive attitudes to diet and exercise.
2 Why do you think that there are higher obesity rates among children in some areas compared to others?

Activity

Exercise and diet in childhood

1 Explain why it is important to set healthy exercise and diet habits in childhood.
2 Identify and explain two ways a parent or **carer** could promote healthy exercise and diet habits in childhood.
3 What does your school do to try to promote healthy exercise and diet habits?

SOURCE E Article from *Mail Online* 16 December 2011

Our attitude to food and fitness 'is fixed at ten years old'

If you struggle to lose weight or to say no to an extra helping of pud, don't blame your willpower – blame your parents. A person's attitude towards food and exercise is largely set by the tender age of ten, a study found. Newcastle University researcher Heather Brown said that healthy eating habits become engrained in childhood and that is the time for parents, schools and governments to intervene.

Piling on the pounds: poor eating habits from childhood are believed to be responsible for wayward eating during adulthood (posed by model)

Her advice follows study of data on hundreds of pairs of American siblings. Some were adults who lived apart from each other, others were aged between ten and eighteen and still living in the family home.

The data was filtered to separate out the effects of influences that don't change over time, such as genetics and upbringing, and those that are more variable, such as the friends that we keep.

The results revealed that the diet and exercise habits we pick up in childhood stay with us throughout life. Dr Brown said our attitudes towards things as simple as whether to have breakfast regularly may be largely set by the age of ten.

'Parents are important role models. If they have an unhealthy lifestyle then their children are more likely to emulate their behaviour and continue these unhealthy habits into adulthood.'

She added that schools should also help children form good habits by providing healthy meals and snacks and sufficient time for exercise.

On the move: similarly, children who exercise often develop their keen interest in fitness as they mature

Writing in the journal *Obesity*, she said: 'This demonstrates the importance of early childhood interventions and prevention programmes to promote a healthier population.'

The study comes a day after official figures for England revealed that one child in three is overweight when they leave primary school at the age of eleven. Almost a fifth are classed as obese, meaning they are so fat they risk knocking years off their lives. And the number of ten- and eleven-year-olds who fall into this category has risen by nearly 10 per cent in just four years, according to the NHS data.

In some towns and boroughs, more than a quarter of children this age are obese. Experts warn that many of these youngsters will stay fat for the rest of their lives, putting them at greater risk of heart disease, diabetes and other serious illnesses.

Tam Fry, of the Child Growth Foundation and National Obesity Forum, said the key to turning the tide is to stop children from getting fat in the first place.

(www.dailymail.co.uk/sciencetech/article-2074799/Attitude-fitness-food-engrained-childhood.html#ixzz4LHQMtlvh)

What are the causes, consequences and impacts on health and well-being of drinking alcohol, smoking and using drugs?

Making unhealthy lifestyle choices can impact on a person's well-being. Here we look at the causes, consequences and impacts of drinking alcohol, smoking and using drugs.

Drinking alcohol

Young people today choose to experiment with drinking alcohol despite restrictions on sales and numerous campaigns to intervene. A report put together by the Church of Ireland estimates that about 80 per cent of young people have consumed alcohol before the age of 16 in Northern Ireland.

Young people are aware of the many health risks associated with alcohol. They learn about it in school, they are bombarded with media messages telling them that alcohol is bad and parents or carers usually warn against the dangers. However, the question remains: if these health risks are so widely known, why is alcohol still so widely used by young people? What causes them to drink? A few reasons why they might take up drinking are shown in the diagram below.

Availability: alcohol is widely available. Some shops, pubs and off-licences are still not as strict as they should be when it comes to asking for ID, so it can be easy for a minor to get their hands on alcohol. People who are legally allowed to buy alcohol have been known to purchase alcohol for younger people.

Packaging: to date, alcohol packaging does not carry any health warnings and young people tend not to stop and think about the dangers of alcohol after purchasing. Alcohol packaging is becoming more and more attractive to young buyers. Alcopops come in a range of colours and flavours which can be very eye-catching to young people.

Peer pressure: young people may be influenced by their friends encouraging or pressurising them to drink.

Culture: young people are growing up in a 'binge-drinking' culture. Young people's views on alcohol and drunkenness are influenced more and more by culture. If they see others drinking and getting drunk around them, they may be more likely to engage in the activity themselves.

Advertising: advertising alcohol is still legal in the UK. Drink adverts can be seen on TV, billboards, posters and magazines.

Price: promotions such as happy hours or buy-one-get-one-free coupled with prices as low as 14p per unit of alcohol have led to government debates about whether alcohol being too cheap encourages young people to drink.

Home environment: approximately 40 per cent of alcoholic drinks sold are drunk at home. The home is a place where young people learn to drink. Parental attitudes to alcohol affect whether or not a young person chooses to drink when they are under 18.

▲ Reasons why young people might take up drinking

UNIT 2 PERSONAL DEVELOPMENT

Consequences of drinking alcohol

As it is illegal to drink alcohol under the age of 18, there is no recommended unit consumption like there is for adults. Depending on how much is taken and the physical condition of the individual, alcohol can have many different health consequences, both long term and short term, as outlined below.

Short-term effects of alcohol:

- Impaired judgement
- Decreased perception and co-ordination
- Unconsciousness
- Headaches
- Coma
- Blackouts (memory lapses, where the drinker cannot remember events that occurred while under the influence)
- Distorted vision and hearing
- Slurred speech
- Drowsiness
- Breathing difficulties
- Anaemia (loss of red blood cells)
- Vomiting
- Upset stomach
- Diarrhoea

Long-term effects of alcohol:

Binge drinking and continued alcohol use in large amounts are associated with many health problems, including:
- Permanent damage to the brain
- Nerve damage
- Emotional health issues such as depression
- Cancer of the mouth and throat
- High blood pressure, stroke and other heart-related diseases
- Alcohol poisoning
- Liver disease
- Vitamin B1 deficiency, which can lead to a disorder characterised by **amnesia**, **apathy** and disorientation
- Ulcers
- Gastritis (inflammation of stomach walls)
- Malnutrition
- Impotence
- Fertility issues

▲ Short- and long-term effects of alcohol on the body

Associated impacts of alcohol

As alcohol can clearly affect a young person's health and well-being and make it more difficult for them to function normally, it is unsurprising that other aspects of a person's life can be impacted, particularly if the abuse of alcohol is a regular occurrence or an addiction. The following could be affected:

Work/school performance

▶ Increased absences: due to hangovers or binge drinking days.

▶ Accidents: in the UK, up to 25 per cent of workplace accidents and around 60 per cent of fatal accidents at work may be linked to alcohol.

▶ Reduced productivity at work or school: performance at work may be affected both by the volume and pattern of drinking. Colleagues/other students may become hostile due to lack of effort.

▶ Disciplinary action or even dismissal or expulsion: this leaves the affected person with reduced income, possibly **debt** and little or no formal education.

Family relationships

▶ Drinking can impair how a person performs as a parent, partner or how they contribute to a functioning household.

▶ There can be an increase in arguments, accidents and violence within the home.

▶ Children can suffer from **Foetal Alcohol Syndrome** if a mother drinks while pregnant, leaving a child with physical and emotional health issues.

▶ Parental drinking can lead to child abuse and impact a child's social development.

▶ A drinker within a family can also cause emotional health problems for other members of the family – for example, fear, anxiety and depression.

- The financial costs of alcohol purchase and loss of wages due to the effects of alcohol can mean that the entire family suffers financially and may have to exclude themselves from social occasions.

Economic costs

- Alcohol-related accidents, long-term treatment plans for alcohol-related illnesses and treatment for addicts cost the health service millions every year.
- Increased policing costs as a result of binge drinking add to this.
- Some people argue that this money could be better spent, for example on education.

Activity: The impacts of alcohol

1 Using the internet, research Foetal Alcohol Syndrome and answer the following questions:
   a What is Foetal Alcohol Syndrome?
   b How can alcohol reach an unborn baby?
   c What are the symptoms of Foetal Alcohol Syndrome?
   d How is Foetal Alcohol Syndrome diagnosed?
2 'A person can stop drinking at any time. I have no sympathy for an alcoholic.' Do you agree or disagree with this statement? Provide reasons for your answer.
3 Advertising alcohol can be a contributing factor when a young person decides to drink. Advertisers state that they target the adverts to over-18s. Are you aware of any alcohol adverts? What are they and what makes you remember them?
4 'Advertising alcohol should be banned like the advertisements for cigarettes.' Evaluate this statement.

The causes, consequences and impact of smoking on health and well-being

According to Cancer Research UK:

18 per cent of children under 16 have tried smoking and 40 per cent of regular smokers start smoking before they are 16.
(www.cancerresearchuk.org)

Causes of smoking

Again, the majority of young people know the risks associated with smoking and the warning 'Smoking Kills' could not be missed on cigarette packaging. For young people many of the reasons for taking up smoking are similar to those for drinking alcohol, for example, being affected by parents and peer pressure. Other reasons may include:

- rebellion
- to fit in
- they enjoy it
- experimentation
- to look cool
- to appear more mature
- curiosity
- to control weight
- to deal with stress
- media influence.

UNIT 2 PERSONAL DEVELOPMENT

Consequences of smoking

Cigarette smoking harms nearly every organ of the body, causes many diseases and reduces the health of smokers in general.

Source A summarises some of the consequences of smoking.

SOURCE A How tobacco affects your body

Cigarette smoke has more than 4,000 chemicals.
More than sixty of these chemicals cause cancer. When someone smokes a cigarette, the smoke enters the lungs and the chemicals start traveling through the body causing serious damage.

Brain
Nicotine, the drug that makes tobacco addictive, goes to your brain. Nicotine makes you feel good when you are smoking, but it can make you anxious, nervous, moody and depressed afterward.

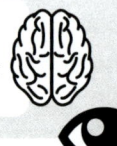

Eyes and Ears
Smoking can cause eye problems and even blindness. Studies show that smoking is also linked to hearing loss.

Skin and Hair
Smoking causes people to get wrinkles and lose hair at a younger age.

Mouth and Teeth
Tobacco makes your teeth yellow and gives you bad breath. It can also cause gum disease and mouth cancer

Throat
Cigarettes, cigars and smokeless tobacco can cause cancer of the throat and larynx (voice box). It can also cause gum disease and mouth cancer

Heart
The nicotine in cigarettes, cigars and smokeless tobacco narrows blood vessels. This forces your heart to work harder and raises blood pressure. Smoking can block arteries, causing heart attacks and strokes (blood clots in the brain).

Muscles and Joints
Smoking keeps oxygen from getting to muscles, making you feel weak. It can also increase the risk of a serious and painful disease called rheumatoid arthritis.

Lungs
The tar in cigarettes increases the risk of lung cancer. Smoking can make you cough. It is also a major cause of bronchitis and emphysema.

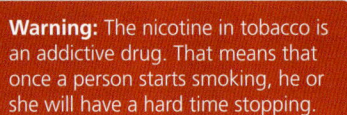

Other Organs
Smoking increases the risk of cancer of the bladder, kidney, pancreas, stomach and reproductive organs.

Warning: The nicotine in tobacco is an addictive drug. That means that once a person starts smoking, he or she will have a hard time stopping.

Associated impacts of smoking

- Work productivity: taking breaks to smoke can slow down productivity. The health effects of smoking could result in increased sick days, causing an employee or student to fall behind in their work and lowering self-esteem.
- Personal hygiene: smoking can result in bad breath and body odour which could result in other people avoiding the smoker. This can result in low self-confidence.
- Social isolation: as a person has to go outside to smoke, smokers can sometimes feel socially isolated at work or school or on nights out when they have to go by themselves to smoke.
- Economic costs: smoking is a huge personal financial strain which can lead to poverty and debt, adding to a person's stress and worry levels. It is also a huge cost to taxpayers. The BBC estimates that smoking-related diseases cost the NHS £5 billion per year.

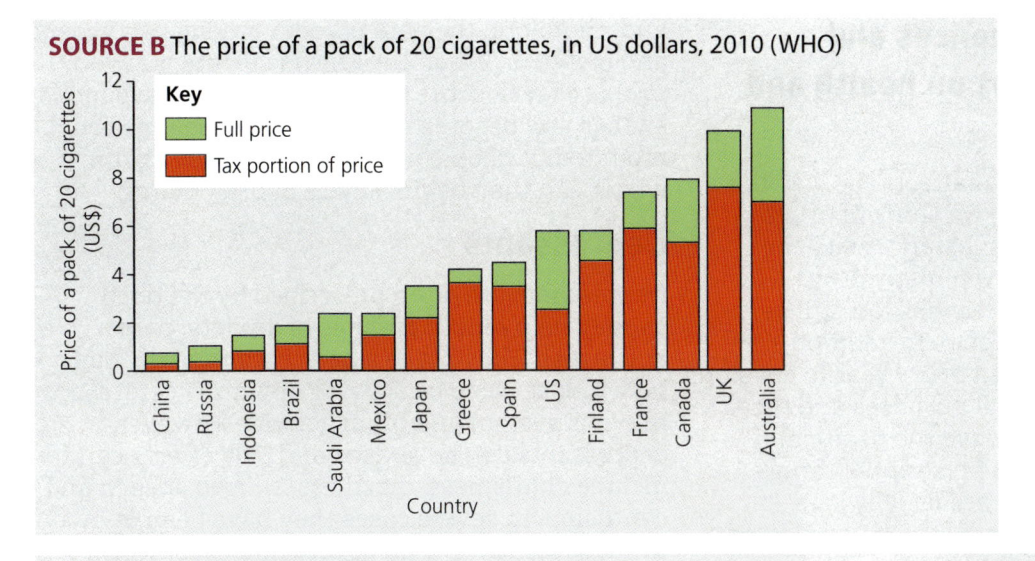

SOURCE B The price of a pack of 20 cigarettes, in US dollars, 2010 (WHO)

Key:
- Full price
- Tax portion of price

Countries (left to right): China, Russia, Indonesia, Brazil, Saudi Arabia, Mexico, Japan, Greece, Spain, US, Finland, France, Canada, UK, Australia

SOURCE C Article from the *Telegraph* 23 June 2016

Ban e-cigarettes in bars and restaurants, leading doctors say

E-cigarettes should be banned from public places like bars and restaurants because of the risks of 'passive vaping', medics say.

Senior doctors said that allowing people to vape openly normalises the habit, and could encourage children to take it up.

But public health officials immediately rejected the idea – saying it could be damaging as it might deter smokers from switching to e-cigarettes.

Speaking at the British Medical Association's annual meeting in Belfast, Dr Iain Kennedy, a consultant in public health from Glasgow, called for a ban, warning that there is no evidence of the long-term safety of the habit: 'It is a myth that there is no such thing as passive vaping.'

He said there was clear evidence that non-vapers living in households with vapers had higher levels of exposure to nicotine.

'There are new potential risks, and we don't yet know the level of those risks,' he said.

'E-cigarettes are probably going to be a very useful tool for helping people quit but we don't want vaping to be seen as a cool activity to take up if they haven't been smoking.'

The doctor suggested the public had been given false reassurance about the safety of e-cigarettes, because their safety was normally compared to cigarettes – 'probably the most harmful manmade product' in existence.

'It is a precautionary principle – until we do the studies and have a better idea of what the risks may or may not be, we should restrict their use in public places,' he said.

The devices were 'undoubtedly safer than cigarettes but that does not mean they are completely 100 per cent safe,' he said.

(www.telegraph.co.uk/news/2016/06/23/ban-e-cigarettes-in-bars-and-restaurants-leading-doctors-say)

Activity — The impacts of smoking

1. Study Source B, which shows the price (and tax charged) on cigarettes globally.
   a. Which country has the cheapest cigarettes?
   b. Which country has the dearest cigarettes?
   c. Which country pays the most tax on cigarettes?
   d. Do you agree with the amount of tax paid on cigarettes in the UK? Give two reasons for your answer.

2. Read Source C and answer the following questions:
   a. Do you agree that e-cigarettes should be banned in public places? Give two reasons for your answer.
   b. Do you think young people could be tempted into smoking e-cigarettes, just because they see someone smoking in a restaurant? Why?
   c. Would you be happy if someone next to you was smoking an e-cigarette in a restaurant? Why?

UNIT 2 PERSONAL DEVELOPMENT

The causes, consequences and impact of using drugs on health and well-being

A drug is any substance that affects the way the body or mind works. When we think of drugs we tend to think of illegal substances such as cannabis or cocaine. However, many drugs are legal in the eyes of the law but can still be dangerous, for example alcohol. In addition, millions of pounds are spent every year to develop drugs to be used for medical purposes and these are then prescribed to improve the health and well-being of others. When prescription drugs are taken as directed, they are usually safe. It requires a trained professional, such as a doctor or nurse, to determine if the benefits of taking the medication outweigh any risks or side effects. But when abused and taken in different amounts or for different purposes than as prescribed, they can affect the brain and body in ways very similar to illegal drugs.

When prescription drugs are abused, they can be addictive and put the person at risk of other harmful health effects, such as overdose (especially when taken along with other drugs or alcohol).

There are three kinds of prescription drugs that are commonly abused:
- Opiates: painkillers, for example codeine.
- Depressants, such as those used to relieve anxiety or help a person sleep, for example Valium.
- Stimulants, such as those used for treating attention deficit hyperactivity disorder (ADHD), for example Ritalin.

Most drugs fall into one of four categories which have different health consequences:

Stimulants

Stimulants speed up the central nervous system and speed up brain activity. They often make you feel more alert, lively, talkative and confident, or euphoric. They postpone the feelings of tiredness and, therefore, they are popular among partygoers and clubbers. When the effects start to wear off, people may become tired and irritable, have mood swings and become restless. These feelings could often tempt people into taking the drug again, which can then begin a cycle of drug taking.

Depressants

Depressants are often prescribed by the doctor as they help reduce feelings of anxiety, panic and stress. They make a person calmer and can help induce sleep by slowing down the central nervous system and brain activity. However, depressants can be abused and side effects can include clumsiness, dizziness, slurred speech and confusion. In severe cases they have been known to cause loss of consciousness and even death.

Hallucinogens

Hallucinogens are substances that affect the senses and alter the drug user's perception. People taking hallucinogenic drugs may see, feel or hear things that in reality are not there and they may have little or no concept of speed or distance. Hallucinations can have an effect on the user's mood; for example, if they have a 'bad trip' it could be terrifying and terrorise their thoughts. Short-term side effects include increased blood pressure, increased heart rate, memory loss and itching. Long-term side effects could include flashbacks, impaired thinking, outbursts of violence and mood swings.

Opiates

Opiates come from the poppy plant. They are very powerful drugs; some can be prescribed by the doctor for pain relief, such as morphine. However, if opiates are abused – for example by using heroin – there can be many side effects. These include feelings of euphoria, dry mouth, vomiting, weak muscles, decreased appetite and thirst, a reduction in heart rate and brain activity and a reduction in breathing rate. Over time, the body can become tolerant of and dependent on the drug and require more to achieve desired results.

Section 1 Personal health and well-being

```
        Legal Drugs  ←——  Drugs  ——→  Illegal drugs
```

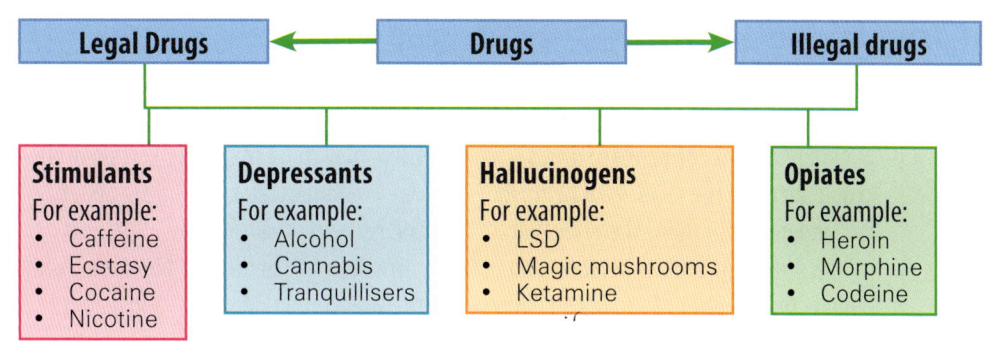

Stimulants	**Depressants**	**Hallucinogens**	**Opiates**
For example:	For example:	For example:	For example:
• Caffeine	• Alcohol	• LSD	• Heroin
• Ecstasy	• Cannabis	• Magic mushrooms	• Morphine
• Cocaine	• Tranquillisers	• Ketamine	• Codeine
• Nicotine			

▲ Four main categories of drugs

Causes of drug experimentation

There are many reasons young people experiment with drugs. These are summarised below:

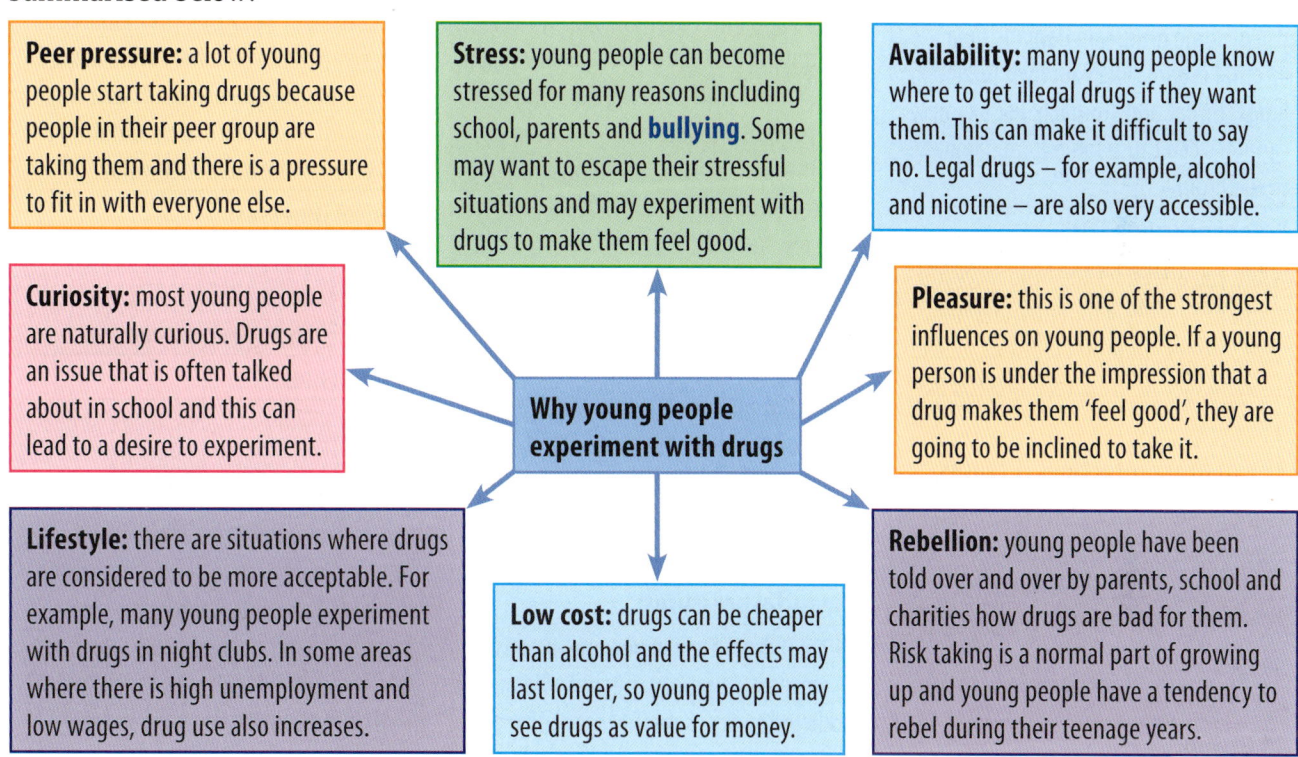

Peer pressure: a lot of young people start taking drugs because people in their peer group are taking them and there is a pressure to fit in with everyone else.

Stress: young people can become stressed for many reasons including school, parents and **bullying**. Some may want to escape their stressful situations and may experiment with drugs to make them feel good.

Availability: many young people know where to get illegal drugs if they want them. This can make it difficult to say no. Legal drugs – for example, alcohol and nicotine – are also very accessible.

Curiosity: most young people are naturally curious. Drugs are an issue that is often talked about in school and this can lead to a desire to experiment.

Why young people experiment with drugs

Pleasure: this is one of the strongest influences on young people. If a young person is under the impression that a drug makes them 'feel good', they are going to be inclined to take it.

Lifestyle: there are situations where drugs are considered to be more acceptable. For example, many young people experiment with drugs in night clubs. In some areas where there is high unemployment and low wages, drug use also increases.

Low cost: drugs can be cheaper than alcohol and the effects may last longer, so young people may see drugs as value for money.

Rebellion: young people have been told over and over by parents, school and charities how drugs are bad for them. Risk taking is a normal part of growing up and young people have a tendency to rebel during their teenage years.

▲ Why young people choose to experiment with drugs

Activity — Reasons for drug taking (SM)

1 Place the reasons why young people experiment with drugs in the diagram above in order of importance, with 1 being the most likely cause. Give three reasons for your answer.

85

Associated impacts of drug taking

Physical injuries:
As drugs impair the mind a person might do things they normally would not. This can increase your chances of getting hurt or having an accident.

Violence:
Some drugs can increase the likelihood of violent behaviour. Drug-induced violence can lead to serious injury to a person and those around them.

Internal damage:
Use of some drugs can damage your internal organs, like your liver, brain, lungs, throat and stomach. For example cannabis can cause long-term damage to the brain.

Pregnancy and STDs:
While you are under the influence, you might be less likely to remember to have safe sex. Unprotected sex can lead to pregnancy or the spread of **STDs** like **HIV/AIDS**.

Risk of other infectious diseases:
Sharing needles from injecting certain types of drugs can put you at major risk of getting diseases like **hepatitis C**, **hepatitis B** and HIV. These diseases are spread through the transmission of body fluids like blood.

Addiction:
There is a chance that a user could become dependent on drugs. This means that they might feel like they cannot operate without drugs in their system. They might also have **withdrawal symptoms** when they stop using the drug. If they use drugs often, their tolerance to the drug might increase, causing them to need to take a greater amount to get the same effects.

Safety:
Being under the influence of drugs could increase the chances of being in a dangerous situation. The effects of some drugs can cause a person to do things they might not usually do. They may also be putting themselves at risk of overdosing. Buying drugs or trying to get the money to buy drugs can also put a person at risk.

School work:
A person might not immediately notice the impact that drug taking is having on their school work, but regular drug use can prevent a person from focusing on their responsibilities, like homework or concentrating in class. Grades will suffer as a result.

Employment:
Drug use can also affect a person's ability to concentrate at work. The side effects of using drugs, like a hangover or a 'coming down' feeling, can reduce a person's ability to focus. Poor performance at work could lead to a person losing their job.

Financial pressures:
Regular drug use can become expensive. In extreme situations, people who are addicted to drugs might try anything, including illegal activities like theft, to secure money to get their next fix.

Homelessness:
Spending money on drugs might not leave much money to cover your living expenses, like rent, food or utility bills. If a person cannot pay these necessary costs, they could lose their home or have it **repossessed**.

Stress:
Users may think that using certain drugs will help them relax and forget about the issues that cause stress. But long-term drug use can have a big impact on the way your brain works, and lead to increased anxiety and stress.

Depression:
Feeling low after using some drugs, including alcohol, is common. Users might feel depressed because of the drug itself, or because of something that happened while they were using it. Sometimes people use drugs as a way to cope with their depression, but drug use can often make them feel worse.

Mental illnesses:
Scientists generally agree that there is a link between drug use and serious mental illnesses like schizophrenia.

Legal issues:
Making, selling or having illegal drugs in your possession is against the law. It is also against the law to give prescription drugs to people who do not have a prescription from a doctor. Punishments for breaking these laws include having to go to court which might result in being sent to jail, having to pay hefty fines, or enter a **rehabilitation** programme.

Relationships:
When drug use becomes a larger part of a person's life, relationships suffer. Conflict and breakdowns in communication can become more common.

Drugs and legal highs

Legal highs or designer drugs are terms often used for 'New' Physcoactive Substances (NPS). While they might be referred to as legal highs they are illegal. They are called 'New' because they began to emerge in the UK around 2008.

Some young people may wrongly think they are safer than other drugs because of their branding and packaging. NPS contain a cocktail of chemical substances which produce similar effects to drugs such as ecstasy, cocaine and cannabis. They are sold as powders, pills, capsules and mixtures for smoking.

Their street names include Spice, China White, Clockwork Orange, Cherry Bomb, Bliss, Mary Jane and Pandora's Box. While, the drug packaging may contain a list of ingredients the user cannot be sure the information is accurate.

The effects

The main effects of NPS can be classified into four main categories:

- 'uppers' stimulants – increase users' energy levels and make them feel euphoric
- 'downers' or sedatives – can make users feel relaxed, sleepy and euphoric
- psychedelics or hallucinogens – alters the user's perceptions of reality. They may experience hallucinations, feel enlightened and detached from the world
- synthetic cannabinoid – has similar effects to natural cannabis but is more potent

The risks

People should consider the risks when making decisions about taking illegal highs.

- Users do not know what is in the product.
- They have not been tested in the way other pharmaceutical products are.
- There is limited research into the risks if using NPS.
- NPS can affect people differently.
- There is uncertainty about the side effects of taking NPS with other substances such as alcohol.
- They all have serious short and long term side effects including dependency on the users physical and mental health and well-being.

Legislation

One of the ways the governments use to deal with the problem of NPS is by passing legislation. In May 2016, the UK Government passed the Psychoactive Substances Act. The Act criminalises the production, distribution, sale and supply of NPS.

Activity — Legal highs

Read the article in Source A and answer the following questions:

1 Use the internet to research:
   - Which groups of people in society are most vulnerable to using illegal highs?
   - The effects and risks of these drugs on users.
   - UK and Northern Ireland statistics on illegal highs
   - The Physcoactive Substance Abuse Act 2016

2 Use the information from your research to create a presentation on NPS or create an information leaflet for students or write a report for your school magazine/news paper.

3. Evaluate the effectiveness of the Physcoactive Substance Abuse Act 2016 in reducing the use of NPS.

UNIT 2 PERSONAL DEVELOPMENT

What are the causes, consequences and impacts on physical and mental health of poor hygiene, stress, unequal work/life balance and low income?

There are many lifestyle factors and personal behaviours that can affect a person's health and well-being. On this page and on page 89, there are four lifestyle factors with their associated causes, consequences and impacts on a person's health and well-being.

	Causes	**Consequences**	**Associated impacts**
Poor hygiene	• Depression • **Dementia** • **Physical disability** • Lack of support at home • Neglected by a parent/carer • Teenage rebellion • Chronic illnesses such as ME which could leave someone too fatigued to wash	• Body odour which could lead to social isolation and loneliness • Bad breath and dental problems leading to low self-confidence and self-esteem • General illnesses due to transportation of germs and infections • Boils due to build-up of skin bacteria, lowering self-confidence • Body lice	• Depression is one of the indirect consequences of poor personal hygiene. It begins from a common feeling of low self-esteem plus low self-worth brought about by poor hygiene. The affected person does not feel good about themselves. • Social problems: when a person ignores the cleanliness and care of the body, they may find themselves isolated by family, friends and society. A repulsive smell from your body, tooth decay or dirty and unhygienic clothing may adversely affect situations like finding a date and making friends. • Employment troubles: due to the above, it may be difficult to find a job or hold on to a current job, resulting in financial worries.
High stress levels	• Being unhappy in a job/school • Having a heavy workload or too much responsibility • Working long hours • Working under dangerous conditions • Having to give speeches in front of colleagues/peers • Facing discrimination or harassment at work/school • The death of a loved one • Divorce • Loss of a job • Increase in financial obligations • Getting married • Moving to a new home • Chronic illness or injury • Emotional problems (depression, anxiety, anger, grief, guilt, low self-esteem) • Taking care of an elderly or sick family member • Traumatic event, such as a natural disaster, theft, rape, or violence against you or a loved one	Short-term • Headache • **Fatigue** • Difficulty sleeping • Difficulty concentrating • Upset stomach • Irritability Long-term • Depression • High blood pressure • Abnormal heartbeat • Hardening of the arteries • Heart disease • Heart attack • Heartburn, ulcers, irritable bowel syndrome • Upset stomach – cramps, constipation, and diarrhoea • Weight gain or loss • Flare-ups of asthma or arthritis • Skin problems such as acne, eczema and psoriasis	• Difficulty concentrating and lack of sleep can decrease performance and productivity at work/school. • Irritability could result in a person snapping at peers and family, causing social isolation. • Increase in consumption of alcohol, cigarettes to cope. See pages 79–82 for the impacts of doing this. • Loss of sense of humour which again can be socially isolating. • Increase of sick days resulting in missing school and lowering grades. • Lower self-esteem and self-worth due to skin problems or weight gain.

Section 1 Personal health and well-being

	Causes	**Consequences**	**Associated impacts**
Poor work/ life balance	• Increased working hours • Increased workload • Poor time management skills • Taking work home to do/finish • Pressure from management	• Exhaustion: when you work long hours on a frequent basis and fail to establish boundaries between your work and home life, you end up suffering from physical and mental exhaustion. • Absence: when you fail to establish boundaries between your work and home life, you end up missing important family events, causing feelings of guilt which can lead to anxiety and mental health problems. • No friendships: by spending all of your time focused on your career, you do not dedicate any time to nurturing and growing your friendships, causing social isolation and related mental health issues. • Stress: see above for health and associated impacts.	• Breakdown of family relationships as work is always a priority. • Workload increase. The more hours a person works at the office and the more consistently it occurs, the more work a person will receive. This will only serve to exacerbate the work/life balance. • Low levels of job satisfaction resulting in stress and depression.
Low income	• No job • Low-paying job • Single-parent family	• Low income could result in a person buying cheaper goods, which are often less healthy. Lack of a balanced diet can result in illnesses and deficiencies. • Low income can lead to stress and depression due to constant financial worries. • Having a low income usually excludes a person from such things as taking out gym memberships or receiving complementary therapies, resulting in illnesses and lower life expectances. • People with low incomes often live in areas that have levels of pollution that cause illness.	• Lower income could result in low-quality housing leading to common illnesses, including respiratory illnesses. • People on low incomes may work long hours to get more money. This leaves less time to visit the doctor if they are ill, which can then lead to more severe illnesses which will involve time off work. • Infant mortality rates tend to be higher in low-income families. Many cannot afford transportation so miss out on necessary health checks after the birth. • Lack of job opportunities due to not being able to afford transport or clothing for interview.

▲ Effects of hygiene, stress, income and work/life balance on physical and mental health

Activity — Work/life balance

1. Suggest five tips for someone with a poor work/life balance because they work too hard.
2. Copy and complete the table below for someone who pays less regard to work and more to life.

Poor work/ life balance with the emphasis being on 'life'	Causes	Consequences	Associated impacts

3. Read the table above and re-classify the consequences and associated impacts into physical and mental health problems. Copy and complete the table to the right.

	Physical health effects	Mental health effects
Poor hygiene	Boils Common illnesses	Loneliness Low self-esteem Low self-confidence
High stress levels		
Poor work/ life balance		
Low income		

89

Developing a healthy mind: how can people deal with the causes and consequences of anxiety, stress and depression?

Part of our health and well-being involves our mental health and in an increasingly pressurised society experiences of anxiety, stress and depression are commonly experienced by young people. How to recognise and deal with these issues is an important step towards developing a healthy mind.

Anxiety

Anxiety is when a person feels uneasy and has worries or fears. It can be accompanied by nervous behaviour such as pacing back and forth. It can be mild (being anxious about an exam) or severe (when people find that the emotion is taking over their lives).

Causes of anxiety

It is difficult to know why some people experience anxiety as a mental health problem and others do not. It has been suggested that some people experience it because of childhood experiences, their personality, effect of drug use or genetics. There are many cited causes of anxiety which include:
- stress at work or school
- financial pressures
- emotional trauma such as the death of a loved one
- experiencing a serious medical illness
- side effect of medication.

Consequences of anxiety

Anxiety can affect a person physically and mentally:
- **Physically:** nausea; tense muscles and headaches; pins and needles; faster breathing; irregular heartbeats; difficulty sleeping; churning in your stomach
- **Mentally:** feeling tense, nervous and on edge; having a sense of dread; feeling your mind is really busy with your thoughts; dwelling on negative experiences; feeling numb; feeling like the world is speeding up or slowing down; feeling restless

Dealing with anxiety

A person who experiences anxiety can attempt to help themselves get through the emotion by:
- talking to someone: this can help alleviate the worries and fears and a trusted person can provide reassurance
- breathing exercises: breathing properly can limit the chances of developing a panic attack and settle a bout of anxiety
- shifting focus: listening to music or doing some exercise can take a person's mind off the emotion and release happy endorphins
- thinking positively: by thinking that things will be okay, that anxiety is causing the feelings and that it will pass, can help to manage anxiety
- keeping a record of events: keeping a diary of bouts of anxiety could help identify triggers which can help manage anxiety
- complementary therapies: massage, reflexology and other therapies can help a person sleep better and reduce the symptoms of anxiety
- joining a support group: a support group can give a person the opportunity to share common experiences and ways of coping with others who are facing similar challenges. It is sometimes comforting for a person to know that they are not alone.

Self-help does not work for everyone. If symptoms continue to deteriorate it is important to seek help from a GP who could then refer someone for talking therapies or Cognitive Behavioural Therapy (CBT), or prescribe medication.

Stress

Stress is the feeling of being under too much emotional or mental pressure. Pressure turns into stress when a person is unable to cope with all the demands put on them. A person's nervous system responds to pressures by releasing a flood of stress hormones, including adrenaline and cortisol. People have different coping abilities and what one person finds stressful, another person could find motivating.

Causes of stress

Many of life's demands can cause stress – for example, exams, financial worries or life changes, such as moving to university.

Consequences of stress

The table below shows common physical consequences of stress:

How a person with stress might feel	How a person with stress might behave	The physical effects of stress
• Irritable • Overburdened • Anxious • Afraid • Racing thoughts • Depressed	• Find it difficult to make decisions • Avoid situations that are troubling • Snap at people • Bite nails • Pick skin • Unable to concentrate	• Shallow breathing • Tired all the time • Grinding teeth at night • Headaches • High blood pressure • Indigestion • Dizziness or feeling faint

▲ Physical consequences of stress

Dealing with stress

Stress is not an illness itself, but it can cause serious illness if it is not addressed. It is therefore important that a young person is aware of ways to deal with stress. A person could:

- identify the triggers and try to avoid or limit these triggers as much as possible
- plan out their time, stick to a schedule or to-do list, and avoid distractions
- address the cause of stress: if it is financial worries, they could seek financial help; if they have too much work to do, they could speak to the teacher or employer about the pressures
- accept the things that cannot be changed: it might not be easy but it will allow a person to focus on things that they might actually be able to do something about
- seek out complementary therapies: massage, reflexology and other therapies can help people to de-stress and remain calm.

If a person is still finding it hard to cope with stress then they should talk to a GP who could refer them for talking treatments, medication or **ecotherapy**.

Depression

Depression has been mentioned several times in this chapter as a consequence of lifestyle factors and the use of drugs and alcohol. But what actually is depression? Depression is a mood disorder characterised by low mood and a wide range of other possible symptoms shown below. This illness can develop quickly or gradually, and can be brought on by life events or changes in body chemistry. Symptoms of depression include:

- sadness and feeling weepy
- numbness, tiredness and a loss of interest in activities once enjoyed
- loss of appetite or eating for comfort
- irritability and aggression
- feeling that you cannot cope
- asking yourself what the point of living is.

UNIT 2 PERSONAL DEVELOPMENT

Causes of depression

There is no single cause of depression. You can develop it for different reasons and it has many different triggers. The diagram below presents some commonly cited causes of depression.

▲ Causes of depression

Consequences of depression

Depression is considered a disease as it has associated physical health effects. These physical symptoms include:

- chronic fatigue
- physical aches and pains that have no apparent source
- increased susceptibility to disease.

Being depressed can feel like a physical disorder because it is so exhausting, and because it can actually hurt. Other effects of depression can include:

- substance use and abuse which could lead to addiction
- social and family withdrawal
- decreased performance at work or school
- self-injury or suicide
- reckless behaviour.

Dealing with depression

- **Stay in touch with family and friends:** a person should not withdraw from life. Socialising can improve the mood of someone who is depressed and means that there will be someone there to listen when the person is feeling particularly low.
- **Be active:** as exercise releases **endorphins**, it can improve a person's mood.
- **Face fears:** someone with depression should not avoid the things they find difficult. By facing up to difficult situations, in time, the situation will become easier to cope with.
- **Avoid alcohol:** alcohol is a depressant and will serve to make the problem worse. Becoming reliant on alcohol can lead to addiction, which again could exacerbate the problem.
- **Eating a healthy diet:** some people do not feel like eating when they are depressed and are at risk of becoming underweight. Others find comfort in food and can put on excess weight. Anti-depressants can also affect appetite. Eating healthily will allow the body to be physically healthy which can promote overall well-being.
- **Have a routine:** when people feel down, they can get into poor sleep patterns, staying up late and sleeping during the day. They should try to get up at their normal time and stick to their routine as much as possible. This will allow social interaction, which can promote emotional well-being.

Seeking help for depression and mental health issues

If a person is feeling depressed and has tried the above strategies but does not feel better, it may be time to visit a GP. The GP may set out treatment plans which could include talking therapies, anti-depressants and self-help. Helplines such as the Samaritans are available for 24-hour confidential, non-judgemental emotional support.

> **Activity** — **Dealing with depression** WO PS
>
> 1 What is meant by talking therapies?
> 2 What is meant by self-help?
> 3 A friend has confided that they have a close family member who they feel might be depressed. In pairs, come up with at least five points that could help the friend deal with the situation at home.
> 4 Search the websites of the following organisations, which provide help with mental health issues. Write brief notes on each one outlining what support they offer:
>   a Rethink   b Mind   c Sane   d Action Mental Health.

Other organisations available to discuss mental health issues are:

- Rethink advice and information line
- the Mind information line
- SANE
- Action Mental Health.

What support is available to help young people overcome addictions and deal with mental health issues?

If a person is suffering from addiction or mental health issues, it is important to know that there is help available. Designated services, charities and trained professionals are all options if a person finds themselves in this situation.

What is addiction?

Addiction is when a person does not have control over doing, taking or using something to the point where it could be harmful. Addiction is most commonly associated with gambling, drugs, alcohol and nicotine, but it is possible to be addicted to just about anything, including work, social media, computer games, **solvents** and shopping.

Addictions can be created when the body becomes dependent on the chemical within a substance and cannot function properly without it, or from the high encountered by gambling, shopping or winning at computer games.

Dealing with addictions

The first step in dealing with an addiction is admitting that there is a problem. Once a person has admitted there is a problem they should take the following steps:

- **Tell friends about their decision to stop the addictive habit.** True friends will respect the decision and provide support.
- **Ask friends or family to be available when they are needed.** An addict might need to call someone in the middle of the night just to talk about their urges. Addicts should not try to handle things on their own; instead they should accept the help offered by family and friends.
- **Accept invitations only to events that where there is no chance of a relapse.** Addicts should avoid situations where others will be engaging in an activity which is considered dangerous for an addict.
- **Have a plan about what to do if in a place of temptation.** Addicts should establish a plan with parents, siblings or other supportive friends and adults to help remove them from the situation.

An addiction may be so severe that a person may need professional help.

Seeking professional help for addiction

Addiction is a treatable condition. Whatever the addiction, there are lots of ways a person can seek help. For example, most pharmacies will offer support services for people who are trying to give up cigarettes and GPs can refer addicts to specialists which could result in admission to a rehabilitation centre. GPs can also put an addict in contact with an organisation that specialises in helping people with addictions.

There are many local dedicated drug and alcohol support teams available across Northern Ireland. These services provide help and support for those who want to tackle their drugs and alcohol misuse.

Activity

Dealing with addictions

1. Using the internet, find a website that can provide help for computer game addictions. What tips does the website provide for addicts?
2. Using the internet, find a website that can provide help for gambling addictions. What tips does the website provide for addicts?
3. Using www.drugsandalcoholni.info/services-near-you, find the nearest:
   a. local drug service
   b. local alcohol service.
4. Search the websites of the following organisations which help people deal with addictions. Write brief notes outlining the support each one provides:
   a. the National Drug Helpline
   b. Drinkline
   c. Talk to FRANK
   d. Alcoholics Anonymous
   e. Narcotics Anonymous
   f. Alcohol Concern.

A full list of local drugs and alcohol addiction services are available at www.drugsandalcoholni.info/services-near-you. In addition to local services, addicts can seek help from national services which include:

- the National Drug Helpline
- Drinkline
- Talk to FRANK
- Alcoholics Anonymous
- Narcotics Anonymous
- Alcohol Concern.

UNIT 2

PERSONAL DEVELOPMENT

Section 2 Emotions and reactions to life experiences

Key content
- Developing a positive concept of self
- Ways young people can manage emotions and reactions to life experiences
- The impact of change on young people's personal development, including: going to college or university; starting a new job; moving in with a partner or getting married; becoming unemployed
- Managing change in positive ways

This section looks at the formation of **self-concept** and how life experiences (such as starting a new school or job) can affect the management of emotions, reactions and personal development. It looks at common types of emotions young people experience when going through changes and how these can be developed and supported in positive ways.

How can a person develop a positive self-concept?

Self-concept is the image a person holds of themselves. It is formed from the knowledge held about themselves, such as the beliefs they have regarding their personality traits, physical characteristics, abilities, values, goals and roles.

Self-concept can be heavily influenced by the opinions and judgements that others make about that person or how that person compares themselves to other people.

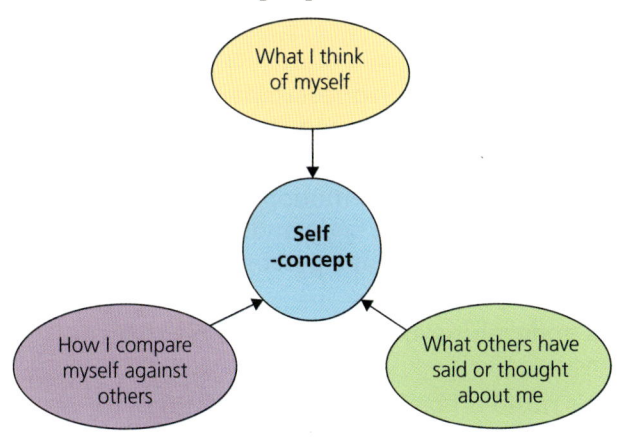

▲ A diagram showing how self-concept is formed

A person can develop a more positive self-concept by:
- getting to know themselves; being aware of their own strengths, weaknesses, talents and potential
- being honest and true to who they are and what they value
- taking responsibility for personal choices and actions
- setting meaningful, achievable and realistic targets that are reviewed regularly for progress
- taking on new challenges
- accepting themselves as a person, being aware that a person can self-improve and develop aspects of themselves.

How can young people manage their emotions and reactions to life experiences?

Emotions are how we feel about things. We all experience both pleasant and unpleasant emotions and reactions to events that take place in our lives. Emotional balance is about getting the balance of pleasant and unpleasant feelings right.

95

When the balance is right, a person will feel happy and get the most out of life.

All too often young people experience unpleasant emotions such as:
- loneliness
- frustration
- sadness.

It is important that when a young person encounters these emotions they are able to manage them so they do not become emotionally unbalanced. Ways of dealing with common emotions are summarised below.

Dealing with loneliness

Loneliness is an unpleasant emotion as a reaction to isolation or lack of companionship. People usually describe feeling lonely for one of two reasons:
- They do not see or talk to anyone very often.
- They are surrounded by people, but they do not feel understood or cared for.

Feelings of loneliness can affect a person's mental and social health so it is important to be aware of the strategies to deal with it before it worsens. A person could:
- form new connections: seeking out social occasions, joining a club or an online forum
- ask their GP if talking treatments are available in their area which could help them to manage the mental health effects of loneliness
- visit online support communities such as Elefriends, a space in which people can open up to others with similar experiences, without fear of judgement.

Dealing with frustrations

Feeling frustrated is being upset or annoyed as a result of being unable to change or achieve something. People can get frustrated for many reasons, for example being let down by other people, life changes or simply sitting in traffic. There are steps that can be taken to avoid feeling frustrated:
- Know and avoid triggers: take a different route to work or school or avoid meeting that person that is always late.
- Breathing exercises: focused breathing can help a person avoid impulsive action or rash words.
- Control expectations of others: we cannot control other people's behaviour, but we can control our reaction to it.
- Think before reacting: check that a response is neither excessive nor insufficient.

Dealing with sadness

Everyone experiences sadness at some point. Sadness sometimes lasts longer than other emotions because we tend to spend more time thinking about it. Strategies to cope with sadness include the following:
- Crying: studies suggest crying and letting the emotion out can release, good feeling, endorphins which can relax the body and allow a person to cope better. It will also show others the pain a person is in and can generate support from others.
- Exercising: exercise releases endorphins and other chemicals that can help fight sadness.
- Distraction: taking someone's mind off being sad can allow them to recover slowly.
- Allowing time: people should allow themselves time to get over sadness.

Section 2 Emotions and reactions to life experiences

- Talking to others: sharing feelings of sadness may make them feel less intense.
- Recognising that if sadness turns into depression then medical help may be needed.

> **Activity** — **Managing emotions** (SM)
>
> Use the internet to help you answer the following questions.
>
> 1 a What is CBT?
>   b When can it be used?
>   c What are the advantages of CBT?
>   d What are the disadvantages of CBT?
>
> 2 a What is ecotherapy?
>   b Give three examples of ecotherapy.
>
> 3 a Watch the video at www.elefriends.org.uk.
>   b Why might someone subscribe to this website?

What impact can change have on a young person's personal development?

Part of self-concept is how we view ourselves to be able to manage and react to emotions. There are many life events that will challenge us in terms of our ability to manage and react to emotions, but it is dealing with these and moving on that will allow us to develop personally.

Below are a list of common life experiences and the associated reactions and emotions encountered by such life changes.

Life change	Typical reactions	Commonly encountered emotions
Starting a new school	<ul><li>May refuse to go</li><li>Be tearful</li><li>Make excuses not to go, i.e. be sick</li><li>Find it difficult to sleep</li><li>Feelings of nausea</li><li>May be nervous</li></ul>	<ul><li>Anxiety</li><li>Loneliness</li><li>Stress</li><li>Fear</li><li>Sadness</li><li>Excitement</li></ul>
Going to university	<ul><li>May be nervous</li><li>May contemplate not going</li><li>May suggest alternatives to going in the hope that they find agreement among peers or family</li><li>Find it difficult to sleep</li><li>Feelings of nausea</li></ul>	<ul><li>Anxiety</li><li>Loneliness</li><li>Stress</li><li>Fear</li><li>Excitement</li><li>Anticipation</li></ul>
Starting a new job	<ul><li>May withdraw until becoming comfortable with surroundings</li><li>May be nervous, become fidgety</li><li>Approach all new tasks with caution and may be slow at doing things first time around</li><li>Find it difficult to sleep</li><li>Feelings of nausea</li></ul>	<ul><li>Anxiety</li><li>Stress</li><li>Fear</li><li>Excitement</li><li>Anticipation</li><li>Happiness</li></ul>
Emigrating to another country	<ul><li>May feel isolated</li><li>Could feel frustrated at the differences in language/culture</li><li>Miss family and friends at home</li><li>Contact home a lot in the beginning</li><li>Get nervous over small but new tasks in the country, for example shopping</li><li>Initially be excited by changes</li></ul>	<ul><li>Loneliness</li><li>Frustration</li><li>Sadness</li><li>Excitement</li></ul>
Getting married/ Moving in with a partner	<ul><li>May initially cause arguments as a person will be getting used to another person's routines</li><li>Initially be nervous as a person is experiencing a new environment with another person in it</li><li>Experience contentment as a person is now sharing their life with another</li></ul>	<ul><li>Frustration</li><li>Anxiety</li><li>Happiness</li><li>Excitement</li></ul>

▲ Reactions and emotions associated with life changes

UNIT 2 PERSONAL DEVELOPMENT

Unfortunately there are changes that occur in life that are unplanned for. When this occurs, it could severely affect how a person manages change. Below are life events which are usually unplanned.

Unemployment

A person who has worked for a long time and suddenly becomes unemployed may question their self-worth. They could feel resentment towards their employer and become frustrated at the situation they have found themselves in. Their self-esteem could be affected, particularly if unemployment came as a result of a redundancy or if they have suffered a series of rejections from posts they have applied for. If the person was to sit around the house they could develop emotional health issues such as depression.

Developing a serious illness or having a family member diagnosed with a serious illness

When this occurs a person could question why this has happened to them. Their religious beliefs could be affected; they could turn away from their religion in bewilderment or turn towards it seeking solace. Illness can result in the person that is sick being a burden on family members and this could cause them to feel angry and stressed at the situation they have found themselves in. Similarly, family members of a sick person could feel under a burden, resulting in stress and frustration.

Bereavement

Dealing with bereavement is very difficult. A person might enter a state of shock and disbelief. They may experience feelings of guilt over things not said or done with a loved one before their passing. Anger and frustration at the huge loss could result in a person lashing out at those closest to them. This could all result in a sense of loneliness and emptiness.

Learning how to manage emotions and reactions to a range of problems and being able to deal with these in a mature fashion will inevitably enable a person to develop personally and improve their self-image and self-concept.

Activity — Dealing with life changes

1 Copy and complete the table below, explaining how a person could deal with the emotions associated with each life-changing event examined above. Choose two emotions from above for each life event.

Life event	Emotions		Strategy to deal with the emotion	
Starting a new school	Emotion 1:	Emotion 2:	Strategy 1:	Strategy 2:
Going to university	Emotion 1:	Emotion 2:	Strategy 1:	Strategy 2:
Starting a new job	Emotion 1:	Emotion 2:	Strategy 1:	Strategy 2:
Emigrating to another country	Emotion 1:	Emotion 2:	Strategy 1:	Strategy 2:
Getting married/Moving in with a partner	Emotion 1:	Emotion 2:	Strategy 1:	Strategy 2:
Developing a serious illness	Emotion 1:	Emotion 2:	Strategy 1:	Strategy 2:
Having a family member diagnosed with a serious illness	Emotion 1:	Emotion 2:	Strategy 1:	Strategy 2:
Bereavement	Emotion 1:	Emotion 2:	Strategy 1:	Strategy 2:
Unemployment	Emotion 1:	Emotion 2:	Strategy 1:	Strategy 2:

2 Evaluate the impact of a young person going to university.

How can changes be managed in positive ways?

As outlined in the table on the previous page, life is full of change. How a person views change can influence how they deal with it. For example, if a person views change to be a good thing, they will be more receptive to embracing change. If they view it as being a bad thing, it is more likely to cause stress. If the change is something that has been unplanned and was not a choice, taking away the person's control of the situation can cause frustration, anger and resentment (for example, being diagnosed with a serious illness).

Dealing with change as it occurs is important so that a person can come to terms with it and move on, limiting the chances of becoming unwell in the process. Strategies a person could adopt to help with managing change include the following:

- Talking to friends and family about feelings: it can be comforting to talk to someone who is going through a similar change. Sharing and discussing these feelings can help a person work through change.
- Finding out as much as possible about the change and impacts it could have. This could relieve stress of the unknown.
- Seeking professional support: if change is causing emotional health problems such as anxiety or stress, professional help could be sought. A GP could refer a person to talking therapies or prescribe medication.
- Considering practical ways to deal with change: distraction techniques such as exercising or listening to music can help a person relax. Complementary therapies could also assist with relaxation and acceptance of change.

UNIT 2 — PERSONAL DEVELOPMENT

Section 3 Relationships and sexuality

Key content
- The positive factors which contribute to healthy family, peer-group and sexual relationships
- The different types of sexual identity and the impact these can have on an individual and their relationship with others
- The physical and emotional effects that unhealthy relationships may have on individuals
- Types of support available for people in unhealthy relationships

This section defines what a healthy relationship is and identifies the positive factors that contribute to it. It looks at unhealthy relationships and the effect they can have on the health and well-being of those involved, and outlines where people in negative relationships can get help. The section concludes by investigating what is meant by sexual identity and how sexual orientation and gender can impact an individual and their relationships with others.

What are the positive factors which contribute to healthy family, peer-group and sexual relationships?

A relationship is a connection a person has to another person. Throughout our lifetime we will form, maintain and break relationships with many people including friends, family, partners, classmates, colleagues and members of our local communities. Relationships can be fleeting, lasting only a short time, but some can last a lifetime. This section looks at what positive factors can contribute to the development and maintenance of common relationships young people have, for example, family relationships, peer relationships and sexual relationships.

Families

Family relationships can include the relationships we have with our parents and our brothers and sisters but also our extended families such as grandparents, aunts, uncles and cousins.

In general, family relationships are built on unconditional love where parents, siblings, etc. love you for who you are and stand by you through good times and bad. In turn, we love, respect and trust them. Sometimes, however, the relationships we have with family members can be taken for granted and frequently they can become strained, especially as we grow up.

Friendship

Throughout life people establish friendships. The term 'friendship' is used to define the mutual trust, co-operation and support between two people. Friendships can range from short-term casual relationships or acquaintances, to long-term friendships lasting a lifetime. Friendships tend to be made with others with similar interests or jobs, from the same class or the same local community.

Some types of friendship relationships include:
- **close friend/best friend:** someone you trust explicitly and share common goals with
- **companion:** someone who is in your wider network of friends, whom you do not consider a close friend

- **acquaintance:** someone you know but do not spend much time with
- **e-pal/pen pal:** someone with whom you correspond via social networking sites or email/letters.

Sexual relationships

As young people mature they begin to become more interested in the opposite sex and embark on romantic or sexual relationships. Developing and exploring romantic relationships often begins during teenage years when two people form a bond based on attraction. This bond can be used as a basis for developing feelings of love and the intimacy required for a longer-lasting commitment such as a sexual relationship or marriage.

Positive factors affecting relationships

There are several factors that can make a relationship stronger and last longer:

- **Trust:** trust is vital in a relationship. Building up trust can be difficult, particularly if one person has been hurt before. If you trust someone you can tell them everything and depend on them. Without trust one or both partners in a relationship can feel insecure.
- **Mutual respect:** this means that each person values the other person for who they are and understands that the other person has boundaries which should not be challenged.
- **Honesty:** honesty is an essential part of building trust within a relationship. If one person withholds information from the other for any reason then this can weaken the relationship. Concealing information can lead to feelings of guilt and betrayal if discovered.
- **Communication:** communication – verbal or non-verbal – is important for expressing opinions, values, beliefs, ideas, feelings and thoughts and is a two-way process.
- **Degree of independence:** people need to grow and develop individually, and the space and time to do this should be built into every relationship.
- **Compromise:** you need to have give-and-take in a relationship. It is important that all decisions in a relationship are made together and that compromises – decisions where you 'meet in the middle' – are made.
- **Tolerance:** everyone has bad habits and no one is perfect. Being tolerant of someone means putting up with things that annoy you.
- **Willingness to accept responsibility:** it is the responsibility of both people in a relationship to ensure that everything that happens will not be regretted in the future. It is important to not play the 'blame game' and hold other people responsible if something goes wrong.
- **Commitment:** being committed is when two people make a pledge to stay together through good times and bad times and do not give up easily. If the two people involved are committed then the relationship will be more stable and more likely to last.

Activity — Factors affecting relationships

1. Look at the factors affecting relationships and try to identify the *three* most important factors that you think every relationship should have. Explain your answer.
2. 'It is important that a child has two parents who have a good relationship.' Do you agree or disagree with this statement? Identify and explain *three* reasons for your answer.
3. Analyse the effects of a lack of trust in a relationship.
4. Describe one way in which mutual respect can help to maintain a healthy relationship.

What different types of sexual identity are there and what impacts can they have on an individual and their relationship with others?

Sexual identity is a self-concept which consists of an individual's sexual orientation and what gender they consider themselves to be. It is a label that people adopt to signify to others who they are as a sexual being. In order for a person to identify fully their sexual identity, a person usually identifies their gender.

Gender identity

Gender is defined at birth (male/female) but gender identity is what an individual perceives their gender to be and what they call themselves. This can be different from the gender they are born into. Transgender is a term used to describe a person who identifies with a gender that is different from the one they were assigned at birth. A person could also identify themselves as being genderless.

A person's gender identity is usually expressed through behaviour, clothing, haircut and voice and may not conform to socially defined behaviours associated with being male or female. If a person struggles with identifying their gender they could be diagnosed with gender dysphoria. This is when a person suffers significant distress as their birth gender is not the one which they now identify with.

Sexual orientation

In addition to identifying gender, a person usually identifies their sexual orientation when considering their sexual identity. Sexual orientation is the term used to describe what gender a person is attracted to. These attractions can be summarised under the following headings:

- **Heterosexuality:** an attraction or engagement of sexual behaviour between people of the opposite sex or gender.
- **Homosexuality:** an attraction or engagement of sexual behaviour between people of the same sex or gender. Men who are romantically or sexually attracted to other men are called gay. Women who are romantically or sexually attracted to other women can be called gay as well, but are usually called lesbians.
- **Bisexuality:** an attraction to or engagement of sexual behaviours towards both men and women.
- **Asexuality:** when a person lacks sexual attraction to others.

Reactions to differences in gender orientation

Thankfully, people of all genders and sexual orientations are protected by law and many people live a fulfilling life because they are happy and true to themselves. However, a minority of people in society find it difficult to accept people that are different from them and this can lead to the following:

- Homophobia: this encompasses a range of negative attitudes and feelings toward homosexuals or people who are identified or perceived as being bisexual or transgender.
- Hate crime: this is when a person is targeted because they belong to a certain group who are being victimised.
- Discrimination: whereby a person is treated differently, in this case because of their gender or sexual orientation.
- Bigotry: whereby a person faces intolerance from another person; in this case it would be based on their gender or sexual orientation.
- Bullying because of perceived differences.
- Rejection by family and friends who cannot accept differences.
- Judgement: particularly from those who believe that homosexuality and gender changes are against their religion.

The impact of sexual orientation or gender identity on a person

Being subjected to the negative reactions to differences in sexual orientation outlined above could impact on a person's health and well-being, particularly if these take place regularly. Effects could include the following:

- **Physical effects:** a person could become injured as a result of a hate crime or bullying. They could lose sleep as they fear for their safety and become run down and unwell.
- **Emotional effects:** stress, post-traumatic stress, depression, feelings of anxiety and fear could accumulate as a result of this treatment.

- **Social effects:** a person could isolate themselves in case an issue arises or could be socially isolated by others who would be worried that they could face the same treatment.

The impact of sexual orientation or gender identity on a person's relationship with others

Most people will go through life having no issues with others as a result of their sexual orientation or gender identity. However, a minority of people could turn their back on someone they perceive as being different and will not form friendships or relationships with them. This includes family members. Reasons for this could include:
- lack of understanding
- religious beliefs
- fear of social stigma – that they could be considered as having the same orientation or gender identity as the friend/family member
- family beliefs and how they were brought up.

SOURCE A Article from the *Belfast Telegraph* website, 16 October 2016

Homophobic hate victim James Hall speaks out after attack in Belfast

A young gay man has spoken out after being a victim of a homophobic hate crime after a night out in Belfast. James Hall (24) claims he was attacked by a man in an unprovoked incident after he responded to him when he was called an offensive homophobic name in the early hours of Sunday morning.

He says that he was standing at a bar in Little Donegall Street area when two men walked past him and began to call him names. Mr Hall told the *Belfast Telegraph*: 'Granted because I was drunk, I said to them, "What's your problem?" But just because I said that, one of them came up and literally just started to hit me. Why?'

He says he was beaten about the face and has bruises and cuts around his eyes.

'This just has to stop,' added Mr Hall. 'I mean, it's 2016 and this is still happening. It's disgusting. Not just to me because I'm gay but all hate crime. This needs to be addressed.' Earlier, Mr Hall had been socialising with friends in the Boom Box nightclub where he met the *Hollyoaks* star and Blue star Duncan James who was making a personal appearance.

He reported the attack to the police and says he will seek medical help today. Police have confirmed that they are treating the attack as a hate crime.

Inspector Antony Frazer said: 'We are appealing for information following the report of an assault on a man in the Little Donegall Street area of Belfast at approximately 3.00am this morning, Sunday, 16 October.'

(www.belfasttelegraph.co.uk/news/northern-ireland/homophobic-hate-victim-james-hall-speaks-out-after-attack-in-belfast-35134430.html)

Activity — Homophobic violence

Read Source A and answer the following questions:
1. What does the term 'unprovoked' mean?
2. What is meant by the word 'homophobic'?
3. What is mean by a 'hate crime'?
4. Using the local and global citizenship section of this book (see pages 7–64) and/or the internet, list the laws that are in existence to protect people from discrimination based on gender assignment or sexual orientation.

What are the physical and emotional effects that unhealthy relationships may have on individuals?

An unhealthy relationship is one which brings more stress into a person's life than happiness. In an unhealthy relationship tensions are usually high, arguments occur and a person may not feel comfortable around the other person any more. The effects of this unhealthy relationship can impact other areas of the person's life, for example, in lack of concentration at work or school.

Signs of an unhealthy relationship include:

- pressure to change for the other person
- worry about disagreeing with the other person
- feeling pressure to stop activities previously enjoyed
- always having to justify your actions, for example where you go or who you see
- a lack of privacy; always having to share everything
- arguments that are not settled fairly
- shouting or violence
- manipulation
- controlling behaviour, for example controlling how a person should dress
- a lack of time spent with each other
- constant criticising.

Having one or two of these characteristics does not necessarily mean that the relationship is doomed, but being aware and recognising some of them within a relationship could allow a couple to improve upon them, which will ultimately benefit the relationship.

However, if a relationship contains many of these characteristics it may affect a person's physical and emotional health and, when this occurs, it might be in the best interest of the people involved to end the relationship. The table to the right outlines how an unhealthy relationship could affect a person's well-being:

Effects of unhealthy relationships
Physical effects
• If the relationship is violent, a person may experience bruises, fractures or burns
• A lack of sleep through worry or fear could affect a person's immunity
• Studies suggest that people in a negative relationship are more likely to suffer a cardiac event
• Those in an unhealthy relationship are more likely to suffer from high blood pressure
• Substance abuse is also a potential risk for people in unhealthy relationships
Emotional effects
• A person could question their self-worth
• Reduced self-esteem
• Reduced self-confidence, which could lead to avoidance of social situations
• Feelings of fear and anxiety
• A person who has received a physical injury could isolate themselves from others
• Stress
• Depression
• Post-traumatic stress
• Self-harm
• Suicidal thoughts

▲ The physical and emotional effects of unhealthy relationships

What support is available for people in unhealthy relationships?

The following strategies could be used in order to improve a relationship:

- Talk things through with the other person and try to come up with an agreed way forward.
- Spend more time together.
- Use talking therapies, for example a marriage guidance counsellor or an adviser at a local church.
- Contact Relate (www.relate.org.uk/relationship-help). Relate offers counselling services for every type of relationship.
- Contact Accord NI (www.accord-ni.co.uk). Accord NI assists with marriage guidance.
- Contact Marriage Care (www.marriagecare.org.uk). Marriage Care assists with marital issues and breakdowns.

Section 3 Relationships and sexuality

If these strategies do not work a person may want to:
- contact a solicitor to determine their legal rights
- contact the Citizens Advice Bureau for free help on entitlements
- contact National Family Mediation (www.nfm.org.uk), which can help couples make joint decisions
- contact Divorce Aid (www.divorceaid.co.uk) for assistance with divorce arrangements
- contact It's Finished (www.itsfinished.com) for support on dealing with a break-up.

If the relationship has become violent a person should:
- contact the police on 101 or 999 for emergencies
- seek temporary accommodation or stay with friends/relatives
- seek help from the National Domestic Violence Helpline, Refuge, Women's Aid and Rights of Women (if the victim is a woman)
- seek help from Men's Advice Line, ManKind Initiative, Survivors UK, Everyman Project, M-Power (if the victim is a man).

Activity — Seeking help with relationships

1 Copy and complete the table below which details the support available from each of the organisations listed in this topic.

	Telephone number	Website	Summary of services offered
Relate			
Accord			
Marriage Care			
National Family Mediation			
Divorce Aid			
It's Finished			
National Domestic Violence Helpline			
Refuge			
Women's Aid			
Rights of Women			
Men's Advice Line			
ManKind Initiative			
Survivors UK			
Everyman Project			
M-Power			

2 Explain the possible benefits of a relationship ending in divorce.
3 Evaluate the impact of a couple separating.

PERSONAL DEVELOPMENT

Section 4 Personal safety and well-being

UNIT 2

Key content
- Causes and consequences of risk-taking behaviour
- Assessing and managing risk in real-life contexts
- The benefits and misuse of social media
- Different forms of abuse: physical, emotional, sexual and neglect
- Personal and social strategies to deal with: abuse; sexual exploitation, including sexual assault, rape, prostitution, female genital mutilation; and trafficking
- Personal and social strategies to deal with bullying (including cyberbullying and homophobic bullying)
- The physical and emotional effects of abuse on a young person's personal development, health and well-being

This section looks at what risk-taking behaviour is and the causes and consequences of it. It summarises the different forms of abuse that a young person could encounter and ways to deal with it. This section investigates the physical, emotional and social effects of abuse on a young person and outlines ways of dealing with various types of bullying.

What are the causes and consequences of risk-taking behaviour?

Risk-taking behaviour is when a person takes on a challenge that may or may not have a desirable outcome. It is possible to take calculated risks – for example, an entrepreneur taking on a new business venture. A certain degree of risk taking is also essential for personal development. Taking risks allows a young person to test their limits, learn new skills and assume greater responsibility for their life.

However, more often than not, risk taking is used to describe uncalculated and unhealthy behaviour. Some risk-taking behaviours can have long-term consequences on health, for example taking drugs, and some can even put others' lives in danger. Examples of common, unhealthy risk-taking behaviours are shown on the right:

▲ Common risk-taking behaviours

106

Causes of risk-taking behaviours

Despite being aware of the dangers of risk-taking behaviour, sometimes young people engage in this behaviour regardless.

Boredom: boredom may tempt a young person into doing something they deem to be exciting. They may partake in activities that seem fun initially, but could be risky. For example, pier jumping.

Peer pressure: the main source of inspiration for young adults to take risks is peer pressure and a desire to impress those within the same peer group. Young people aspire to be unique but also have a strong need to be accepted. This need can result in adopting the values and beliefs of a peer group and taking part in activities that would normally be considered immoral or risky.

Rebelling against parents: it can be argued that acting out against parents is a natural part of growing up. Our parents are possibly the biggest influence on our early development and control most of what we do. If this controlling is seen as negative and restrictive it can lead to young people acting out or taking a risk to prove a point or gain attention.

Being under the influence of alcohol or drugs: being under the influence of substances such as alcohol and drugs can alter brain activity and cloud judgement. Not being able to think clearly and rationally can make people more open to suggestion and less likely to consider the consequences of their actions.

The media: what we read in newspapers, hear on the radio or see on TV can lead to us taking risks, especially if it is perceived that they are low risks and will be fun. For example, we often hear of celebrities with drug problems in the media, which may influence young people to try drugs also.

School: school is designed and structured to be a place of learning and development for all but sometimes can be seen as restricting, tedious, repetitive and boring to some pupils. It is often difficult to express individuality at school so pupils may act out and rebel which can lead to suspension or expulsion.

Curiosity: young people like to experience new things and this could lead to them indulging their curiosities about alcohol and drugs.

▲ Why do young people take risks?

Consequences of risk-taking behaviour

Engaging in risk-taking behaviour can have negative effects on a young person. Risk-taking behaviour could lead to:
- ▶ injury or harm to the young person
- ▶ injury or harm to others
- ▶ criminal charges
- ▶ negative effects on a young person's relationships with others
- ▶ feelings of regret.

Assessing and managing risks in real-life contexts

As a young person grows up they tend to become increasingly independent of their parents. A maturing young person will often find that they have more time to spend with their friends, have relaxed curfews and could find that parents check up on them less. With this independence comes responsibility. A young person has the responsibility to behave in a way that would not put their (or others') health or life at risk.

Any of the risk-taking behaviours outlined on page 106 could seem tempting to some young people at a particular time in their life, but it is the responsibility of the young person to assess and manage the risks presented to them. As a child, parents or guardians would have done this for you – if you were playing with a dangerous object, it would have been taken away.

UNIT 2 PERSONAL DEVELOPMENT

As a young adult, this assessment and management of risks becomes a personal responsibility. In other words, a young adult has the responsibility to consider the risks and weigh them up against the perceived benefits to make a responsible decision.

The diagram below summarises the thought process a young person should go through before taking a risk.

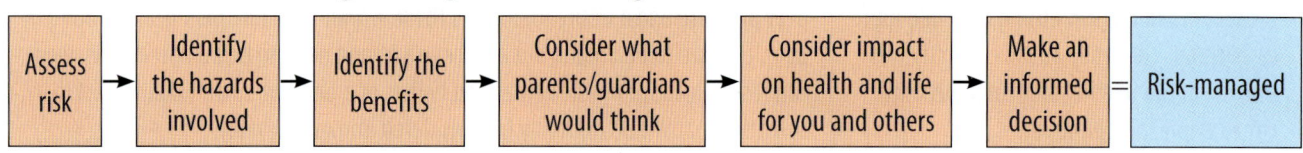

Assess risk → Identify the hazards involved → Identify the benefits → Consider what parents/guardians would think → Consider impact on health and life for you and others → Make an informed decision = Risk-managed

▲ How to make a risk-managed decision

Activity — Risk-taking behaviours

1. Part of assessing and managing risk in real-life situations involves considering the consequences of risky behaviour. Copy and complete the table below, which explains the causes of risk-taking behaviours and their consequences, with possible examples of the risk-taking behaviours given on page 106. The row on dangerous driving has been completed for you as an example.

Risk-taking behaviour	Causes	Possible consequences	Explanation
Dangerous driving	Curiosity Boredom To impress peers Attention seeking Influenced by drugs Adrenalin rush	Injury or harm to the young person Injury or harm to others Negatively affecting a young person's relationships with others Experiences of regret Criminal charges	Dangerous driving could lead to a crash which could injure or kill the people in the car or bystanders. Family or friends could turn their back on the young person, resulting in the breakdown of relationships. If injury or death occurs the young person will have to live with this for the rest of their life and may experience feelings of regret. The young person could be charged and then have a criminal record which could involve time in a young offenders' institution.
Unprotected sex			
Deliberate self-harm			
Severe or excessive dieting			
Compulsive over-eating			
Anti-social behaviour			

2. Explain one way a young person could avoid engaging in anti-social behaviour.
3. Analyse the effects of excessive dieting on a young person.
4. Suggest and justify the reasons a young person may use an extreme diet.

What are the benefits and misuse of social media?

Social media is a collection of websites and applications that enable users to create and share content or to participate in social networking. There are many commonly used social networking sites which include Facebook and Twitter, but new social networks pop up daily and are forever evolving.

Benefits of social media

Social media platforms can help individuals make new friends or build business connections. These connections could help a person find a new job, promote or advertise a business venture, find a romance, access news in real time, share photographs, receive support from like-minded individuals and share political beliefs. With 35 million people in the UK using social media platforms there is no doubt that people find it a useful tool, with many benefits. Unfortunately, social media can also be abused and used in ways that it was not initially designed for.

Misuse of social media

There is evidence to suggest that social media has been misused in the following ways:

- **Cyberbullying:** individuals target someone online and bully them by posting comments, sending messages or uploading photos that are malicious.
- **Sexual exploitation:** children and young people need to be aware of the risk of sexual exploitation when using social media. People on line may not be who they claim. There is a risk of meeting sexual predators. These people use social media to meet children and young people and may manipulate them to perform sexual acts.
- **Identity theft:** someone uses a name and previously uploaded photos that are not their own to create a fake profile/account. This can become very problematic for the person whose identity has been stolen, particularly if views and opinions are posted that are very different from their own. Furthermore, people often use fake accounts if they have malicious intentions, for example if they plan to be a sexual predator.
- **Addiction:** people have reported that they are now addicted to social networking and it consumes much of their time. This can lead to a deterioration of social skills and real-life friendships. School work can also suffer as a result of too much time being spent online.
- **Lack of privacy:** any information posted online creates a 'digital footprint' which cannot be easily erased. Many sites have privacy settings but these are sometimes overlooked. This can affect employment prospects or leave a person vulnerable to identity theft.

What forms of abuse can people experience?

Abuse is defined as any action that intentionally harms or injures another person. There are many different types of abuse but the four that this topic addresses are physical abuse, emotional abuse, sexual abuse and neglect.

Physical abuse

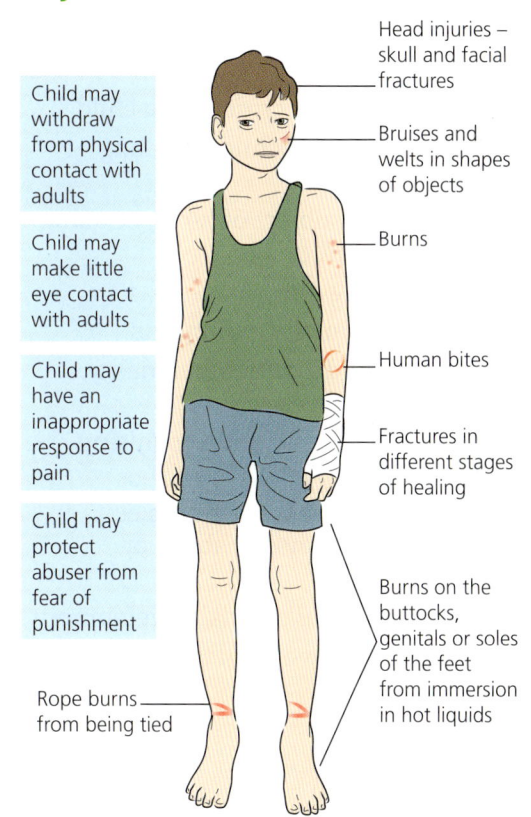

▲ Signs of physical child abuse

Over 9,000 children and young people contacted Childline about physical abuse last year.
(Bentley, H. *et al.*, 2016, How Safe Are our Children?)

Physical abuse is deliberately hurting a child or young person, causing injuries such as bruises, broken bones, burns or cuts. Physical abuse is not accidental. Children who are physically abused suffer violence such as being hit, kicked, poisoned, burned, slapped or having objects thrown at them. Less well-known forms of physical abuse include shaking or hitting babies, which can cause non-accidental head injuries, or when parents or guardians make up an illness in their child and then give them medicine they do not need, making them unwell. This is known as fabricated or induced illness.

Physical abuse causes serious, often long-lasting, harm and in severe cases death.

Emotional abuse

Emotional abuse is the ongoing emotional maltreatment or emotional neglect of a child. (www.nspcc.org.uk)

Emotional abuse is sometimes referred to as psychological abuse and can seriously damage a child's emotional health and personal development. According to the NSPCC emotional abuse includes:

- humiliating or constantly criticising a child
- threatening, shouting at a child or calling them names
- making the child the subject of jokes, or using sarcasm to hurt a child
- blaming, scapegoating
- making a child perform degrading acts
- not recognising a child's own individuality, trying to control their lives
- pushing a child too hard or not recognising their limitations
- exposing a child to distressing events or interactions, such as domestic abuse or drug taking
- failing to promote a child's social development
- not allowing them to have friends
- persistently ignoring them
- being absent
- manipulating a child
- never saying anything kind, expressing positive feelings or congratulating a child on successes
- never showing any emotions in interactions with a child, also known as emotional neglect.

Emotional abuse can sometimes be difficult to spot. However, young people may:

- use language, act in a way or know about things that you would not expect at their age
- struggle to control strong emotions or have extreme outbursts
- seem isolated from their parents
- lack social skills or have few, if any, friends.

▲ Illustration of emotional abuse

Sexual abuse

One in twenty children have been sexually abused in the UK (Radford, L. et al., 2011, Child Abuse and Neglect in the UK Today). Sexual abuse is when a child is persuaded or forced to take part in sexual activity. A child might not understand or be aware that what is happening to them is abuse and they may not even know that it is wrong. There are two different types of child sexual abuse. These are called contact abuse and non-contact abuse:

- Contact abuse involves touching activities where an abuser makes physical contact with a child, including penetration.
- Non-contact abuse involves non-touching activities, such as grooming, exploitation, persuading children to perform sexual acts over the internet and flashing.

Young people who are sexually abused may:

- stay away from certain people, for example those who have sexually abused them
- show sexual behaviour that is inappropriate for their age, for example become sexually active at a young age
- have physical symptoms, for example Sexually Transmitted Infections (STIs).

Neglect

Neglect is the most common form of child abuse and is the ongoing failure to meet a child's basic needs. A child may be left hungry or dirty, without adequate clothing, shelter, supervision, medical or health care. They might not get the attention and care they need from their parents. A neglected child may also suffer from other types of abuse

Section 4 Personal safety and well-being

and neglect can result in long-term damage or even death. The NSPCC highlight four main types of neglect:

- **Physical neglect:** failing to provide for a child's basic needs such as food, clothing or shelter. Failing to supervise a child adequately, or provide for their safety.
- **Educational neglect:** failing to ensure a child receives an education.
- **Emotional neglect:** failing to meet a child's needs for nurture and stimulation, perhaps by ignoring, humiliating, intimidating or isolating them. It is often the most difficult to prove.
- **Medical neglect:** failing to provide appropriate health care, including dental care, and refusal of care or ignoring medical recommendations.

Dealing with abuse

If you are gravely concerned about the welfare of a child or young person you can ring the police directly on 101 or contact the children's social care team at your local council. If you are worried about a child, even if you are unsure, you can phone the NSPCC helpline on 0808 800 5000 to report or get advice about any concerns.

If you feel that you would like help with any of the issues mentioned in this section please speak to someone you trust, for example a teacher, or phone Childline (0800 1111) or call or email the NSPCC (help@nspcc.org.uk/0808 800 5000).

Activity

Child abuse in Northern Ireland

Read Source A and answer the following questions:
1 Why do you think people in Northern Ireland are 'more aware of the tell-tale signs of abuse'?
2 Peter Wanless suggests that 'It's a big decision to involve health and social care trusts.' Why might it be difficult for some people to report a concern they have regarding child abuse?

SOURCE A Article from the *Belfast Live* website, 13 October 2016

NSPCC helpline flooded by abuse and neglect calls in past year

People in Northern Ireland have become more aware of the tell-tale signs of child abuse, an NSPCC chief said yesterday. Peter Wanless was speaking out as it was revealed suspected cases recorded by a phone helpline and passed to police and government agencies have soared by 35 per cent. The charity has seen a surge in contacts it refers to external bodies 'such as health and social care agencies and the PSNI'.

Figures from its 24-hour Helpline which takes calls from across the UK showed 547 from Northern Ireland were passed on in 2015/16 – more than 10 per week – compared with 405 in 2012/13.

Across the UK, 33,333 contacts were passed on in 2015/16 – nearly 100 a day – compared to 23,733 in 2012/13.

Speaking in Belfast, Mr Wanless said: 'These figures show people here are more alive to the issues of child abuse following high-profile scandals such as Savile and the Historical Institutional Abuse inquiry. People in Northern Ireland have become increasingly concerned and aware of the tell-tale signs of abuse and neglect in children and our helpline is an invaluable service. It's a big decision to involve health and social care trusts or police and our counsellors will only act when there is genuine concern for the welfare of a child.'

The Northern Ireland figures show:

- Contacts from the public concerned about neglect of a child which were referred rose from 181 in 2012/13 to 238 last year – up 31 per cent.
- Referrals due to physical abuse rose from 89 in 2012/13 to 120 in 2015/16 – a 35 per cent rise.
- Contacts passed on because of emotional abuse increased by 65 per cent – from 43 in 2012/13 to 71 in 2015/16.

Adults can contact the helpline on 0808 800 5000, by texting 88858 or by visiting the website.

(www.belfastlive.co.uk/news/nspcc-helpline-flooded-abuse-neglect-12017949)

What personal and social strategies are available to deal with abuse, sexual exploitation, sexual assault, rape, prostitution, female genital mutilation (FGM) and human trafficking?

Some children and young people's circumstances may make them vulnerable and at risk to sexual exploitation and other forms of sexual abuse. This section considers the different forms of sexual abuse and the personal strategies children, young people, and social strategies that wider society can use to deal with these.

Sexual Exploitation

Sexual exploitation involves the abuser using their relationship, position or authority to take advantage of children and young people and coerce them to perform sexual acts. The abuser may offer gifts, money, alcohol or drugs in exchange for sex or they may intimidate or use violence. Sexual exploitation can also led to child prostitution.

Abusers may also make use of technology and social media to make contact with children and young people. The abuser may try to persuade them participate in sexual conversations in text or online, they may coerce them to send or post sexually explicit images or to participate in sexual activities via the webcam. The abuser can use this information to blackmail the child or young person and may threaten to share the images of conversations with their friends and family. A young person could use some of the personal strategies to deal with sexual exploitation:

- Be aware and understand what sexual exploitation and unhealthy relationships mean.
- Be able to recognise and identify situations where there is a risk of sexual exploitation.
- If the young person is in a situation where they feel they can't say no they should ask themselves are they in a safe situation.
- Be aware of accepting money, gifts, drink or other things from people they do not know.
- Avoid situations, which may put them at risk, e.g. being with a group of adults who they do not know and going with adults to hotel or private rooms.
- Remain in control of situations. Avoid becoming drunk or taking drugs.
- Be safe online. Be careful who you friend and chat to on social media. People may not be who they say they are.
- Do not meet people you know only from social media sites unless accompanied by a friend. Young people should also talk to and inform their family about the meeting.
- Do not post or share sexually explicit personal images on the internet and social media. Abusers can use this information to blackmail young people. The abuser may threaten to share the images with others unless the young person does what they want.
- Do not stay silent. If the young person feels they are at risk or being sexually exploited they should talk to a friend, close relative or someone else they trust.
- Young people can contact the police
- In Northern Ireland, they could contact:
  - Childline
  - NSPCC
  - Barnardo's
  - Samaritains
  - Childnet
  - Child Exploitation and Online Protection Centre (CEOP)

Sexual assault, including rape

A sexual assault is any sexual act that a person did not consent to or is too young to consent to, or is forced upon them. It is a form of sexual violence and includes rape (a form of sexual assault that involves penetration of the vagina, anus or mouth) or other sexual offences, such as groping, forced kissing or the torture of a person in a sexual manner. If a young person receives something such as a gift, money or affection as a result of a sexual assault, it is considered sexual exploitation.

Personal strategies

If you feel you have been subjected to a sexual assault please seek help by confiding in a trusting adult or contact:

- a GP/nurse/A&E department
- a voluntary organisation such as Women's Aid, Victim Support, the Survivors Trust
- the Rape Crisis team on 0808 802 9999
- a local GUM clinic (Genitourinary Medicine)
- the NHS on 111
- the police (101 or emergency 999).

> **Activity**
>
> **Dealing with abuse and sexual exploitation**
>
> 1 Many organisations were mentioned in this topic. Using the internet, make notes on whom each of the organisations listed work with and the type of work they do.
>
>   a Women's Aid
>   b Victim Support
>   c the Survivors Trust
>   d Rape Crisis Team
>   e Sexual Health NI
>   f Women's Project Centre
>   g Nexus
>   h Lifeline.
>
> 2 Suggest and justify reasons why a young person may enter prostitution.

Prostitution

Prostitution is the business or practice of engaging in sexual relations in exchange for money or another benefit. It is a form of sexual exploitation. It is estimated that in the UK there are 80,000 people involved in prostitution and Home Office figures show that 70 per cent of prostitutes spent time in care and many are homeless, and 95 per cent of street prostitutes are on heroin or crack.

Usually people who engage in prostitution become reliant on the money or are forced to continue this illegal activity and find it difficult to stop. There is help available for people in this situation. The personal strategies a young person could use in this situation include:

- go to the police to seek protection from those forcing them into prostitution
- seek medical help from a GP or GUM clinic, social services or Sexual Health NI
- contact the Department for Social Development to access a full range of benefits available to people which could stop a person becoming reliant on the income gained from prostitution
- seek debt advice from many of the voluntary organisations that provide it, for example the Citizens Advice Bureau; alleviating the burden of debt could mean that a person no longer has to engage in prostitution
- contact the Inspire Women's Project Centre which can help women get back on track after a criminal conviction
- contact Women's Aid who could provide support or even accommodation if prostitution is being forced by a partner
- visit the Belfast Drop-in Service for Commercial Sex Workers which provides a safe and non-judgemental environment
- seek counselling, for example by Nexus and Lifeline.

Female Genital Mutilation

Sexual abuse can also involve genital mutilation. Female Genital Mutilation (FGM) is a procedure where the female genitals are deliberately cut, injured or changed for no medical reason. It is usually carried out before puberty starts and is illegal in the UK. An estimated 200 million girls and women alive today are believed to have been subjected to FGM.

FGM can be carried out for various cultural, religious and social reasons within families and communities in the mistaken belief that it will benefit the girl in some way. Below are some reasons as to why the procedure is carried out.

- FGM is carried out as a way to control women's sexuality, which is sometimes said to be impossible to control if parts of the genitalia, especially the clitoris, are not removed. Some communities believe that FGM will ensure virginity before marriage and fidelity afterwards.
- FGM is seen as part of a girl's initiation into womanhood and as part of a community's cultural heritage. Sometimes myths about female genitalia (e.g. that an uncut clitoris will grow to the size of a penis) reinforce the practice.
- In some communities, the external female genitalia are considered dirty and ugly and are removed to promote hygiene and aesthetic appeal.
- Although FGM is not endorsed by either Islam or Christianity, supposed religious doctrine is often used to justify the practice.
- In many communities, FGM has to take place before marriage or sometimes before a woman and her husband can inherit.

The effects of FGM depend on a number of factors, including the type performed, the expertise of the practitioner, the hygiene conditions under which it is performed, the amount of resistance and the general health condition of the girl/woman undergoing the procedure. Complications may occur in all types of FGM, but are most frequent with infibulation.

Immediate complications include severe pain, shock, haemorrhage, infection, urine retention fever and septicaemia. Haemorrhage and infection can be severe enough to cause death. Long-term consequences include complications during childbirth, anaemia, the formation of cysts and abscesses, urinary incontinence, sexual dysfunction, hypersensitivity of the genital area and increased risk of HIV transmission, as well as emotional effects, for example post-traumatic stress.

A key challenge is not only protecting girls who are currently at risk but also ensuring that generations to come will be free from the dangers of the practice. This is especially important considering that FGM-concentrated countries are generally experiencing high population growth and have large youth populations. Young girls from certain communities that practice FGM are vulnerable and at risk of FGM. However, it is important that young girls realise that they are at risk. They can prevent FGM but only by taking action. Some examples of the personal strategies a young girl could use to prevent FGM include:

▶ Be informed about FGM and the risks to their health and welfare.
▶ Where there is immediate danger contact the police.
▶ Talk to someone they trust eg a friend, close relative, school nurse, doctor or teacher.
▶ School have a designated teacher responsible for Child Protection. They could find out who this is. Tell them about their concerns. The teacher is not there to judge but to offer advice and support.
▶ In Northern Ireland they could contact:
  ▶ African and Caribbean Support Northern Ireland
  ▶ Women's Aid
  ▶ Childline
  ▶ NSPCC
  ▶ Barnardo's
  ▶ Samaritans

Trafficking

Human trafficking is the trade of people, mostly for the purpose of sexual slavery, forced labour or prostitution. Statistics suggest that there were 2,744 potential victims of human trafficking encountered in the UK in 2013 and sexual exploitation accounted for 41 per cent of the cases. The three most prevalent countries of origin for potential victims of trafficking in Europe were Romania, Poland and the UK.

Human trafficking can be incredibly hard to detect, but if a victim does come forward or is found, their needs are complex and they often require the involvement of many services to address their trauma and medical needs. Victims may need:

▶ emergency medical treatment through, for example, A&E
▶ emergency shelter
▶ social services involvement
▶ employment advice and help through the Department of the Economy
▶ legal representation through legal aid
▶ counselling.

> If you suspect that someone is a victim of trafficking, contact the police on 101 or 999 for an emergency situation.

Social Strategies

One of the main aims of the governments of most countries throughout the world is to protect the health and well-being of its citizens. One way they do this is by developing and implementing social strategies to prevent, educate and protect children and young people from the different forms of sexual abuse. These strategies commonly include:

▶ Pass and enforce specific laws to target each different type of abuse.
▶ Develop and implement government policies throughout government departments and public bodies.
▶ Establish mutli-agency approaches to tackle each of the various forms of sexual abuse. A multi-agency approach is when people from different government departments and bodies work collaboratively to tackle forms of sexual abuse.
▶ Interventions by public agencies to protect children and young people from sexual abuse. In cases where children and young people are at risk of sexual abuse the police can remove the child or young person from the family home.
▶ Train those involved with children young people to:
  ▶ identify the signs of sexual abuse
  ▶ identify children and young people who may be at risk
  ▶ support children and young people at risk
▶ Raise public awareness about forms of sexual abuse and their consequences for individuals and society.

- Educate and inform children and young people about different forms of sexual abuse and where they can access support.
- Provide support services to help children and young people who are at risk of sexual abuse.

What personal and social strategies are available to deal with bullying?

There are many different types of bullying that can be experienced by children and adults alike; some are obvious to spot while others can be more subtle. The diagram below summarises the four types of bullying:

Physical bullying Physical bullying includes tripping, hitting, kicking or damaging someone's property.	**Social bullying** Social bullying takes place behind a person's back. It involves ruining someone's reputation or causing humiliation. It includes lying and spreading rumours, playing nasty jokes or encouraging others to exclude someone socially.
Verbal bullying Verbal bullying includes insults, teasing, intimidation, homophobic or racist remarks.	**Cyber bullying** Cyber bullying can be private or public and uses digital technologies to target the victim. Cyber bullying can include: abusive or hurtful texts, emails or posts, images or videos, deliberately excluding others online, nasty gossip or rumours, intimidating others online or using their log-in details.

Why do some people bully?

There are lots of different reasons to explain why some people become bullies. They may have:
- family problems
- been bullied themselves
- no friends and feel lonely
- bad feelings about themselves and want to make other people feel bad too
- insecurity issues and bullying gives them power
- joined a bullying gang and have gone along with things just to keep on the bully's good side.

Bullies use 'differences', e.g. 'wearing glasses', 'too good at exams' and 'too creative' as an excuse for their bad behaviour. It is not the 'difference' in the victim that is the problem, it is the bullies who have the problem because they may be afraid, jealous or lack understanding of the issue. There are two typical bullying issues caused by perceived 'differences':
- Homophobic bullying: homophobic bullying occurs when people behave or speak in a way which makes someone feel bullied because of their actual or perceived sexuality. People may be a target of this type of bullying because of their appearance, behaviour or physical traits, or because they have friends or family who are lesbian, gay, bisexual or transgender.
- Racist bullying: racist bullying occurs when people behave or speak in a way which makes someone feel bullied because of the colour of their skin, the way they talk, their ethnic group or their place of birth.

Strategies to deal with bullying and where to get help

A person who finds themselves a victim of bullying should:
- rise above it and walk away; the bully may get bored
- hold the anger; bullies crave an emotional response and will continue to bully if they get it
- stand up for themselves but avoid a physical reaction; if an incident gets physical someone could get seriously injured – there are other ways they can stand up for themselves, for example being assertive
- practise confidence by rehearsing how to verbally respond to the bully
- tell a trusted adult, for example a teacher or school counsellor
- stay within a group if they are feeling unsafe
- keep a record of all incidents or nasty messages received
- increase security settings to restrict contacts, block the bully or unfriend them on social media.

UNIT 2 PERSONAL DEVELOPMENT

If these strategies do not work, there are other sources of help and support for young people. It is important not to suffer in silence. A young person could contact the following:

- Childline (0800 1111): Childline's website has a useful section on how to cope with bullying: www.childline.org.uk/info-advice/bullying-abuse-safety. A section of their website is also dedicated to racist bulling: www.childline.org.uk/info-advice/bullying-abuse-safety/crime-law/racism.

- Bullybusters (0800 169 6928): Bullybusters operates a free anti-bullying helpline for anyone affected by bullying. Its website also has message boards to seek support. Bullybusters is funded by Sefton, Liverpool and Knowsley local authorities and services are only available to residents in these geographical areas.

- Bullying UK (0808 800 2222): Bullying UK offers practical advice and its website has a section on bullying at school: www.bullying.co.uk/bullying-at-school.

- EACH (0808 1000 143): a charity for young people affected by homophobic bullying. They also provide training and consultancy on all matters connected with gender identity or sexual orientation.

  www.each.education

- Stonewall is the lesbian, gay, bi and trans equality charity, campaigning for acceptance without exception for LGBT people in Britain and abroad. You can learn more about Stonewall and its work, including that in schools, at www.stonewall.org.uk.

Activity — Dealing with bullying

1. Research and produce a report on the social strategies used to tackle bullying (including cyber bullying.
2. Evaluate the effectiveness of the social strategies used to tackle bullying (including cyber bullying.
3. Visit www-bullying co.uk./bullying at school. Explain the ways this organisation supports victims of bullying.
4. Explain the effects of bullying on the physical and emotional health and well-being of a young person.

What are the physical and emotional effects of abuse on a young person's personal development, health and well-being?

Abuse has short- and long-term effects on a young person's personal development, health and well-being. The table on page 117 summarises some effects of each type of abuse. It is important to note that if a person displays one or two of the effects it does not automatically mean that they are being abused.

Section 4 Personal safety and well-being

Type of abuse	Effects on physical health and well-being	Effects on emotional health and well-being
Physical abuse	Unexplained injuries: burns, scalds, bruises, fractures Problems sleeping Develops addictions to drugs and alcohol	Anxiety and becomes withdrawn **Obsessive behaviour** Thoughts of, or engagement in, self-harm Suicidal thoughts Post-traumatic stress Depression Low self-esteem Difficulty trusting others Bullies others
Emotional abuse: emotional abuse is the most difficult form of child abuse to identify and stop. Emotional abuse leaves many hidden scars	A child living in continuous fear and sorrow cannot eat well to grow well. They will be vulnerable to diseases and health complications	Affects self-concept: a young person may view themselves as being unworthy of love and find it hard to bond with others Affects a child's mental development. Their intelligence and memory development can be affected, resulting in mental problems and disorders Greater risk of developing one or more behavioural problems. These may include learning difficulties, difficulty with socialising and rebellious behaviour Anxiety Insecurity Low self-esteem Depression Anger Lack of empathy
Sexual abuse	Anal or vaginal soreness An unusual discharge STIs Pregnancy	Sleep problems or nightmares Depression or withdrawal from friends or family Refusal to go to school Behavioural problems Unusual aggressiveness Extreme fear or anxiety Thoughts of, or engagement in, self-harm Suicidal thoughts Post-traumatic stress Depression **Promiscuity** Low self-esteem
Neglect	Poor hygiene: unwashed clothes, body odour Decaying teeth Recurring or untreated health problems due to poor nutrition Skin sores, rashes, flea bites, **scabies** or **ringworm** Anaemia and tiredness Undiagnosed hearing or sight problems Addiction to drugs/alcohol	Post-traumatic stress Risk-taking behaviour: running away from home or engaging in criminal behaviour Depression Low self-esteem

▲ The physical and emotional effects of different kinds of abuse

Activity — The effects of abuse

1 Using the table above, write down one short- and one long-term effect on the *physical* health and well-being of someone experiencing:

   a physical abuse
   b emotional abuse
   c sexual abuse
   d neglect.

2 Carry out the same task as outlined in question 1, but this time for the effects on the *emotional* health and well-being of someone experiencing each of the four types of abuse.

PERSONAL DEVELOPMENT

Section 5 Responsible parenting

UNIT 2

Key content
- The roles and responsibilities of parents, children and young people within different family structures
- The social, emotional and economic impact of becoming a parent
- The opportunities in and challenges of parental responsibility for carer, single, same-sex, teenage, young, older and/or step-parents
- The role of parenting in a child's physical, social, emotional, intellectual and moral development

This section looks at the roles and responsibilities of different types of parents, for example a single-parent family or a family with a **step-parent**. It looks at the varying responsibilities of children and young people within different family structures, for example when a child is a carer. It discusses the opportunities and challenges of parental responsibility and the social, emotional and economic impact of becoming a parent. The section concludes by looking at the role of parenting in a child's overall development.

What are the roles and responsibilities of parents, children and young people within different family structures?

Becoming a parent is not an easy time. Whether a parent is part of a couple, a single parent, a teenage parent, a step-parent, an older parent or a carer, the changes a child brings can be very challenging. The UNCRC outlines the rights each child should have (see page 36). A parent or carer should ensure that their child's rights are being met and they have a responsibility to make sure this happens. The main roles and responsibilities of a parent are shown on page 119.

In healthy families, every member is responsible for fulfilling certain roles. It is important to discuss, as a family, each member's understanding of the roles he or she has been assigned. In healthy families, children and young people are required to take on appropriate roles of responsibility within the family. The role of a child or young person within a family could change depending on the family structure they are part of. There are many different types of family structures that exist in today's society. The traditional family structure consists of two married individuals providing care for their children, but this type of structure is becoming more uncommon.

Section 5 Responsible parenting

1. A parent is expected to provide a **safe environment**. For example:
- keep the child safe from abuse
- keep unsafe objects away from the child
- child proof the home.

2. A parent is expected to provide a **loving environment**. For example:
- spend time with the child
- communicate with the child
- show an interest in the child
- be affectionate towards the child.

3. A parent is expected to **support** the child **financially**. Until the child turns 18 a parent is expected to spend money on the needs of the child. For example, lunch money, money for school trips and money for the basic needs of the child.

9. A parent is expected to **discipline a child**. For example:
- reward good behaviour
- be consistent with punishing bad behaviour
- be fair.

8. A parent is expected to **encourage and foster interests and skills**. For example:
- encourage a child to participate in a club
- acknowledge achievement in their interest
- set realistic expectations
- make an interest or a skill into something fun, not something that they dislike doing.

4. A parent is expected to help support a child's **educational needs**. For example:
- communicate regularly with the school
- help with homework
- celebrate the child's achievement at school
- have conversations with the child about what goes on at school.

5. A parent is expected to provide for the child's **basic needs**. For example, ensure the child has:
- water
- food
- clothes
- shelter
- a warm bed
- medical care.

7. A parent is expected to provide **opportunities for social development**. For example:
- organise play dates
- encourage making friends
- encourage the child to talk about their feelings
- bring the child to places where there will be other children – for example, the park.

6. A parent is expected to assist with the **development of a child's morals and values**. For example:
- teach the child the difference between right and wrong
- lead by example and show the importance of values such as honesty, respect, patience, generosity and forgiveness.

▲ The roles and responsibilities of a parent/carer

Roles and responsibilities

Below is a selection of some family structures that can be found in society and what a child/young person's roles and responsibility could be within them.

Child or young person is a carer

A young carer is someone under the age of 18 who helps look after a relative who has a disability, an illness, a mental health condition or an addiction. A young carer may have to look after a parent, a younger brother or sister, or both. They will have extra roles and responsibilities in the home such as cooking, cleaning or helping someone to get dressed or move around. They may have to give a lot of physical and emotional help to the person they are looking after and provide similar support for a younger brother and sister if the parent is unable to.

Some young people start caring at a young age and do not realise they are carers; others can become carers overnight. Although young carers should not be doing the same things as adult carers, the burden can still be very heavy especially when a young person has school to attend, homework to do and a life of their own to lead.

Child or young person is being looked after by a carer

A child who is being looked after by their local authority is known as a child in care. They might be living with foster parents, at home with their parents under the supervision of social services, in residential children's homes or in other residential settings like schools or secure units. Being in care and not being in your own homely environment can be very difficult for a young person to accept. The settling-in period can also be difficult for the carer. A young person has to remember that they have been placed in care by well-trained people who believe it is in the best interest of that young person. It is therefore the responsibility of the child or young person to:

- follow the rules that have been set
- try to get to know the people that they have been placed with
- carry out any chores or duties that have been assigned
- behave in an acceptable manner
- attend school, behave and work well
- speak up if they are unhappy
- speak up if they deem something to be unfair or unjust and give the carers a chance to rectify the situation.

Child or young person is being looked after by a single parent

In 2014 there were 2 million single parents in the UK. We have different sorts of single parent families in today's society: headed by mothers, headed by fathers and even headed by a grandparent raising their grandchildren. Life in a single-parent household can be stressful for the adults and children. A single parent may feel overwhelmed by the responsibility of juggling a job, household finances and chores with caring for a child or young person. It is therefore the responsibility of a child or young person to help out a parent as much as they can (within reason) without complaining. A child should help out at home with chores, help out with siblings, behave in an acceptable fashion in and outside the home, ensure a parent does not have to worry about school by doing the work/homework given, respect the parent and acknowledge the hard work put in by a parent on a daily basis. A young person may also have to be conscious that, because there is only one parent, there may be only one income and as such a child or young person may not always get everything they want.

Child or young person is being looked after by a step-parent

When families 'blend' to create step-families, things may not progress smoothly. Some children and young people may resist changes, while parents and step-parents can become frustrated when the new family does not function like their previous family. Within this family structure a child or young person's roles and responsibilities may change. A young person will have to:

- be receptive to change
- attempt to get to know a step-parent and their family and be welcoming to them
- respect the step-parent and their family
- do chores around the house
- behave in an appropriate manner
- attend, work well and behave at school
- speak up if unhappy
- speak up if they deem something to be unfair or unjust and give the step-parent a chance to rectify the situation
- allow time for a settling-in period and be aware that things will not be perfect straightaway.

Child or young person has an older parent or parents

More and more people are putting off having children until later in life. Some children are also cared for by grandparents. Both of these situations could mean that a young person's parent/carer is older than the parents of their peers. A child or young person in this situation could have specific roles and responsibilities which could include:

- accepting that their parent or carer is older and not being embarrassed by the issue
- accepting that their parent or carer may have traditional views
- being aware that as a parent gets older they may not physically be able to do as much and that a young person may have to help out more
- being aware that a parent/carer could experience more health problems than the parents of their peers
- being aware that an increased age gap can lead to communication issues and trying to find ways to address this
- being respectful of generational differences
- speaking up in a respectful manner if a young person feels that something is unfair, unjust or traditionalist.

SOURCE A An article from the *Mirror* website by Gerard Crouzens, 18 October 2016

Mum who gave birth aged 62 pictured smiling as she leaves hospital carrying her one-week-old daughter

Spanish doctor Lina Alvarez faced criticism after announcing she was pregnant with her third child, but says she feels 'phenomenal'.

Proud 62-year-old mum Lina Alvarez poses with her week-old daughter as she leaves hospital after her caesarian. The Spanish doctor shed tears as she admitted: 'I couldn't feel happier' on the steps of Lucas Augusti Hospital in the Galician city of Lugo.

Lina, whose daughter shares her name, sparked debate in her home nation by announcing last month she was eight months pregnant with her third child. The new arrival was born two weeks ahead of schedule last Monday weighing 5.2lbs after her mum was admitted for observation when she began to suffer high blood pressure. Lina's eldest son Exiquio, 28, who is disabled after a medical error left him injured during her pregnancy, and her second son Samuel, 10, met their sister shortly after her birth.

She insisted today she felt 'phenomenal' as she left the hospital which has been her home for just over the past week and agreed to pose with her baby daughter for waiting photographers.

(www.mirror.co.uk/news/world-news/mum-who-gave-birth-aged-9073405)

▲ Lina Alvarez, a 62-year-old doctor, has recently given birth to a baby girl

---

Activity — Parenting later in life

Read Source A and answer the following questions:

1 Analyse the effects of having an older parent on a young person.
2 Suggest and justify reasons why people may put off having children until they are older.
3 Evaluate the impact of a young person becoming a carer for a parent.

What are the social, emotional and economic impacts of becoming a parent?

Raising children is one of life's most rewarding roles, but it can also pose numerous challenges. Parents in their teens often face the most difficult challenges as they are still maturing themselves. Over time many young parents may face emotional, social and financial issues.

Emotional issues

Having a baby can be an emotionally trying time for any parent but can be especially difficult for young parents. Studies show that they are more likely to face issues such as postnatal depression, stress and fear of failure.

Social issues

Having a baby can lead to many changes in a parent's life, particularly in relation to their social standing and activity.

Social stigma

Being a teenage parent is more socially acceptable now than it would have been in the past. However, some young parents or single parents still feel that they are frowned upon by society. Some people feel that a young parent is unable to care for a child when they are still a child themselves. Young parents or single parents are often seen as a drain on the welfare system and many working adults feel resentful about paying taxes to support these parents. There are also people who think young parents are foolish to get themselves into such a situation in the first place, while some older members of society may feel that having a child without being married is shameful. Social stigma can also cause emotional issues as it can lower self-confidence and self-esteem.

Social life

Once a baby is born it takes up copious amounts of time and energy. A parent will not be able to interact with friends or take part in the same social activities as they used to. Finding someone to look after the child may also prove difficult and therefore time spent socialising can be dramatically reduced, which could lead to isolation and affect emotional and social health.

Financial issues

Raising a child can be very expensive. Costs such as clothing, food, nappies, childcare, prams, cots, toys, medical care and everything else that children require very quickly mount up. New parents may have to rely on family, friends and benefits to help with costs and also childcare, which can add to stress and be emotionally challenging.

Career prospects

The job market is a highly competitive place. Women who take maternity leave to have children may feel that they have missed out on promotional opportunities or experience and may feel that their career prospects have been lessened. If a parent is a teenager they may find it difficult to find a job without previous work experience and qualifications. Staying in full-time education can be difficult for young parents and they may need to forsake long-term career plans to take any available employment.

School/university

A young parent's education will be dramatically affected by having a child. During pregnancy a young woman may find it difficult to attend school/university as often as they would have done and may fall behind. If this happens before important exams they may not fully achieve their goals and reach their academic potential.

After becoming a parent, a young woman may be unable to attend school/university at all as the child will become their main priority. Those who try to balance parenthood with school will be at a disadvantage as time spent at home will be centred on the child and homework may become neglected. Most infants do not settle into regular sleeping patterns until they are older and this could mean that the young parent will be sleeping less at night. This will affect how often the young parent can come to school and will also affect concentration while at school/university.

Section 5 Responsible parenting

Activity — Financial impacts of having a baby

1 Every newborn requires essential items. In pairs, copy and complete the table below to decide the financial implications of a newborn using a catalogue or the internet to help you. Add rows to your table to include any other items you feel you would like for a child.

Non-consumables

Item	On a budget	Luxury budget
Cot	Seller: Cost:	Seller: Cost:
Change mat	Seller: Cost:	Seller: Cost:
Steriliser	Seller: Cost:	Seller: Cost:
Bottles	Seller: Cost:	Seller: Cost:
Seat/bouncer	Seller: Cost:	Seller: Cost:
Car seat	Seller: Cost:	Seller: Cost:
Pram/buggy	Seller: Cost:	Seller: Cost:
Baby bath	Seller: Cost:	Seller: Cost:
Baby gym	Seller: Cost:	Seller: Cost:
Baby monitor	Seller: Cost:	Seller: Cost:
Total:		

Consumables (per year)

Item	On a budget	Luxury budget
Nappies (six per day)	Seller: Cost:	Seller: Cost:
Nappy cream (one tube per two weeks)	Seller: Cost:	Seller: Cost:
Formula (one tub per week)	Seller: Cost:	Seller: Cost:
Baby bubble bath (one a month)	Seller: Cost:	Seller: Cost:
Baby shampoo (one a month)	Seller: Cost:	Seller: Cost:
Total:		

2 Are you surprised by how expensive babies are?

3 What costs might be incurred later in a child's life?

What are the opportunities and challenges associated with parental responsibility?

Many new parents say that having children changes everything. Becoming a parent presents many challenges. However, as the newness of parenthood passes, many parents adjust to the changes and find that their lives are enriched by the presence of a child. Different types of parents (carer, single parent, parent in same-sex relationship, teenage/young parent, older parent or step-parent) will experience a distinct range of opportunities and challenges which are summarised on pages 24–25.

UNIT 2 PERSONAL DEVELOPMENT

	Opportunities	**Challenges**
Parent	• Turns a couple into a family and gives a sense of completeness • Enriches a person's life • Can improve mental well-being in the long term as parents have to look beyond themselves in caring for another • Parents tend to look after themselves more in a bid to improve health and lifespan to look after a child • Potentially a parent will have someone to look after them when they are older	• Financial commitment • Time commitment • Reduced social life • Reduced free time/time for yourself • Being responsible all of the time • Pressures of a child can cause relationship issues

	Additional opportunities	**Additional challenges**
Carer	• Self-satisfaction that you are improving the life of another • Benefits are available to carers (foster reward payments and carers' allowance) • Becoming an asset to the community will improve self-confidence, self-esteem and self-worth • Foster care can be a temporary arrangement which means a carer might only have to commit for short periods of time • Develop links with other carers through training which sets up a support network • 24-hour support for foster carers if a carer encounters difficulty	• As a foster carer, the child will not remain with you forever. Forming an attachment and then giving the child back can be traumatic • Dealing with children with emotional issues can be difficult • Family may find it difficult to accept a new child • The child may find it difficult to fit in with a new family, causing stress for all involved • A carer may find it difficult to bond with a child that is not their own
Single parent	• No arguments or misunderstandings on who does what as a parent • No other parent to undermine authority • Limited misunderstandings on parenting styles and rule setting • More motivated as the rearing of the child is done by one person which could spur that person on • Strong parental bond as a result of being the only parent	• Only one income • May not be able to work as a single parent will have the responsibility of looking after a child • Reduced social life as there is only one person caring for the child • Being alone can be isolating and cause depression • One person is fully responsible if something goes wrong • Multi-tasking (doing chores, working, completing both parenting roles) can cause pressure and stress on a person • Possible social stigma as the parent does not have a partner • If becoming a single parent is a new development the single parent could face negativity or behavioural issues from the child/children
Parents in same-sex relationship	• Parents in same sex relationships are likely to be caring and committed parents because they have made a conscious decision to have children, promoting improved self-confidence, self-esteem and self-worth • Likelihood that having a child was a well-considered and planned decision so the parents will be able to provide for all the needs of the child or children	• Social stigma as some people find same-sex relationships difficult to accept or understand • The worry that a child may be subjected to bullying because of parents' sexual orientation • Some same-sex parents find it difficult to explain their relationship status to school professionals, medical professionals and children's friends/parents, as well as explaining relationship status to children

	Additional opportunities	Additional challenges
Teenage/ young parent	<ul><li>Being closer in age could create a closer bond</li><li>A young parent could identify more with their child as they may have a better understanding of the challenges young people face in today's society so a young person may find it easier to turn to their parent(s) for advice</li><li>A younger parent may be fitter, healthier and more energetic which could allow for more shared activities</li><li>Young parents may adapt quicker to the upheaval a new child brings</li></ul>	<ul><li>A young parent may feel like they have lost out on their carefree youth, particularly when comparing their lives with peers</li><li>There may be a feeling of inexperience which can become overwhelming</li><li>A young parent could feel lonely and isolated if they cannot socialise with their peers as much</li><li>Depending on how young the parent is, they may feel embarrassed due to social stigma</li><li>A young parent will still be growing up and maturing when raising a child</li><li>A young parent may not be financially stable and may therefore face financial difficulties</li><li>The education and career of a young parent will most likely have to be put on hold in order to raise a child</li><li>Postnatal depression is prevalent in young parents, particularly if the child is unplanned</li></ul>
Older parent	<ul><li>There is a distinct possibility that the child has been planned for so the parent(s) will be financially stable, possibly giving the child a better quality of life</li><li>An older parent will be more mature and have more life experience which could be passed on to the child</li><li>Older parents tend to have finished their education and have stable employment, allowing financial stability to continue long term</li><li>Older parents usually have more stable relationships and have the ability to communicate and compromise. This is a healthy environment in which to bring up a child</li></ul>	<ul><li>May have health and energy issues to contend with when raising a child</li><li>A child could be embarrassed about their older parent</li><li>An older parent may find it more difficult to identify with their child as they are older and grew up at a different time. This could cause friction or bonding issues</li><li>A child could get teased or bullied because of an older parent and the rules imposed by them</li><li>Depending on how old a person is, they could be placing a burden on their child in terms of caring for them when they are old</li><li>Some people consider old parents to be selfish as the child may have many parentless years ahead of them if a parent was to pass away</li><li>Some older parents can struggle with the loss of independence when they have been used to it for so long. This could cause stress, resentment towards the child and depression</li><li>Some older parents become isolated from their community, friends and even family as they have concentrated on furthering their careers. This could result in having little or no support network when the baby arrives</li></ul>
Step-parent	<ul><li>Step-parents have usually taken time to consider parenthood before taking it on, creating more stability</li></ul>	<ul><li>A step-parent could face bonding issues as the child is not their own</li><li>A child could resent an additional parental figure in their lives, leading to arguments and additional stresses</li><li>If the step-parent has children of his or her own, they could find it difficult to treat step-children in the same way. This could result in resentment</li></ul>

Activity — Parental responsibility

1 Describe one challenge of being a step-parent bringing up a family.
2 Analyse the effects of having a baby on a young person.
3 Suggest and justify reasons a person would consider becoming a foster carer.

UNIT 2 PERSONAL DEVELOPMENT

What is the role of parenting in a child's physical, social, emotional, intellectual and moral development?

A parent has many responsibilities when raising a child. Part of their responsibility is to ensure that they help their child to develop physically, socially, emotionally, intellectually and morally.

▲ The different aspects of child development

Strategies for ensuring development in each of these areas are outlined below and on page 127.

Physical development

A parent should ensure that a child's basic needs are met so they can physically thrive. They should lead by example and ensure the child is fed a balanced diet and that exercise is promoted. If a child is clean, cared for and looked after they are more likely to thrive physically. A parent should ensure that their child is seen by medical professionals for the recommended health visitor checks and when they are ill.

Emotional development

Emotional intelligence in a child can be developed in many ways. In order to help a child's emotional development, a parent should model the skills they would like to see their child develop. Many emotional skills are developed over time, and some adults are stronger in this area than others; this will usually be reflected in the child.

A parent should encourage:
- **self-awareness:** ensuring the child knows their strengths, what they are good at and what they can improve upon

- **identification of emotions:** if a child is upset or annoyed, a parent should help identify and acknowledge their feelings and encourage the child to come up with ways that would make them feel better (self-soothe)
- **social awareness:** being aware of the emotions of others and the effect a child can have on others. A parent should encourage a child to deal with conflict themselves, for example, promoting sharing and compromise. A parent can do this by managing their own emotions, listening to their child talk about their emotions, providing opportunities for a child to solve their own problems and giving positive feedback when a child does these things themselves.

Social development

A parent is expected to provide opportunities for social development. For example:
- organising play dates
- encouraging the child to make friends
- encouraging the child to talk about their feelings
- taking the child to places where there will be other children, for example the park.

Intellectual development

Intellectual development is the process of a child acquiring intelligence and increasingly advanced thought and problem-solving ability. Children develop cognitively at a pace. A parent can enhance a child's intellectual development by:
- encouraging them to think and solve problems for themselves
- encouraging learning through play, i.e. puzzles or educational games
- reading often with or to the child
- encouraging independence, i.e. cleaning up after themselves, dressing themselves
- taking an interest and supporting the work that is going on in school, at home.

Moral development

Moral development shapes a child's decision-making process when choosing between what is right or wrong and what is fair or unfair. A parent plays a significant role in instilling the morals within a child that they feel are valuable. From honesty and respect, to generosity and kindness, the parenting techniques used can help shape a child into a moral adult. A parent should:
- teach a child the difference between right and wrong
- lead by example and regularly display their own morals so a child can watch, learn and imitate
- create a moral environment so that all siblings treat each other morally
- praise a child when good moral decision making has taken place
- correct a child if they believe that the child is being immoral
- a child may see immoral behaviour from others outside the house. A parent can use this as a learning experience and ask a child what should have been done differently.

Activity

Child development

1 Describe how a parent could help develop a child socially.
2 'A teenager should be in charge of their own intellectual development.' Evaluate the validity of this statement.

PERSONAL DEVELOPMENT

Section 6 Making informed financial decisions

UNIT 2

Key content:
- managing a budget
- the consequences of poor budgeting
- making financial decisions based on research, advice and the credibility of information
- protecting against fraud and identity theft
- making financial decisions, and advantages and disadvantages of consumer choices
- the advantages and disadvantages of using comparison websites for car and home insurance, electricity, gas and oil
- sources of financial advice and consumer protection including relevant consumer legislation

This section looks at how a person could make more informed financial decisions. It looks at consumer choices including quality versus price, cash versus **credit** and buying versus renting. It investigates the merits of a budget, managing a budget and the consequences of poor budgeting. The section explores making a whole range of financial decisions based on research, advice and information. Ways of assessing the credibility of financial information, particularly understanding how to detect bias and non-bias information, is also explored. Methods for protecting against fraud and identity theft when paying electronically are covered as well as online scams which are now becoming increasingly common. The section concludes by examining the advantages and disadvantages of using financial comparison websites and outlines sources of financial advice in relation to the Consumer Credit Act and the Sale of Goods Act.

How can consumers manage a budget?

Budgets are an invaluable tool for managing finances. They are used by governments and businesses to manage **income** (money coming in) and **expenditure** (spending) on a weekly, monthly and yearly basis. A budget is a money plan and can be used on a smaller scale by individuals to manage their own finances. This section looks at what information a budget contains, how to stick to a budget, the advantages of using one and the consequences of not.

Making and using a personal budget

There is no right or wrong way to make a budget, but most contain a list of all available income and all expenditures whether necessary or optional. Necessary spending includes things that we need, for example, rent or food. When essential things have been paid for, the money left (**disposable income**) can be used for things we want, like new clothes or a holiday. As we get older, sources of income and expenditure change (e.g. mortgage repayments or car repairs).

	Week 1 (£)	Week 2 (£)	Week 3 (£)	Week 4 (£)	Monthly total (£)
Income					
Wages from part-time job	20	20	0	20	60
Pocket money	5	5	5	5	20
Selling items online	10	0	0	25	35
Benefits	0	0	0	0	0
Other	80	0	0	10	90
Total income	115	25	5	60	205
Spending					
Mobile phone bill	10	10	10	10	40
Savings	20	0	0	0	20
Food	10	10	10	10	40
Clothing	60	0	0	0	60
Entertainment	5	10	5	5	25
Other	0	0	0	0	0
Total expenditure	105	30	25	25	185
Net Income	10	-5	-20	35	20

▲ An example budget for a young person

Net income is calculated by subtracting total expenditure from total income. In order to save money on a regular basis or help get out of debt, total expenditure should be greater than total income. If net income is negative then income needs to be increased somehow or spending reduced. In the example shown above, net income at the end of the month is £20.

Budgets are flexible. Many are updated on a monthly basis but it can sometimes be easier to break them down into weeks or even days to obtain a better understanding of how much you spend. The more often a budget is updated the more likely it is to be accurate and the more beneficial it will be.

Advantages of budgeting

Some of the advantages of making and keeping a budget include:

- ▶ makes it easier to track and control spending
- ▶ shows where you are spending too much
- ▶ can relieve money-related stress
- ▶ can help with debt management
- ▶ can help free up and save money
- ▶ can help with investing money
- ▶ can help prepare for emergencies
- ▶ can help share financial information with others – for example, couples can track spending or have it to hand if such information is required when applying for a loan or mortgage.

UNIT 2 PERSONAL DEVELOPMENT

Keeping to a budget

Keeping to a budget can be difficult; however, the diagram below gives some tips on keeping on track. Finally, do it now rather than later. Creating a budget sooner rather than later can set you on the way to achieving your goals.

Consider quality vs price: cheaper items can sometimes be inferior quality and better-quality items tend to cost more. It is important to research items to see if you can save money elsewhere and what represents the best value for money. This is covered in more detail on page 106.

Keep your budget up to date: keeping track of spending on a daily basis can help keep your budget up to date. Regularly checking and updating the budget will help keep you focused on your goals but will also allow you to make any necessary changes.

Treat yourself: it is important to socialise and put aside money for the fun things in life. If you are making a budget it is important to factor in time and money for entertainment which can help keep you motivated. Additionally, it is important to set yourself regular rewards especially if your budget is spread out over a long period of time.

Sticking to a budget

Motivation: when creating a budget and trying to stick to it, it is important to keep in mind the motivation you have for changing your spending habits and the goals you want to achieve.

Be realistic: when creating a budget it is important to be realistic about what you can afford to save or pay off. Trying to save too much can mean taking money away from other expenditures.

Self-discipline: perhaps the hardest thing to do is to be self-disciplined. Changing your spending habits takes a lot of willpower but over time it is possible to adjust to the lifestyle your budget calls for.

▲ How to stick to a budget

Activity — Managing a budget (ICT) (M) (PS)

1. Create a table detailing your own income and spending for:
   - a today
   - b this week
   - c this month.

   What is your net income at the end of each of these periods?

2. 'A budget is a beneficial financial tool that makes life easier.' Evaluate the impact of a budget on a young person's life.

3. Refer to the sample budget on page 129.
   - a What could the person do to increase income?
   - b What could the person do to decrease spending?
   - c If the person lost their part-time job, but carried on spending at the same level, how would this affect their net income?

4. Identify and explain three expenditures adults might have that a young person would not.

5. Using the internet or the Glossary (pages 215–219), put the following terms into your own words:
   - a income
   - b expenditure
   - c budget
   - d disposable income
   - e net income
   - f **overspending**
   - g debt
   - h **bankruptcy**
   - i **eviction**
   - j credit rating
   - k **loan sharks**.

130

Section 6 Making informed financial decisions

What are the consequences of poor budgeting?

A budget will help you live within your means and guide you in achieving your short- and long-term financial goals. Not having a budget is like not having a financial map or plan for your life. The diagram below depicts some of the consequences of not having a budget, which include **spending leaks**, overspending and debt.

Activity

Poor budgeting

1. Identify the consequences of poor budgeting.
2. Evaluate the need for a budget for a 16-year-old.

Could result in:
- bankruptcy
- eviction
- emotional health issues
- poor credit rating/unable to get credit
- resorting to desperate measures, e.g. loan sharks/theft

No budget → Spending leaks → Overspending → Debt (credit cards, overdraft, loans, payday loans)

Which contribute to ↑

Spiralling debt

Resulting in:
- Interest rate charges

▲ Possible consequences of not having a budget

How can good financial decisions be made based on research, advice and credible information?

When making any financial decision it is very important to shop around and make a decision based on research, advice and credible information. For example, if you were purchasing a car it would make financial sense to check out similar models at other car showrooms before making a hasty purchase. This will allow you to compare prices and get the best deal.

Many of us will have to make personal financial decisions in our lives and common decisions will include the following:

- Where is the best place to do my online shopping?
- What provider should I use for a **personal loan**?
- Which **internet banking** provider should I use?
- Which **current account** should I choose?
- Who has the best saving scheme?
- Which provider has the most competitive **ISA (Individual Savings Account)** scheme?

Before making any of the financial decisions above, it is important to gather all the research, advice and information from as many sources as possible which will result in an informed decision being made. It is worth noting that financial trends change on a day-to-day basis and the best offer today might be different from the best offer tomorrow. The research, advice and information gathered usually has a short shelf-life and would need to be repeated if the financial decision is delayed.

Sources of advice, information and research

Financial decisions	Sources of advice, information and research
Best place to shop online Best personal loan Top internet banking provider Most competitive current account Best savings scheme The most competitive ISA	The Money Advice Service: www.moneyadviceservice.org.uk The Money Saving Expert: www.moneysavingexpert.com/banking/compare-best-bank-accounts Financial comparison websites: • www.gocompare.com • www.comparethemarket.com • www.moneysupermarket.com • www.uSwitch.com Financial adviser **Citizens Advice Bureau** Bank manager/employee Local building societies Online bank providers Research undertaken in a local branch of a bank Price comparison websites: • www.idealo.co.uk • www.pricerunner.co.uk Friends and family

131

UNIT 2 PERSONAL DEVELOPMENT

How can consumers assess the credibility of financial information and advice?

There is a wealth of financial advice available both online and on the high street. Some of this advice may be biased. This means that the advice provider might not always have the best interests of the consumer at heart and may have their own agenda. For example, a bank manager may receive **commission** if they sell a certain product (i.e. a loan); therefore they might push advice on a consumer, without fully considering their needs.

It can be very difficult for a consumer to wade through all the biased information in order to find out what might truly be the best financial product for them. It is very important that a consumer is aware of potential biased sources so that they can gather information from the most non-biased sources in order to make a fully informed decision.

On this page and on page 133, some common sources of financial information are shown:

Source:	Financial comparison websites
Verdict:	Usually non-biased
Reasoning:	Using comparison websites is a must in trying to find the cheapest deal, although you will have to use multiple comparison websites in order to compare the products fully as not all of the sites list every company. Some companies do not use comparison websites at all, so you will have to contact them directly in order to view the products they offer. For example, Hughes Insurance NI do not use comparison websites. Some websites have been criticised as they display a big headline price which distracts from the small print which contains crucial product features.

Source:	The Money Advice Service
Verdict:	Non-biased
Reasoning:	The Money Advice Service is a UK-wide, independent service set up by the government to improve people's financial well-being. They pride themselves on delivering impartial and quality advice which is consistent and delivered by qualified professionals. They are independent from any sales process and can therefore be considered non-biased.

Source:	The Money Saving Expert
Verdict:	Non-biased
Reasoning:	The editorial code on their website, www.MoneySavingExpert.com, states that their main aim is to 'help the consumer'. They remain independent from commercial objectives and therefore could be considered as non-biased.

Source:	Financial adviser
Verdict:	Usually unbiased if they are registered, qualified and independent
Reasoning:	Financial Advisers comply with the **Financial Conduct Authority** whose work is defined by the **Financial Services and Markets Act 2000**. Their advice should be non-biased and have the best interests of the consumer at heart. However, advisers sometimes face a conflict of interest. Instead of acting only in the client's best interest, advisers sometimes make recommendations which are influenced by third parties who pay them commission, rendering the advice biased. Furthermore, there are financial advisers that are considered **'restricted' advisers** – they will only recommend a suitable product for you from the range of products they sell. A restricted adviser does not have to tell you that you could buy a similar product from another company at a cheaper price.

Source:	Citizens Advice Bureau
Verdict:	Unbiased
Reasoning:	The Citizens Advice Bureau complies with the Financial Conduct Authority. They are independent and give advice in an unbiased way.

Source:	Bank/building society employee
Verdict:	Biased
Reasoning:	An employee of a particular bank/building society will most likely only make product recommendations based on the products sold within their organisation. This will not take into account the products of competitors and therefore will be biased information.

Section 6 Making informed financial decisions

Source:	Friends and family
Verdict:	Biased
Reasoning:	Not only are friends and family usually unqualified and unregistered, they will usually make recommendations based on what they have tried and tested. This may not take into account your financial situation or requirements and will therefore be biased.

Source:	Price comparison websites, e.g. Price Runner
Verdict:	Non-biased
Reasoning:	**Ofcom** has an accreditation scheme and members who are listed on their website are considered non-biased. Accredited price comparison websites must show a good selection of providers (covering at least 90 per cent of the market). There is no requirement to show absolutely all deals in the market so using multiple websites is recommended.

Source:	Online banking website/local branch research
Verdict:	Biased
Reasoning:	An online bank or local branch will most likely only make product recommendations based on the products sold by their bank/website. This will not take into account the products of competitors and therefore will be biased information. There might be an abundance of attractive marketing material and literature available online or in a local branch, but again this is to encourage a sale and will not take into account competitors' products.

Activity — Assessing financial information

1 Using the websites in the table above, provide a website summary using the following websites:

Website	What services are offered?	Who might use this website?	Is this website useful or not? Why?
www.moneyadviceservice.org.uk			
www.gocompare.com			
www.comparethemarket.com			
www.moneysupermarket.com			
www.uSwitch.com			
www.idealo.co.uk			
www.pricerunner.co.uk			

2 Using the internet to guide your decision making, look at the scenarios below and choose the best two sources of information, advice and guidance for each financial decision.

   a I am looking to buy a new Dyson V6 vacuum cleaner and looking for value for money. There are too many websites to sift through to find the cheapest price.

   b I am buying a new car but do not have enough money to purchase it outright. I want to know the best personal loan deals out there.

   c My mother and father keep bugging me to open an ISA. I do not even know where to begin looking for the best one on the market.

   d I am fed up with the charges my bank bill me for at the end of every month. Surely there are cheaper current accounts out there. I need to find out the best current account on the market.

   e I spend all my money in my account every month as I do not have a savings account. I really should get my act together. I wonder what banks offer the best interest rates at the moment?

3 What is an ISA?

4 Explain the role of a financial adviser.

5 Using www.comparethemarket.com, answer the following questions:

   a What savings account has the highest interest rate?

   b Which branch-based bank has the lowest interest rate for a Cash ISA?

133

How can consumers protect against fraud and identity theft?

Identity theft happens when **criminals** access enough information about someone's identity (such as their name, date of birth, current or previous addresses) to commit identity fraud. **Identity fraud** can be described as the use of a stolen identity in criminal activity to acquire goods or services by deception.

▲ Online identity theft is on the rise

Criminals commit identity theft by stealing your personal information. This is often done by taking documents from your rubbish, theft of credit or debit cards or by making contact with you and pretending to be from a legitimate organisation.

With the ownership and use of credit and debit cards and **contactless payments** increasing, identity theft and crime is on the rise.

▲ Contactless payment can be made with a debit or credit card

What is meant by contactless payment?

Contactless is a fast, easy and secure way to pay for purchases costing £30 and under. Contactless payments are becoming increasingly common on a range of devices including:

- debit and credit cards
- stickers
- key fobs
- wearable devices, such as watches and wristbands
- mobile devices (with Apple Pay being the most popular), such as smartphones and tablets.

▲ The contactless payment icon found on credit and debit cards with contactless capability

The contactless device contains an antenna so that when it is touched against a contactless terminal, it securely transmits purchase information. No PIN is needed.

You can tell if you have a contactless card if you see the logo on the front or back of your card.

Protecting yourself against identity theft and fraud when using credit or debit and contactless payment methods

Criminals are using increasingly sophisticated methods of obtaining personal details to commit identity theft and fraud, but there are small steps that can be taken to protect yourself.

Section 6 Making informed financial decisions

- Don't throw away anything with your name, address or financial details on it without shredding it first.
- If you receive an unsolicited email or phone call from what appears to be your bank or building society asking for your security details, never reveal your full password, login details or account numbers. Be aware that a bank will never ask for your PIN or for a whole security number or password.
- If you are concerned about the source of a call, wait five minutes and call your bank from a different telephone making sure there is a dialling tone.
- Check your bank statements carefully and report anything suspicious to the bank or financial service provider concerned. Sometimes criminals will start by taking out minimal amounts that could easily be missed.
- Know when your bank or credit card statement is due and if it doesn't arrive, tell your service provider.
- If possible, set your account preferences to only receive online statements.
- If you move house, ask Royal Mail to redirect your post for at least a year.
- Never keep your PIN saved on your phone, or close to where you keep your cards.
- Shred documentation containing PIN codes or online banking login details.
- Immediately report the loss of any payment method or device to the bank or credit provider.
- If possible, securely protect your contactless device with a PIN.
- Carry your contactless payment methods securely when shopping.
- When using the pin or contactless facility while shopping, do not hand over your card to the shop assistant. The technology is designed so that you are the only person that handles the card or device.
- Take measures to cover or disguise the PIN you type in when using chip and pin facilities or ATMs.

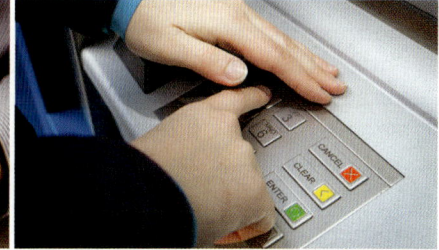

▲ Online banking on a mobile device   ▲ Contactless payment devices   ▲ Cover your PIN

Protecting yourself when online banking

More and more people are turning to the internet to bank. As a result losses from online banking fraud rose by 48 per cent in 2014 compared with 2013. The rise can be attributed to the increased use of computer malware and fraudsters trying to trick people out of their financial details. When banking online you should:

- beware of scam emails asking you to divulge your username and passwords
- have a secure password that cannot be easily guessed
- always type in the URL instead of searching for it to ensure you are on the correct webpage
- install free security software offered by most banks such as Trusteer Rapport
- make sure that your computer has up-to-date software, anti-virus, anti-spyware and a firewall.

Activity

Protecting against fraud and identity theft

1. Debit and credit card fraud can take place by **shoulder surfing** and **card skimming**. With a partner, discuss and write down what you think is meant by each of these terms.
2. Suggest six ways that you can protect yourself against identify theft when using a debit card.

UNIT 2 PERSONAL DEVELOPMENT

Protecting yourself against identity theft and fraud shopping online

A 2015 Sales Index (IMRG Capgemini eRetail Sales Index) estimated that 27% of retail sales now take place online – and forecasted 11% growth in 2016.

Customers often have to trust websites to protect personal data and payment details, in order to protect them from identity theft and fraud. There are several steps that can be taken to minimise the risk of identity theft and fraud when shopping online.

- Make sure the retail stores you buy from are legitimate. As far as possible always manually type URLs. Simply searching for a store can lead to you visiting unauthentic websites.
- Use a credit card rather than a debit card as some credit cards will protect you against fraud. It is more difficult to recover lost funds on a debit card.
- Use PayPal or Google Wallet or similar software. Repeatedly typing in credit and debit card numbers increases the risk of theft.
- Before typing in payment details, make sure you have a secure connection. Look for the image of a lock in your browser window, an address that starts with 'https' (rather than 'http'), the wording 'Secure Sockets Layer' (SSL), or a pop-up box that says you are entering a secure portion of the website.
- Create strong passwords that include upper and lower case letters, numbers, symbols and punctuation marks, and update them regularly to help prevent hacking, particularly on websites that have stored your credit or debit card information.
- Protect against **malware (malicious software)** by regularly updating your browser, operating system and security software. Setting your browser security high enough to detect unauthorised downloads and using pop-up blockers will also help.

Investment scams

Many of us receive **spam** (or junk) email on a daily basis, which clutters our inboxes. Much of it is unwanted junk sent to many email addresses at once. Unfortunately, criminals are using email to try and scam unsuspecting victims. Scam emails can take many forms, for example, you could receive an email from someone pretending to be a distant relative offering you a share in an inheritance.

Some of these junk emails are known as **phishing emails**. Phishing is a method used by criminals to access valuable personal details, such as usernames and passwords, which can then be sold on, making money for the criminals. Very often the emails appear to be authentic and from legitimate organisations, but embedded links within the message direct you to a hoax website where login or personal details are requested. Common phishing emails include:

- emails pretending to be from a bank or trusted establishment, such as PayPal or Apple
- emails pretending to be from HM Revenue and Customs (HMRC) about tax refunds.

From: Revenue & Customs [mailto:philatelic.ries@r&c.gov.uk]
Sent: 28 March 2016 10.36
To: Mr Jones
Subject: Revenue & Customs tax refund

Revenue & Customs

Tax Refund - Act Now

Dear Mr Jones

Our records show that you have made an overpayment on your income tax for year ending 2015. Revenue & Customs have issued a I29 form to issue a repayment for the overpayment of **£656.30**. Please click on the link below to reclaim your overpaid tax.

Get Started

For security reasons we will record your IP address, time and date. Please insure all information is input correctly or you may be liable to a penalty fee and possible criminal prosecution and legal action.

Revenue & Customs

▲ A phishing email claiming to be from a revenue and customs department

Protecting yourself against scam emails

These small steps can be taken to ensure that you are not caught out by an email scam.

- Do not open emails sent from an unrecognised email address.
- Ignore emails where the sender's email address does not correspond to the trusted organisation's website address.
- Do not respond to threatening emails saying, for example, 'act immediately or your account will be closed'.
- Disregard emails that ask you to give personal details.
- Disregard emails that contain spelling and grammatical errors.
- Do not click any links contained within suspicious emails.
- Do not reply to the senders of suspicious emails.
- Ignore any attachments that come with suspicious emails.

If in doubt about an email at all, it is best to report it and send it immediately to your junk or spam folder.

Source A shows how easy it is to be caught out by a phishing scam.

SOURCE A *Belfast Telegraph* February 2016.

Money returned to internet banking scam pensioner Michael McCartan

A Belfast pensioner who was cruelly duped of nearly £1,000 in an internet banking scam has claimed victory over the faceless thieves who stole his money. Michael McCartan has received all of the money back that was taken from his and his wife's Christmas pension payments in a cyber con.

Danske Bank – where Mr McCartan had banked for over 46 years – initially told him that it would not refund the stolen £970 as he had failed to protect himself sufficiently from online criminals. But after the bank managed to recover most of the money stolen from the 72-year-old in what it described as 'complex case of fraud', Dankse has made up the balance.

The money was taken from Mr McCartan's bank in several transactions after he was stung in the phishing scam around December 16 last year. Scammers used his bank details to buy concert and flight tickets and to move money within Western Union in the US.

Phishing is a growing online crime in Northern Ireland where the victim receives an email purportedly from a reputable company in order to get them to reveal confidential details, such as bank information or address online, which are then fraudulently used. Mr McCartan mistakenly updated his bank account details to what he believed was a genuine request to update his Amazon account or it would be suspended.

'I'm delighted with the news,' Mr McCartan, who cares for his bed-bound wife Eileen, told Radio Ulster's On Your Behalf.

'Danske hasn't really told me the full story but the manager asked me to come down and meet her and the branch manager. 'They went through the whole thing with me, that some of the money had been recovered, that they were working on transactions and were hopeful that these could be recovered but in the meantime that it was within the branch manager's remit to make up the shortfall and give me all the money back.'

▲ Michael McCartan in his Dunmurry home

Danske Bank said: 'We can confirm that Mr McCartan has had lost funds credited to his account. This was a complex case of fraud, and like all other such cases, it was reviewed on an individual basis by the bank.' Mr McCartan was initially told by Danske Bank that his money would not be refunded as he had failed to protect himself sufficiently from online criminals.

Last month a spokesman said: 'Every case is looked at on its own merits. Unfortunately, under the terms and conditions of his account, this customer is not entitled to a refund from the bank because by giving away his card details he effectively authorised the transaction.' However, Mr McCartan had referred his complaint to the Financial Ombudsman as he claimed that Danske should have picked up on unusual purchases on his account.

(http://www.belfasttelegraph.co.uk/news/northern-ireland/money-returned-to-internet-banking-scam-pensioner-michael-mccartan-34476452.html)

Activity — Phishing scam

1 Study Source A.
   a What steps could Mr McCartan have taken to protect himself online?
   b On this occasion, Mr McCartan was reimbursed. Do you think he should have been reimbursed? Give two reasons for your answer.

UNIT 2 PERSONAL DEVELOPMENT

What are the advantages and disadvantages of consumer choices?

A consumer is someone who buys goods and services to use personally. There are a range of choices and decisions that consumers have to make on a daily basis. This section explores three consumer decisions that many of us will face in our lives. The issues that will be investigated are:

1 quality versus price
2 cash versus credit
3 buying versus renting.

Quality versus price

Everyone wants to get the best possible value for their money. It is often thought that the more something costs, the better quality it will be and the longer it will last, but this is not necessarily the case.

If you needed to purchase a tin opener would you buy product A or B? Ask yourself why. Your answer could be an indication of whether you prioritise quality or price.

It is not always the case that something more costly is of higher quality. For example, if you were considering laying a wooden floor; using bamboo would be a cheaper alternative to common hardwoods, and it is just as durable, stylish and easy to maintain.

When making this type of consumer decision it is important to know how much you can afford, then shop around to get the best possible quality for your budget.

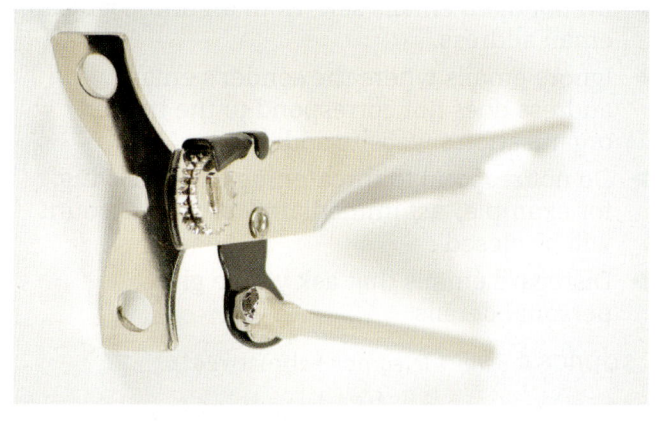

▲ Product A, priced at £1.75

▲ Product B, priced at £6.80

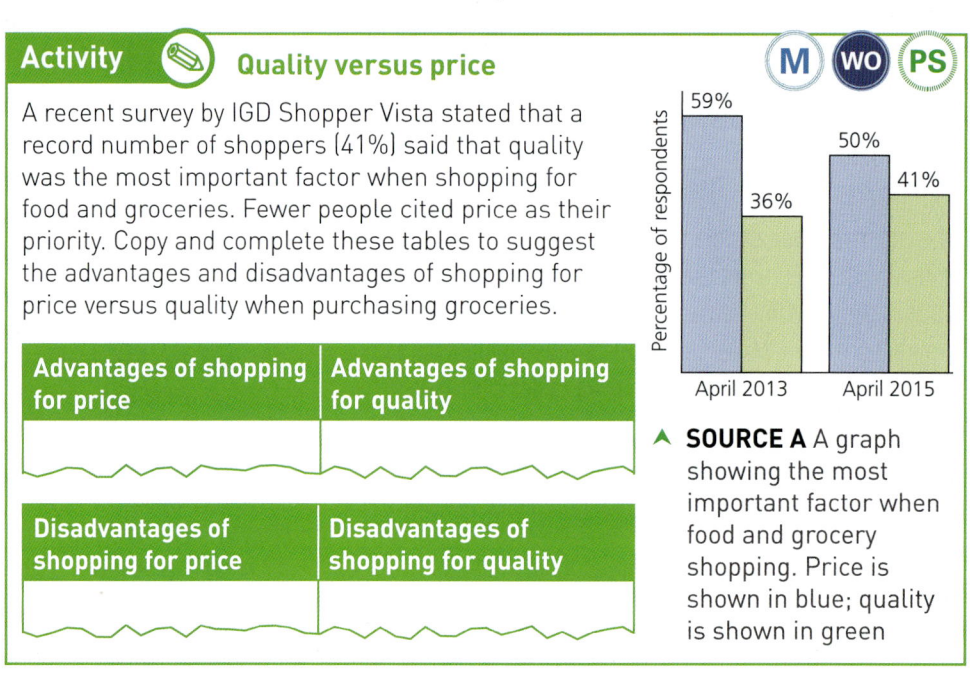

Activity — Quality versus price

A recent survey by IGD Shopper Vista stated that a record number of shoppers (41%) said that quality was the most important factor when shopping for food and groceries. Fewer people cited price as their priority. Copy and complete these tables to suggest the advantages and disadvantages of shopping for price versus quality when purchasing groceries.

Advantages of shopping for price	Advantages of shopping for quality

Disadvantages of shopping for price	Disadvantages of shopping for quality

April 2013: 59%, 36%
April 2015: 50%, 41%

▲ **SOURCE A** A graph showing the most important factor when food and grocery shopping. Price is shown in blue; quality is shown in green

Cash versus credit

Most retailers or service providers have facilities to pay by cash or by credit or **debit card**. But what do these terms mean?

Credit

Credit is a term used to describe obtaining goods or services without paying for them immediately. There are a number of different types of credit, which include loans, **credit cards** and store cards.

▲ Commonly used credit cards

Credit cards

Credit cards are a commonly accepted form of payment for goods and can also be used to withdraw cash from ATMs. Organisations such as MasterCard and Visa agree to give people credit up to an agreed limit and, in turn, send out monthly bills stating a minimum amount to be repaid. If credit card bills are paid off in full each month then there is little or no charge for the consumer. However, if the consumer fails to pay off the full balance then they are charged interest on the money they owe, which adds to their debt. Some credit cards can be useful when purchasing items online as they offer the consumer more protection. For example, if something you bought online was not delivered, the credit card company would issue a refund.

Debit cards

When debit cards are used they take out (debit) the value of the goods or services from the bank account that is linked to the card. When using a debit card it is possible to spend more money than is in the linked account. This would mean that the consumer would go into their overdraft.

The table below lists the advantages and disadvantages of paying for goods or services by cash and credit.

Advantages	Disadvantages
Cash	
can make budgeting and accounting easier	less convenient, as you might have to search for an ATM
handing over cash tends to lead to less spending	if you lose your wallet or purse, any cash in it might never be returned
less likely to be subject to identity fraud	carrying a large amount of cash can make you a target for criminals
Debit cards	
more convenient than cash	can lead to overspending if not managed carefully
can track spending with online banking	can be subject to criminals stealing account information or identity fraud
can be used to shop online	some retailers and ATMs charge for using a debit card
can be replaced if lost or stolen	doesn't have same payment protection as a credit card
Credit cards	
more convenient than cash	can lead to overspending if not managed carefully
credit can be easily obtained	can lead to debt
can track spending online	some companies charge a monthly fee
buyer protection means you are less likely to be subject to online scams	can be expensive if **interest rates** are high
can be replaced if lost or stolen	credit cards can be an easy target for criminals
good credit history can make it easier to obtain a loan or mortgage	onus is on customer to resolve any credit history disputes

▲ Advantages and disadvantages of cash, debit cards and credit cards as methods of payment

UNIT 2 PERSONAL DEVELOPMENT

> **Activity** — **Cash versus credit** (M) (PS)
>
> 1 'Using a credit card is useful when you are short of money.' Do you agree or disagree with this statement? Justify your answer.
> 2 Look at the following statistics from uk.creditcards.com, a website containing consumer credit and debt statistics:
>   - 75% of all spending in the UK retail sector was made using plastic cards as at the end of November 2013.
>   - During November 2015, domestic spending on debit cards amounted to £38.9 billion, compared to £34.9 billion spent in November 2014.
>   a Do you think the UK could soon become a cashless society.
>   b In pairs, consider the advantages and disadvantages of a cashless society. Draw up a table to list your findings.

Buying versus renting

Generally it is possible to rent most goods such as televisions, fridges or cars if you don't have enough money to buy them outright. There are advantages to renting goods, for example paying a few pounds a week to rent a television means you don't have to worry about it breaking down as the rental company would replace it. However, it also means that you do not own the item and so would lose out on any potential *profits*, should you ever need to sell it.

The decision to buy or rent is an important one when it comes to accommodation or housing.

Many people aspire to own their own home, but for many it makes more economic sense to live in rented accommodation. Numerous factors affect decision-making when it comes to buying or renting accommodation and some of these are shown in the diagram on the right.

Buying a house or property can be very stressful and can take several months to complete. It involves numerous parties other than the buyers and sellers, including estate agents, surveyors and solicitors. Buying is a long-term commitment and carries with it many advantages and disadvantages, as shown in the diagram below.

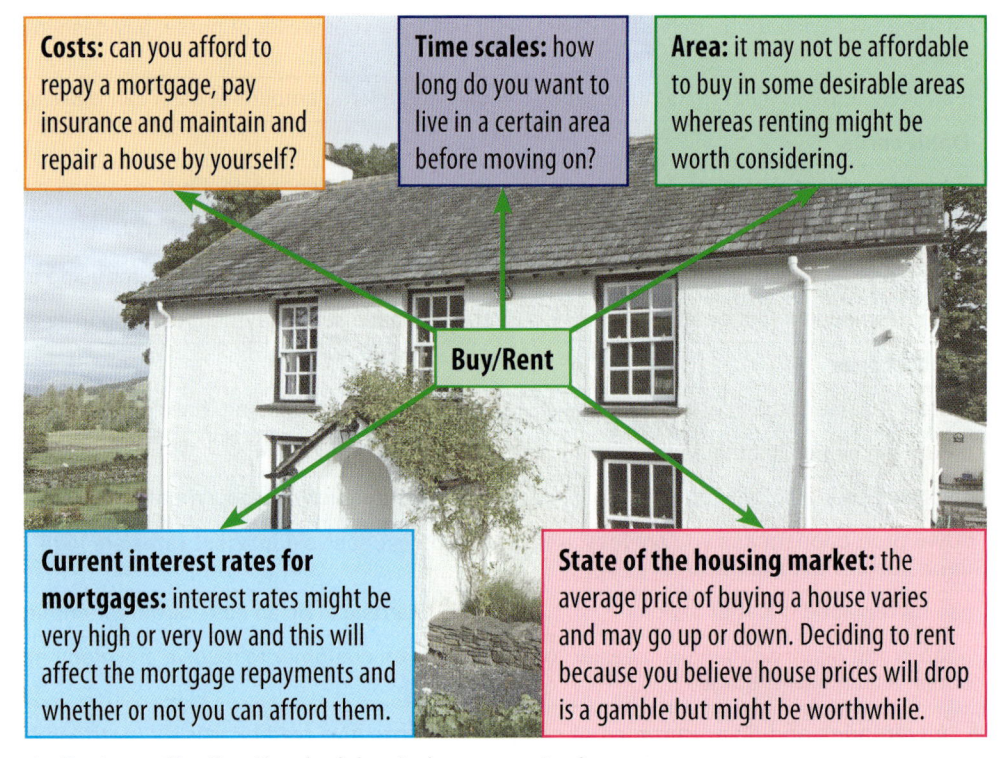

Costs: can you afford to repay a mortgage, pay insurance and maintain and repair a house by yourself?

Time scales: how long do you want to live in a certain area before moving on?

Area: it may not be affordable to buy in some desirable areas whereas renting might be worth considering.

Buy/Rent

Current interest rates for mortgages: interest rates might be very high or very low and this will affect the mortgage repayments and whether or not you can afford them.

State of the housing market: the average price of buying a house varies and may go up or down. Deciding to rent because you believe house prices will drop is a gamble but might be worthwhile.

▲ Factors affecting the decision to buy or rent a home

Section 6 Making informed financial decisions

Advantages
- Greater sense of independence and increased self-esteem.
- You own the property so can make improvements or build extensions.
- It is possible to rent out rooms or your driveway to generate extra income.
- You can turn your house into a business – for example, a B&B.
- Any improvements made are likely to increase the value of the property.
- Selling the house for more than the purchase price can lead to big profits.
- Home owners tend to have a higher social standing.

Disadvantages
- Many people don't have the capital (money) to buy a house and so need to take out a mortgage.
- Mortgage repayment rates can vary and generally have high interest rates so you end up paying a lot more than you borrowed.
- Failing to keep up with mortgage repayments can mean losing your house.
- The value of the house can decrease meaning you would lose money if it was resold. In this case you may be repaying a mortgage for more than the value of the property (this is referred to as 'negative equity').

▲ Advantages and disadvantages of buying a home

Advantages
- Renting is generally cheaper than paying off a mortgage and the rent does not fluctuate.
- Renting is usually short-term, with lease periods of a year or less.
- Landlords are responsible for the upkeep of the property, including plumbing, heating, electrical wiring and sometimes the provision of electrical goods such as fridges and ovens if specified in the lease.

Disadvantages
- You may have to move and seek alternative accommodation when the lease expires.
- You may have to share accommodation with strangers or people you dislike.
- You might not have any say over decoration or renovations.
- You will not own the house and so many people see renting as throwing money away.

▲ Advantages and disadvantages of renting a home

What are the advantages and disadvantages of using comparison websites for car and home insurance, electricity, gas and oil?

Running a home and a car is expensive. It is important to shop around when making investments in electricity, gas, oil, home and car insurance. Many consumers sign up to an energy or insurance provider and stick with that provider for a long period of time, not necessarily because they are getting a great deal, but because it is what they are familiar with and to change providers may seem like an unwanted hassle, particularly as providers often automatically renew contracts.

As insurance and energy providers are constantly reviewing and changing their charges and **tariffs**, as customers, we too should be regularly analysing whether we have the best deal. Switching providers may seem like a hassle at the time, but it could save the customer hundreds of pounds per year!

With 10 million users a year, online comparison websites are a very popular way of helping consumers compare the market for energy and insurance. The table below summarises the advantages and disadvantages of using them.

Advantages of using price comparison websites	Disadvantages of using price comparison websites
Save money: checking quotes with a comparison website will allow you to compare many different providers and enable you to choose the lowest price available on that comparison website	**Not all providers use them:** you could be missing out on a good deal if you exclusively use price comparison websites. For example, Hughes Insurance NI do not use comparison websites; instead you have to go to them individually for a quote
Easy and convenient: rather than manually gathering quotes from multiple providers, you can get a lot of information by just a few mouse clicks	**Initial false quotes:** there is a concern that many insurance providers initially provide a price for no-frills cover so that the provider appears at the top of the results page. But by the time the customer has added all the extras needed to get full coverage, there might not have been a saving at all. Similarly with energy providers, off-peak tariffs may initially lure a customer in but the initial cost increases dramatically when the peak costs are considered
Variety and choice: not only are there a variety of comparison websites you can use to compare the accuracy of figures, using multiple comparison websites will allow you to compare a vast number of providers	**Sponsored results:** most of the commonly used price comparison websites come under regular scrutiny, but some will promote providers that have paid the comparison website money to appear more visually prominently on the website, which may not necessarily provide the best deal
Smaller companies: there are less well-known providers out there that comparison websites could reveal as big money savers. This is particularly useful within the energy provider market where the market is dominated by the 'big six' and smaller providers are less well known	**Commission charges:** the cost that the customer eventually ends up with will include a built-in commission charge which is on average 24 per cent. A provider may be able to forego the commission charge if you go to them directly
	Unavailability in Northern Ireland: some price comparison websites do not cover Northern Ireland when seeking quotes, particularly energy providers
	Details shared: once all the details are typed into a comparison website, sometimes companies will use these details to make contact with you for marketing purposes. This can lead to unwanted emails/texts and calls

Section 6 Making informed financial decisions

Activity — Using price comparison websites

1 Using the internet to assist you with your research, answer the following questions:
   a Go to www.cheapestoil.co.uk/Heating-Oil-NI and find out who is the cheapest provider of oil that will deliver to your area.
   b How much is it for 500 litres?
   c How much is it for 900 litres?

2 Read Source A and use the internet to help you answer the following questions:
   a What is meant by comprehensive cover?
   b Review some of the **cashback websites** mentioned. What is a cashback website?
   c What is meant by **insurance excesses**?
   d What advice does the article offer when using price comparison websites?

SOURCE A An article on comparison websites from the *Telegraph* website, 12 January 2012

Car insurance: the pros and cons of using comparison sites

Price comparison websites say they will get you the best deal. But our investigation found that this wasn't always the case.

When the *Telegraph* put insurance price comparison websites to the test last year, the results were surprising.

In some cases we found that customers could get a cheaper insurance deal by phoning an insurer direct or by going to the insurer's own website. It can also be quicker and you could get free add-ons such as legal cover and more cashback.

One comparison website boss said the rapid growth of the sites had left many insurers out of pocket. He said: 'I believe some insurers are lowering premiums through different points of sale, such as over the telephone.'

We tested four sites, looking for the best quote on a 30-year-old female with a seven-year no-claims discount driving a 1.6L 2007 Ford Mondeo Zetec.

According to one site, the Post Office charged £363.56 for a comprehensive policy, with a £200 excess. Yet by going direct to the Post Office, we found that the cost of insurance could be reduced. We were quoted £357.16 and could reduce this further by using the £25 cashback offered through a number of cashback sites, giving a grand total of £332.16.

Anyone using the leading cashback sites, such as quidco.com, greasypalm.co.uk or topcashback.co.uk, will see links to some comparison sites. But the discounts on offer are far less.

Typically we found that premiums could be reduced by just £1.50; in contrast, by going direct to an insurer's site from a cashback website, you can earn up to £100 off your premium.

This is not the first time comparison sites have come under scrutiny. In 2008 the Financial Services Authority investigated 17 sites and said they needed to make some improvements, particularly in relation to highlighting excesses and making it clear what 'assumptions' had been made about consumers' needs.

In other words, there were concerns that some insurers might be offering 'no-frills' cover, just to cut premiums and propel their brand to the top of the comparison tables.

The comparison sites did not contest our findings, but said they were surprised that lower premiums were found by contacting an insurer direct.

Simon Lamble of confused.com said: 'This is quite an unusual thing to happen and it is not behaviour we would normally expect. We have deals in place with the insurers to ensure that the deals we offer are their best.'

A spokesman for comparethemarket.com said: 'Insurers included on our site are not allowed contractually to offer lower premiums elsewhere. Comparethemarket.com customers can be confident they are getting the cheapest deal through our site.'

The best advice for those buying car insurance is to shop around among price comparison sites and direct-only insurers. In many cases the websites could find you the cheapest quote — and they are quick and convenient to use. But remember to check carefully that the cover offered is exactly what you want — the websites' default choices for aspects of cover, such as the excess, may not be what you expect.

(www.telegraph.co.uk/finance/personalfinance/insurance/motorinsurance/8253330/Car-insurance-the-pros-and-cons-of-using-comparison-sites.html)

What are the available sources of financial advice and consumer protection?

With so many financial decisions to make throughout a lifetime it is good to know that there are numerous sources of financial advice available and that consumer protection has been written into law to guard us from unscrupulous companies.

Consumer protection

The law gives customers protection against unfair selling practices. The consumer has basic legal rights and it is most beneficial to know about two laws in particular:

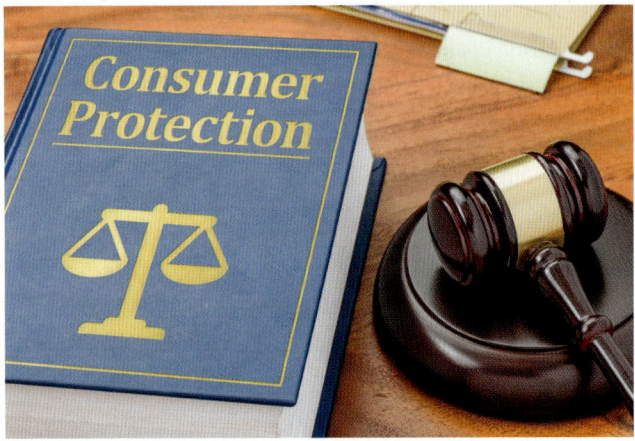

Consumer Credit Act 1974 (amended in 2006)

The Consumer Credit Act gives customers protection when entering into a loan agreement. It also gives customers the right to a cooling-off period. The Consumer Credit Act ensures the following:

- The creditor assesses the customer's credit-worthiness, in other words assesses if it is realistic for the customer to pay back the loan within the agreed timeframe. They can use the information the customer provides and a credit reference agency.
- The customer must be informed of:
  - the nature of the agreement
  - the identity and address of the creditor
  - the type of credit
  - the amount of credit or the credit limit
  - the duration of the agreement
  - the rate of interest charges, the APR and any conditions applicable to the rate
  - the total amount payable
  - the amount and timings of repayments.

This information must be contained in a document headed 'Pre-Contract Information'. Both the customer and the credit provider must sign the agreement and a copy of the agreement must be given to the customer either at the date of signing or within seven days.

▲ A Pre-Contract Information document for a loan

Consumer Protection from Unfair Trading Regulations 2008

The Consumer Protection from Unfair Trading Regulations Act protects consumers from unfair or misleading trading practices. It bans misleading advertisements and aggressive sales tactics.

The law has put in place the following:

- A general ban on unfair commercial practices: this means if practice falls below the good-faith standards of skill and care that is expected in the industry or practice affects the consumers' ability to make an informed decision on whether to purchase a product, then it is deemed to be unfair.
- A ban on misleading and aggressive practices: this means that traders are not allowed to claim something about a product that is not true or advertise goods that do not exist.
- A 'blacklist' of sales practices which will always be unfair and so are banned outright. There are 31 banned sales techniques that are illegal under this act. These include persistent cold calling, pressure selling and aggressive doorstep calling.

144

Consumer Rights Act 2015

The Consumer Rights Act covers the following:

- **Product quality:** the product should be of satisfactory quality, fit for purpose and as described.
- **Returning goods:** consumers have a legal right to reject goods that are of an unsatisfactory quality, unfit for purpose or not as described and get a full refund within 30 days from the date the product is bought. After 30 days consumers are not legally entitled to a full refund if the item develops a fault, although some sellers may offer you an extended refund period.
- **Repairs and replacements:** if you are outside the 30-day right to reject, the customer has to give the retailer one opportunity to repair or replace any goods which are of unsatisfactory quality, unfit for purpose or not as described.
- **Digital content rights:** the Consumer Rights Act defines digital content as 'data which are produced and supplied in digital form'. Just like goods, digital content must be of satisfactory quality, fit for a particular purpose or as described by the seller. If digital content does not conform to these criteria, the customer has the right to a repair or replacement of the digital content purchased.
- **Delivery rights:** the retailer is responsible for goods until they are in your physical possession or in the possession of someone appointed by you to accept them. There is a default delivery period of 30 days during which the retailer needs to deliver unless a longer period has been agreed.

As consumer law can be complicated and difficult to understand there are numerous sources of financial assistance available to help customers interpret and use the law to their best advantage.

Free financial help

There are a number of sources where a customer can obtain information. Free financial help and information can be obtained from:

- charities such as Turn2us
- government-led or government-backed services such as the Money Advice Service
- commercial organisations like comparison websites.

While these services are seen as reliable sources of information, they are not always regulated. This means that if a customer makes a decision based only on their advice the customer is responsible for the decisions made and there will be fewer rights if the product turns out to be unsuitable.

Other useful sources

- Which?: provides some free general advice, but it is a subscription-based service so you have to pay to be a member and to access services such as their money helpline.
- Citizens Advice Bureau: a local service which provides help on many consumer issues including debt. Their website also provides generic financial advice.
- Financial advisers.
- Financial Conduct Authority: provides information on financial products and possible scams. Someone using financial advisers can also check if they are using a regulated financial adviser.
- MoneySavingExpert.com: provides money saving tips and advice.

the Money Advice Service

UNIT 2 PERSONAL DEVELOPMENT

Activity — Consumer rights

1. In pairs discuss the following consumer issues and, using your own knowledge and internet research, discuss what you think the consumer rights would be in each situation.

   a I bought a skirt but when I arrived home I changed my mind. I took it back to the shop the next day but the staff would not give me a refund. Can they do this? Why?

   b I bought new shoes recently but the heel of one shoe broke the second time I wore them. The shop is offering to repair them. Do I have to accept this?

   c I bought an iPhone after seeing a private advertisement in my local newspaper. When I got it home I discovered that it wasn't working. What are my rights?

   d I received a DVD player for my birthday but it doesn't work properly. The shop manager told me to send it back to the manufacturer, as the fault had nothing to do with the shop. Is this correct?

2. In addition to legislation, there are a number of organisations which have been set up to protect the interests of consumers. Using the internet, copy and complete the following table to summarise what each organisation does.

Organisation	What do they do?
The Consumers' Association www.which.net/campaigns/contents.html	
Trading Standards Service www.economy-ni.gov.uk/topics/consumer-affairs/trading-standards-service	
The General Consumer Council www.consumercouncil.org.uk	

3. Copy and complete the table below. In groups, using the internet to help you, summarise each consumer protection law. You will be required to present your findings to the whole class.

Act	Main details
Sale and Supply of Goods and Services Act 1994	
Consumer Protection Act 1987	
Food Safety (Northern Ireland) Order 1991	
Weights and Measures (Northern Ireland) Order 1981	

4. What is meant by a credit reference agency? What do they do?
5. Give two examples of a credit reference agency.

UNIT 3

EMPLOYABILITY

Section 1 The impact of globalisation on employment

Key content
- The impact of global economic changes on Northern Ireland:
  - **changing employment patterns**
  - migration
  - the growth and impact of new technologies
  - skills shortages in the workforce
  - emerging careers as a result of **globalisation**

This section looks at the impact globalisation has had on Northern Ireland. It explores how global economic changes have led to changes in employment patterns with particular relation to immigration, emerging careers and the growth of new technologies.

What is the impact of global economic changes in Northern Ireland?

How we communicate and share each other's cultures through travel and trade is changing ever more quickly and efficiently. We are in a huge global economy where something that happens in one area can have knock-on effects worldwide. This process is called globalisation.

Globalisation means the world is becoming increasingly interconnected due to increased trade and cultural exchange. Globalisation has increased the production of goods and services. The biggest companies are no longer national firms but multinational companies. Globalisation has been taking place for hundreds of years, but has really been impacting on Northern Ireland over the last few decades.

Globalisation has resulted in:
- increased international trade
- companies operating in more than one country
- greater reliance on the global economy
- freer and wider movement of capital, goods and services
- awareness and growth of companies such as Coca-Cola, McDonald's and Nike.

▲ Globalisation

Globalisation means that Northern Irish companies are expected to compete on a global platform. This means they have to try to sell their products and services to markets outside of Northern Ireland. They may also need to source raw materials from global markets and the Northern Ireland government needs to try to attract global companies to set up and employ people in Northern Ireland. We are part of a world that is now referred to as a **global village**.

> **Activity — A global village**
>
> 1 Using the internet, research what is meant by a 'global village' and write your own definition of the term.
> 2 What is the impact of a global village on Northern Ireland? Think about the advantages and disadvantages.
> 3 Design a poster that shows how the term 'global village' impacts on Northern Ireland.

Changing employment patterns

As part of a global village the **employment patterns** in Northern Ireland have changed greatly. Fifty years ago very few companies from Northern Ireland operated abroad and most of the jobs in Northern Ireland were provided by Northern Ireland-based companies. Today the situation is very different. Many people in Northern Ireland are now employed by global companies or by Northern Irish-based companies that depend on a global market.

When someone is employed it usually means that they are in a paid job with a contract of employment. Employment patterns refer to the types of jobs we do, who employs us and how many of us are employed at a given time. Over the last 50 years, many changes have occurred in employment patterns within the UK and Northern Ireland. These include:

- more women in work
- growth in the number of people employed in the public sector, such as the NHS
- growth in service industries such as banking, IT and tourism
- decline in manufacturing industries such as shipbuilding
- changing employee and consumer demands
- an increase in a **gig economy** of employment.

In Northern Ireland, like elsewhere in the UK, the pattern of employment has changed.

> **Activity — A gig economy**
>
> Use the following links to investigate the term 'gig economy':
> - www.bbc.co.uk/news/business-37384174. 'The gig economy: Opportunity or threat?'
> - www.bbc.co.uk/news/business-37605643. '"Gig" economy all right for some as up to 30% work this way', Rebecca Marston, 10 October 2016.
> - www.theguardian.com/commentisfree/2015/jul/26/will-we-get-by-gig-economy. 'The "gig economy" is coming. What will it mean for work?' Arun Sundarajan, 26 July 2015.
>
> 1 What is meant by a gig economy?
> 2 How does a gig economy impact on employment patterns?
> 3 Evaluate the benefits and drawbacks of a gig economy for Northern Ireland.

SOURCE A Article from the *Belfast Telegraph* website, 26 February 2015

Changes of career the driving force behind job creation in Northern Ireland

Northern Ireland workers are feeling increasingly confident about switching jobs with one global recruitment firm witnessing a 40 per cent increase in the number of permanent positions filled here.

Recruitment giant Hays saw a 25 per cent increase in the number of jobs over the last six months of 2014. That includes both temporary and permanent roles.

The firm has three offices in Northern Ireland, including one in Belfast city centre. And it's the IT sector which has boosted the number of Northern Ireland's workers changing jobs, according to Hays' global finance director Paul Venables.

'Permanent positions are up 40 per cent – the biggest growth was areas in IT, with a big pick-up in programmers, developers and data specialists,' he said.

That increase is in part down to fresh job creation, whereas the bulk is made up of workers jumping ship to new companies.

'There are a lot more of our professional candidates who are more comfortable about changing their jobs,' he said. 'That's a good bellwether. And the big difference in the recovery is that it's areas outside London which are seeing the biggest growth. We have seen a pick-up in SMEs hiring a few more people, but the real job creation is people changing their career. And it's not salary levels that are driving this, but a lack of promotions within the company they are working for.'

Mr Venables said the company had also witnessed an overall boost in the size of pay packets over the last six months.

Hays counts Moy Park, BT and EY among some of its biggest clients in Northern Ireland. And as a result of a more fluid job market and increased workforce confidence, it has expanded its Northern Ireland team to 50.

'As a result of all this, we have increased our own head count in Northern Ireland,' he said.

The latest increase is the second consecutive jump the firm has witnessed in its Northern Ireland arm. The company's UK and Ireland business showed a growth in fees to £135m, while operating profits soared by 113 per cent to £21m. Profits across the company worldwide rose to £81.5m, up from £66.7m in the six months to December.

Meanwhile, dole claimants in Northern Ireland have dropped in number for the 25th month in a row.

(www.belfasttelegraph.co.uk/business/news/changes-of-career-the-driving-force-behind-job-creation-in-northern-ireland-31022180.html)

Activity — Changing careers and job creations

Study Source A on the job force in Northern Ireland.

1 Why do you think there has been an increase in IT jobs in Northern Ireland?

2 Describe why this change in working patterns could be because of globalisation.

3 Evaluate how this change could impact on the Northern Ireland economy.

UNIT 3 EMPLOYABILITY

What is migration?

When someone moves out of a country it is known as emigration and when they move into a country it is known as immigration. People who leave their country to live elsewhere are known as emigrants in their own country and immigrants in the country they go to. This process is called migration.

Our patterns of employment (the jobs we do and how many jobs there are) are influenced by other countries and by people from other countries; this is all part of the growth of globalisation. We rely on USA-based companies to supply employment in Northern Ireland as well as to buy our products and services. We have to understand that we are part of a global economy and the process of migration is a part of this. More and more people are moving countries to find work and we in Northern Ireland must become an important player in the global market if we are to grow and survive.

There are lots of reasons for migration in our global society such as: looking for work, moving to a place where your work skills are required, retirement, reuniting of families and emigrants returning to their country of birth.

Impact of immigration on employment patterns and the economy in Northern Ireland

There has always been movement of people from one country to another and Northern Ireland has always experienced both emigration and immigration. The patterns of migration for Northern Ireland are more like those in the Republic of Ireland than the rest of the UK and since the nineteenth century there have traditionally been more emigrants than immigrants. However, during the 1990s and 2000s there was a significant growth in immigration into Northern Ireland from countries outside the UK.

People from Poland, Romania and the Philippines are just some of the immigrants who have come to Northern Ireland for work. These people bring vital skills that help the economy to grow and flourish. Likewise, many people left Northern Ireland to work in Europe, USA and Australia when their skills were required in these countries in the 1970s and 1980s.

Migrant workers coming to Northern Ireland is good for our economy as migration has meant that skills shortages in the employment market have been filled.

Many migrants work in different industries in Northern Ireland, including food processing, construction, engineering, agriculture, hospitality and healthcare. Workers from different national backgrounds can be found working in any of these industries. However, some patterns are beginning to emerge between nationality and occupation. For example, there are high levels of Portuguese-speaking and Polish workers in food processing factories in Ballymena, Derry/Londonderry, Coleraine, Dungannon and Portadown. The public and private healthcare sector in Northern Ireland benefits particularly from nurses and medical practitioners from the Philippines and India. A large number of Lithuanians have also worked on mushroom farms and in other agriculture businesses in Newtownards, Portadown and the border region.

> **Activity — Migration and Northern Ireland**
>
> Study Source B on immigration in Northern Ireland, and answer the following questions:
>
> 1 What is meant by the statement 'Immigration provides substantial economic and social benefits to Northern Ireland'?
> 2 According to this article, what does migration contribute to Northern Ireland?
> 3 List four of the key findings of the article.
> 4 How do these key findings impact on employment patterns and the economy of Northern Ireland?

SOURCE B

Immigration in Northern Ireland

Two academics from Queens' University Belfast Professor Peter Shirlow and Dr Richard Montague have written a report commissioned by the Centre for Democracy and Peace Building about the impact of immigration on Northern Ireland as part of a response to race hate crimes in 2014. It examined areas such as population, employment, housing, benefits, healthcare, social cohesion, crime, education and economy.

The report states that approximately 4 per cent of the Northern Irish workforce is made up of migrant workers and that migrant workers contribute more in tax than they use in services. It is estimated that migrant workers contributed £1.2 billion to the economy from 2004 to 2008. Migration contributed to sustaining economic growth, filling labour shortages of much needed skills and enriching Northern Irish society through cultural diversity.

Immigration provides substantial economic and social benefits to Northern Ireland through contributions in tax, labour and cultural diversity which all lead to enriching Northern Ireland. The report highlighted the following key findings:

- Migrant workers contributed about £1.2bn to the economy from 2004 to 2008
- 4 per cent of the Northern Ireland workforce is made up of migrant workers
- 3 per cent of the total number of pupils attending school in Northern Ireland are from ethnic minorities
- 81.5 per cent of migrants in the UK are employed
- less than 5 per cent of EU migrants claim Jobseeker's Allowance
- the cost of temporary migrants using the health service amounted to about £12m of the £109bn NHS budget

Professor Shirlow stated that 'the findings of the report are profoundly important because they completely rebut stereotypes that have plagued our migrant population in recent years. People need to be educated about the facts. We frequently hear claims that migrants take our jobs and use up our limited services. Migrants pose no threat to our society. This report will hopefully go some way towards changing the conversation about migrants in Northern Ireland.'

UNIT 3 EMPLOYABILITY

The growth and impact of new technologies

Each one of you uses different technologies every day, from when you wake in the morning until you go to bed at night. Consider what wakens you. How do you get to school? What technologies do you use in school?

Technology such as computers, mobile phones and the internet are part of your everyday life and there are probably quite a few you would find it hard to do without! Technology is constantly changing; each year new products come to the market offering different or improved features such as better graphics or faster download times. The technology timeline below shows when some of the technologies we use today were launched.

1976	Apple I launched – one of the world's first personal home computers
1981	IBM releases its own affordable personal computer (PC)
1982	Compact Discs are launched as a new way to store music
1989	The World Wide Web is invented
1994	Amazon is launched
1995	eBay is launched
2001	Apple launches the iPod
2004	Wikipedia is launched
2006	Facebook is created
2007	Twitter is created
2010	Apple launches the iPhone
2011	Instagram is created
2015	Apple Watch
2016	The iPhone 7 is launched

▲ Technology timeline

Activity — Changing technologies

1 Follow the instructions below.
   a Create a collage using pictures from magazines, newspapers and the internet to show your use of technologies.
   b Take the collage home and ask someone over 50 to pick out technologies they used when they were your age. Did they use any of the same technologies?
   c What can you conclude from your research?
2 a Choose two or three of the items on the Technology timeline and identify ways in which they have influenced our lifestyles.
   b Can you think of other technologies that have influenced our lifestyles? Find out when they were introduced.
3 List the advantages and disadvantages that new technology can have for our lifestyles. An example has been done for you below.

Advantages	Disadvantages
Easy access to information	Pressure to have the latest piece of technology

152

The effect of technology on employment

The growth of new technologies has affected Northern Ireland in a number of ways. It has affected the way we study and work, how we communicate, the way we shop, how we spend our leisure time and our employment patterns. If companies in Northern Ireland want to remain competitive in the global market they must seek out and use the latest technologies in order to keep one step ahead of the competition. This means that people looking for jobs must be adaptable and willing to learn new skills if they are to be employable.

Jobs that were once considered quite common are now becoming obsolete (no longer needed) in Northern Ireland and the rest of the world because of new technologies. Many jobs can be performed much more quickly and efficiently with the help of technology and, therefore, fewer employees are needed in those roles. Some jobs that are no longer needed or are in decline include the following.

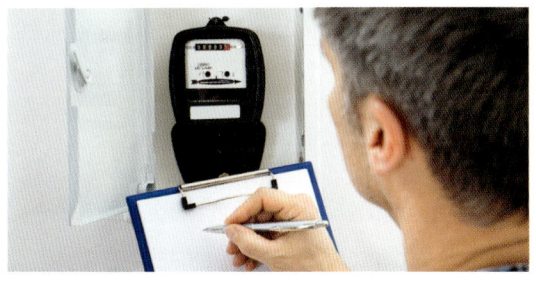

Meter readers: many people are employed by electricity and gas companies to visit domestic and commercial properties to read meters and record the amount of energy that has been used. However, in recent years many customers of electricity and gas have opted to use technology to 'pay as they go'; this means that they do not receive a bill and therefore there is no need for a meter reading. Alternatively, new technology means that meter readings can be tracked digitally.

Travel agents: many people no longer use the services of a travel agent as the internet has provided a vehicle for people to plan, book and enjoy holidays that are tailored to their specific requirements. The contacts or skills of the travel agent are no longer exclusive to the job. Individuals can now purchase flights, accommodation, car hire and insurance using new technology.

Agricultural workers: there have been numerous changes in the agricultural industry because of new technology. At one time, milk from cows was extracted by human hands. Due to technological advances the majority of milk is now extracted using machinery. This means that the volume of milk produced is substantially more than it was in the past. However, this also means that the job of 'milk maid' is no longer an employment option.

Typists: many people who once required a secretary to type and organise files now complete these activities themselves using a computer. This has seen the decline of 'typing pools' (a group of people – usually women – who typed whatever information was required in an organisation/institution).

Telephone operators: a human voice at the end of a phone is increasingly a thing of the past. This job is being replaced by touch-sensitive phones and pre-recorded messages.

UNIT 3 EMPLOYABILITY

Skills shortages in the workforce

In Northern Ireland we need to keep up to date with changing jobs and employment patterns and as part of this we need to be aware of the changes that are ongoing within employment.

Northern Ireland employment is heavily dependent on public sector jobs (health, education, government agencies) and this means that Northern Ireland depends upon the government for jobs and wages. Nearly one in three workers in Northern Ireland is employed by the government compared to nearly one in five in the UK as a whole. As there are more government cutbacks, and as the government plan to shed 20,000 public sector jobs, Northern Ireland needs to find other means of employment.

If Northern Ireland is to grow as an economy and society we need to understand that we have to be a highly skilled population in order to attract jobs and encourage enterprise.

Case study: 2015 CBI/Pearson Education and Skills Survey

More than half of businesses in Northern Ireland fear they will not be able to recruit enough high-skilled workers to succeed in the future, according to the 2015 CBI/Pearson Education and Skills Survey.

A UK-wide survey, which included 61 firms which employ people in Northern Ireland, found that 59 per cent of firms in Northern Ireland need more highly skilled staff, particularly in key sectors such as science and engineering, construction and manufacturing. But 60 per cent are not confident that they will be able to find the high-level skills needed to meet demand and grow. Businesses are already reporting real problems in recruiting people with Science, Technology, Engineering and Maths (STEM) skills – with 15 per cent currently struggling to employ graduates with sufficient STEM skills.

Nigel Smyth, CBI Northern Ireland Director, said:

> While the Northern Ireland economy continues to make headway we must be on our guard as local growth risks being undermined by a shortage of the higher-level skills businesses need to get on, and the situation is only set to get worse.
>
> High-growth, high-value sectors with the most potential are under the most pressure, like science, engineering, digital and manufacturing. We must make sure that our education and skills system is truly responsive to the needs of business and that young people receive much better careers advice, if we are to propel the Northern Ireland economy forward in the years ahead.
>
> Business also wants to see universities doing more to improve the business relevance of undergraduate courses (65 per cent) and help students become job-ready (53 per cent) if the challenge is to be met.

Rod Bristow, President of Pearson's UK business, said:

> Building a world-class school and qualifications system is the best long-term solution for securing sustainable, skilled workers and economic growth.
>
> We must prepare young people for the world of work through closer engagement and collaboration between the business community, universities, schools and further education colleges.

(Adapted from: www.cbi.org.uk/news/skills-crisis-in-northern-ireland-threatens-local-growth-cbi-pearson-survey/)

Activity: Employment prospects

1 Using the internet, find out what is meant by 'STEM jobs'.
2 Make a list of ten STEM-type jobs.
3 Evaluate how STEM jobs are important for Northern Ireland in a globalised world.

Section 1 The impact of globalisation on employment

Changing industries

The increase in new technologies is also part of the gig economy – a fast-approaching new type of job economy that will impact on employment patterns. New technologies are changing how we are employed.

Case study: Uber

Traditionally taxis in Northern Ireland have been supplied by private taxi companies in urban areas and by individual taxi drivers in rural areas. However, due to advances and changes in how we use technology this situation is changing quickly in urban areas. It is no longer necessary to phone a taxi driver or taxi operator to order a taxi. We can now use apps on our smartphones and we can even track where the taxi is and how long it will take to reach us. The latest taxi service to come to Belfast is Uber.

Uber launched in San Francisco, USA, on 31 May 2010 and it is now available in over 500 cities globally. Every week in London, 30,000 people download Uber to their phones and order a car for the first time. Uber is an app which connects taxi drivers with passengers directly, instead of through a centralised booking service. The app – which is available on Android and iOS – pitches itself as a safe and reliable way to get on-demand rides in most of the world's major cities. Using GPS, it detects your location and connects you with the nearest driver. You can also request a specific type of car if you prefer – such as a luxury ride or a straightforward taxi. The app texts you when the driver arrives and you can check the identity of the driver against who actually shows up. The app also gives you a price estimate, and is cashless – you pay through the app, including tips. You can even split the fare between different riders.

The Uber app arrived in Belfast in late 2015 and within a six-month period Uber claim that 30,000 people in the Belfast area have downloaded the app. There are more than 200 Uber taxi drivers working in the Belfast area. Uber plan to be in every town across NI by expanding organically to places like Lisburn and Bangor first.

Emerging careers as a result of globalisation

As outlined in the Uber case study, careers are changing due to technological advances and as part of the process of globalisation. We have seen that traditional careers are disappearing and changing. There are also new careers emerging due to globalisation.

Future job opportunities in Northern Ireland

There are job opportunities across all occupational areas in Northern Ireland but there is higher demand in occupations relating to STEM.

As the world becomes increasingly technology-dependent it is anticipated that the range of businesses emerging around the STEM areas will grow significantly. This will require people to acquire a good education in STEM subjects.

The following areas are extremely important to the Northern Ireland economy:

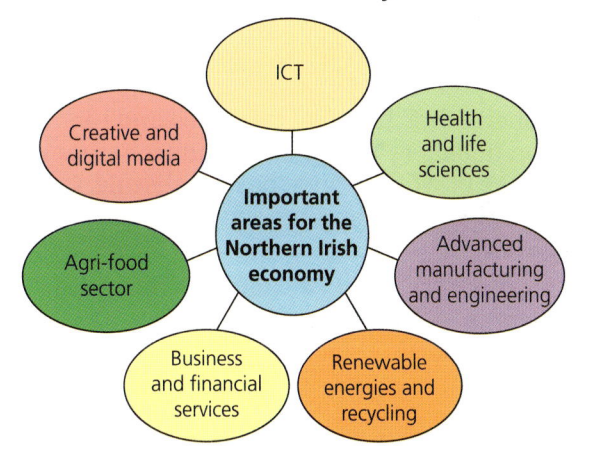

Important areas for the Northern Irish economy:
- ICT
- Health and life sciences
- Advanced manufacturing and engineering
- Renewable energies and recycling
- Business and financial services
- Agri-food sector
- Creative and digital media

▲ Important areas for the Northern Irish economy

Activity: Uber and Northern Ireland

Study the case study on Uber.

1. How has changing technology enabled the growth of Uber?
2. Do you think Uber has a future in Northern Ireland? Justify your answer.
3. How does Uber relate to the idea of a gig economy for employment patterns?
4. How does Uber demonstrate globalisation?
5. Evaluate the impact Uber might have on the taxi industry.
6. What other jobs do you think may change due to advancing technology?

ICT

ICT, particularly software development, database development, systems architecture and internet specialist skills, is very important for all types of businesses and really vital to our daily lives: mobile communication, computer games, touch screen technology and satellite navigation devices are all things we depend on.

Creative and digital media

Digital is everywhere and is extremely important to a growing economy; it helps growth through the development of new technologies and the provision of services to businesses and consumers. It is expected that because of this there will be employment in:

- cloud computing
- mobile technologies
- cross-platform mobile applications
- computer games and digital entertainment
- cyber-security products and services
- green/low carbon IT products.

Agri-food

As one of the largest industries in Northern Ireland, there could be 15,000 potential job opportunities in the next five years within the agri-food sector. Food and drink manufacturing includes the processing of meat and poultry, dairy, fish and shellfish, fruit and vegetables and the production of bakery and drinks products among others. Areas of work include bakery, distillery, creamery and ready meals production. Jobs can include:

- laboratory technicians
- food scientists
- biotech
- machine operatives
- butcher
- supply chain manager.

Business and financial services

There are many different industries within the finance, accountancy and financial services sector. This is an industry that is expected to grow in Northern Ireland. Jobs vary, but include:

- accountants
- bank officials
- underwriters
- insurance and investment brokers
- actuaries and pensions advisers.

Advanced manufacturing and engineering

This includes careers requiring Computer Aided Design (CAD) skills, Computer Numerically Controlled (CNC) machine operatives, mechanical and electrical engineering skills, including people at technician level and strategic marketing level.

Renewable energies and recycling

Global agreements on more energy efficient technology are creating demand for new engineering solutions. Mechanical engineers are at the forefront of designing everything from better forms of green energy and zero emission engines, to the latest breed of nuclear power stations. Careers in this sector include:

- mechanical engineers
- research and development managers
- physical scientists
- design and development engineers
- biological scientists and biochemists.

Activity — Emerging careers

The information on page 157 is from a booklet on the Northern Ireland government website about emerging careers due to technology and globalisation: www.economy-ni.gov.uk/sites/default/files/publications/del/Skills-in-Demand.pdf.

1 Using the information from this booklet, design a presentation to deliver to your class. The presentation should aim to:

- describe the jobs of the future in Northern Ireland
- explain why these jobs will be needed
- explain how these jobs will ensure Northern Ireland is part of the global village
- explain what future employees must do to ensure the employment needs of a future Northern Ireland are met.

Section 1 The impact of globalisation on employment

EMPLOYMENT PROJECTIONS
Top 10 growth sectors (2015-2025)

- Professional, scientific and technical
- Information and communication
- Administrative
- Manufacturing
- Retail
- Hotels and restaurants
- Construction
- Health and social work
- Transport and storage
- Art and entertainment

There will be growth opportunities for all skills levels across a range of sectors, the focus will be predominantly on higher level skills.

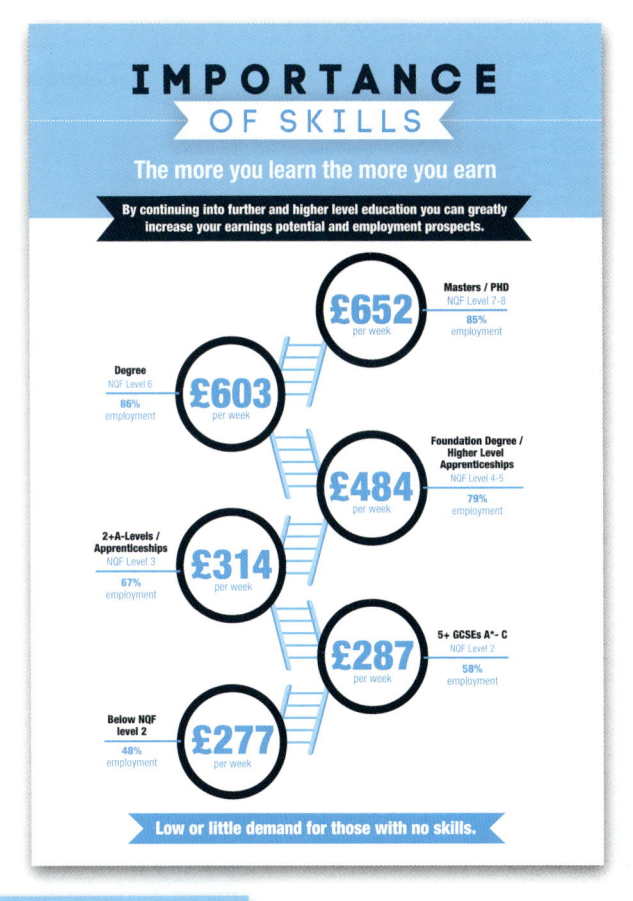

IMPORTANCE OF SKILLS
The more you learn the more you earn

By continuing into further and higher level education you can greatly increase your earnings potential and employment prospects.

- **Masters / PHD** — NQF Level 7-8 — £652 per week — 85% employment
- **Degree** — NQF Level 6 — £603 per week — 86% employment
- **Foundation Degree / Higher Level Apprenticeships** — NQF Level 4-5 — £484 per week — 79% employment
- **2+A-Levels / Apprenticeships** — NQF Level 3 — £314 per week — 67% employment
- **5+ GCSEs A*- C** — NQF Level 2 — £287 per week — 58% employment
- **Below NQF level 2** — £277 per week — 48% employment

Low or little demand for those with no skills.

SUBJECTS IN DEMAND

STEM related subjects will be in most demand reflecting the anticipated growth in the ICT, professional services and advanced manufacturing sectors. STEM qualifications will also be demanded by a wider range of sectors across the economy.

More graduates are needed in the following subject areas:

1. Computer science
2. Civil engineering
3. Electronic and electrical engineering
4. Nursing
5. Information systems
6. Mechanical engineering
7. Physics
8. Mathematics
9. Marketing
10. Chemistry

Our economy needs more people with Foundation Degree Level / Higher Level Apprenticeship qualifications in:

1. Science
2. Nursing
3. Engineering
4. ICT
5. Creative Arts
6. Manufacturing
7. Law and legal
8. Sociology and social policy
9. Building and construction
10. Hospitality and catering

The subjects are listed in priority order of demand.

▲ Information on the Northern Irish economy and skills from www.economy-ni.gov.uk

EMPLOYABILITY

UNIT 3
Section 2 Preparing for employment: recruitment and selection

Key content
- The skills, qualities and attitudes required for a successful career
- The importance of **lifelong learning** in achieving your personal and professional potential
- Ways employers assess candidates' suitability for a job:
  - Filling a job vacancy
  - Application forms
- Preparing for an interview
- Researching the job and employer
- Preparing responses to potential questions, including providing examples to demonstrate experience
- Participating in a mock interview
- **Self-evaluation** and **reflection** on interview to improve future performance

This section looks at the skills, qualities and attitudes that are required to have a successful career or careers. It explores the term lifelong learning and the importance of being adaptable and flexible in employment. It examines how employers assess the suitability of candidates for jobs and it looks at ways employees can be self-evaluative and reflect on their interview skills in order to improve future interview performance.

What are the skills, qualities and attitudes required for success in a career?

In a **competitive job market** with changing employment patterns operating in a global world certain skills, qualities and attitudes are extremely important for employers. Skills can be learned and they can always be improved on. The process of acquiring skills is therefore a lifelong process.

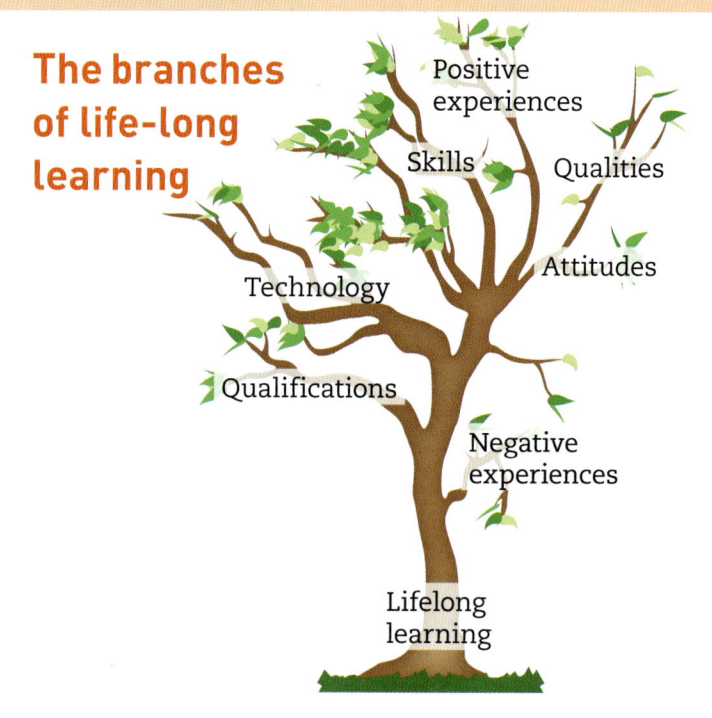

The branches of life-long learning

Tree diagram labels: Positive experiences, Skills, Qualities, Attitudes, Technology, Qualifications, Negative experiences, Lifelong learning

Section 2 Preparing for employment: recruitment and selection

Skills for success

SKILLS
A skill is the ability to do something, and the following are very important to employers:

- communication: the ability to communicate well through talking and listening, reading and writing

- ICT: the ability to use technologies such as email and social media, operate and interrogate a database and spreadsheet and use word processing

- numeracy: the ability to manipulate numbers and figures and decode diagrams and graphs

- problem solving: the ability to work through a problem in a systematic and connected way to offer solutions

- critical thinking: the ability to think clearly and analyse (break down) patterns using evidence to work towards a conclusion

- working with others: the ability to work in a team to achieve shared targets or goals.

QUALITIES FOR SUCCESS
Qualities are characteristics that we all have, which can also be learned and improved on. They include:

- punctuality: being on time for all aspects of a job

- responsibility: being able to deal with situations and being in control even when things are difficult

- initiative: being able to come up with ideas and trying to perform tasks in different ways.

ATTITUDES FOR SUCCESS
Attitudes are the ways we think and feel about things and these too can be changed. They include:

- flexibility: being able to adapt skills, time and resources to make sure all resources are being used in the best way possible

- commitment: being able to stick with tasks even if they are difficult and time consuming

- resilience: being able to recover quickly from difficult times

- positivity: being eager and ready to try and do your best at all times.

▲ The skills, qualities and attitudes valued by employers

UNIT 3 EMPLOYABILITY

The importance of skills, qualities and attitudes for successful careers

All of the skills, qualities and attitudes discussed on page 159 are very important for a successful career because they are vital for secure and successful employment. Employers need their workers to be highly skilled with good qualities and positive attitudes so that they can remain competitive and stay in business. Other attributes that they are looking for are shown below:

▲ What employers want

Activity: What employers want

All of the points in the table below are considered to be important to employers when they are looking for employees. Using your knowledge of what employers are looking for, copy and complete the table and decide, using the scale 1–10 (1 being the most important), what employers' priorities might be when looking for employees. Justify your prioritisation.

Important to employers	Explanation	Priority 1–10	Justification
Self-direction	Know what you want Willing to work for what you want Have goals and targets		
Previous success	Demonstrate successful achievements		
Ability to recognise strengths	Know what you are good at		
Independent thinker	Have your own ideas		
Problem solver	Demonstrate when you have worked out solutions		
Have ambition			
Be proactive			
Want to learn			
Work well in a team			
Be responsible			

Why is lifelong learning important in achieving personal and professional potential?

When you are employed by someone you usually have a contract of employment that sets out your terms and conditions such as pay, hours, holidays, the type of job you will do and the leave period you need to give or can expect to receive when your employment ends. You will also usually have a job description which outlines your role and responsibilities in more detail. However, increasingly, because of the fast pace of change in technology, people's duties, responsibilities and ways of carrying out the job often have to change, even though the job title may remain the same.

All those in employment (or looking for employment) should be willing to learn throughout their life. This can be learning about new technologies or adapting skills to suit the type of job they are required to do. Lifelong learning is the idea that learning new knowledge, understanding and skills is important throughout your life, both during and beyond your school years. Every single day, children, young people and adults learn new things. This is because we can always learn something new or a different and better way of doing something we have been doing for a long time.

Think about your ability to read and write. When you were five could you have read and understood this book? Probably not! Your reading skills have continually developed and improved. Likewise, if you think about your ability to solve problems, it too will have improved and this skill will continue to improve as you learn and mature.

Activity — Lifelong learning

1. Look at the photographs below – they show just some of the new things a nurse and mechanic might have to learn about and change their working practices as a result of. Choose a different job and make a list of things that you think might change that the employee would have to learn about.

2. Think of five things you have learned in the last 24 hours and record them in your own version of the following table.

Things learned	Where	Why

3. Do you think you stop learning when you leave school or college? Explain your answer.

4. Do you think that once you get a job, you stop learning? Explain your answer.

5. Considering what you have learned about changing employment patterns in Section 1 of this unit, explain why lifelong learning is so important in our society.

new practices
new drugs
new health and safety rules
new information about diseases

new technologies
new health and safety rules
new models of cars

UNIT 3 EMPLOYABILITY

Some of the lifelong skills needed for employment

An employer will only employ you if you are knowledgeable and skilled, but they will also expect you to continue to learn and develop existing and new skills by retraining. Employers want their employees to be adaptable, flexible and multi-skilled (able to do more than one job).

Below is a list of skills, qualities and attitudes that employers are looking for when they recruit someone (give someone a job), but employers also want their employees to continue to improve and adapt these skills as their business needs change.

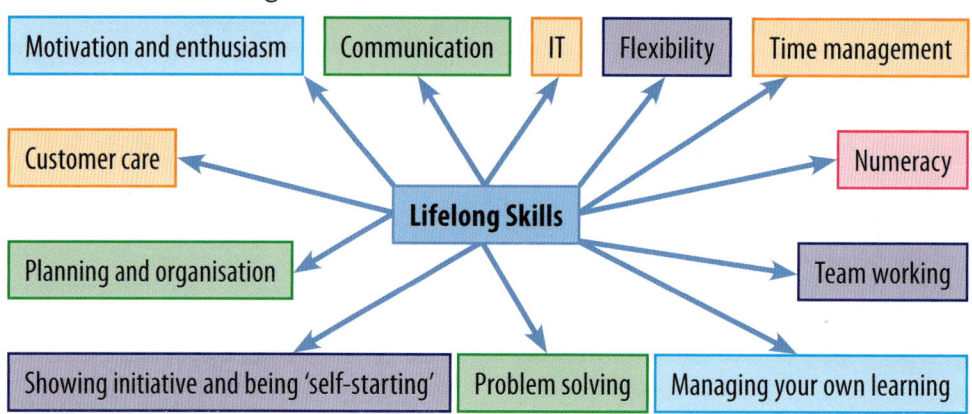

Lifelong Skills:
- Motivation and enthusiasm
- Communication
- IT
- Flexibility
- Time management
- Customer care
- Numeracy
- Planning and organisation
- Team working
- Showing initiative and being 'self-starting'
- Problem solving
- Managing your own learning

▲ Lifelong skills

Activity — Traits, qualities and attitudes for employment

1. In groups, select the two traits in the spider diagram above that you think are most important to employers.
2. Brainstorm what is involved in these traits and think about how they can be learned and improved throughout life.
3. For each trait write a short explanation that includes:
   - a definition
   - an example
   - how it can be learned throughout life.
4. Share your explanations with the rest of the class. One example has been given for you below.
5. Justify your reasoning.

Motivation and enthusiasm

We think motivation and enthusiasm are the two most important lifelong learning skills for employers because both of these skills can help other people in a team and workplace. Employers need their employees to continue to look for motivation in their job so that they are always doing a good job.

Section 2 Preparing for employment: recruitment and selection

The value of lifelong learning

You have learned that lifelong learning is required by employers, but why do they think it is so important and why are some employees reluctant to get involved in lifelong learning? The table below shows some advantages and disadvantages to lifelong learning. Can you think of any more?

Advantages	Disadvantages
Allows people to develop the skills they have already	It can be expensive
Lets people develop new skills	It can be time consuming
Gives people the opportunity to gain more qualifications	May mean people miss out on family time and social engagements
Allows people to meet the needs of an ever-changing employment market	People may be disappointed as may not always lead to promotion
Enables people to gain **promotion** and perhaps a better salary	Can leave the learner feeling tired and stressed
Encourages people to feel more motivated	
Helps people to have more job satisfaction	
Allows people to have higher self-esteem	

Activity — Importance of lifelong learning

Get into groups of four, and then into two pairs (Pair A and Pair B).
1. Carry out the role plays below depending on which pair you are.
2. Act out your role play to the other members of the group.
3. A pair from each group could act out their conversation for the whole class.

PAIR A

One person in the pair is the employer and one person is the employee in Cartoon 1 below. The employer thinks that lifelong learning is a good idea and is trying to convince the employee that they should be involved in lifelong learning.

PAIR B

One person in the pair is the employer and one person is the employee in Cartoon 2 below. The employee thinks that lifelong learning is a good idea and is trying to convince the employer that the business should be involved in lifelong learning.

▲ Cartoon 1

▲ Cartoon 2

163

UNIT 3 EMPLOYABILITY

> ### Activity — What employers want
>
> Look at the skills and qualities below.
>
> 1 Which ones would an employer want an employee to have, and which ones would they not want? Give reasons for your choices.
> 2 What other skills and qualities might an employer be looking for? Produce a list in groups.
>
> - nervous
> - lazy
> - reliable
> - uncaring
> - unpunctual
> - boisterous
> - selfish
> - rude
> - fun
> - kind
> - literate
> - illiterate
> - numerate
> - innumerate
> - worried
> - committed
> - unreliable
> - reasonable
> - thoughtful.

Training is important in lifelong learning and an important part of employment because as the needs of society change, the needs of employers change, and employees need to be allowed to develop new skills to meet these changes.

Look at the photographs below. They illustrate how the way we watch movies and TV at home has changed over the years.

A VHS video

A Sky Box

A DVD

A laptop

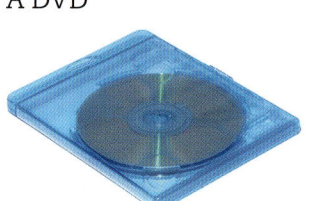

A Blu-Ray

An Amazon Firestick

▲ Ways of watching a film – through the years

Each of these changes has meant people involved in the TV and film distribution industry have had to retrain and adapt their skills to provide films and TV in different formats and to meet new challenges such as how to combat illegal methods of watching TV and films.

The example above shows the impact that technology has had on the need to change and adapt, but other influences, such as the economy, also mean people in employment must be adaptable and prepared for change.

Case study: Andrea's case study

Andrea left school at 18 with a Level 3 Qualification in Business Management. She did not want to attend university as she wanted to earn some money to start saving to buy a house. Andrea embarked on full-time employment in a busy high street retail jewellers. She worked there for eight years and was promoted from sales assistant to assistant manager. During this period she developed her customer care and organisation skills and her adaptability. However, after eight years Andrea decided that she wanted to earn more money and she wanted a change in her career path.

Andrea used her retail experience as well as her Level 3 Qualification gained at school to gain employment with a well-known training company. At the age of 25 she became part of a large training team who had responsibility for training new retail recruits across different high street shops. This involved the use of skills, attitudes and qualities that Andrea had developed while working in retail. During this time she was constantly learning about how to train staff and about new retail initiatives being introduced due to technological advances in **merchandising** and **stock control**.

After two years she was approached by another, similar training company and offered a better role with a better salary, a company car and access to training for herself. She accepted this job and continued to develop her skills in the areas of communication, problem solving and working with new technologies. Andrea remained with this company for five years and also gained a Level 4 Qualification for teaching in the further education sector.

However, as the high street economy slowed with a recession and the increase in online shopping, Andrea found her training career in **jeopardy**. She knew that she enjoyed working with young people and was good at explaining things, patient and understanding. She realised that she had always wanted to use her caring and compassionate nature as a major driving force in her job choice. This was coupled with a desire to be her own boss. So Andrea set about retraining herself as a childminder. This involved:

- training in child protection – getting Access Northern Ireland-checked
- training in childcare learning and development at Level 3
- training in running a business
- developing a business strategy
- developing workplace policies
- learning about employment legislation
- learning about marketing
- investing in equipment and resources
- changing her home to meet government guidelines
- changing her car.

Andrea began working as a childminder when she was 33. She loved the work and being her own boss, but after much deliberation Andrea decided that childminding was not for her. Due to personal reasons (unemployment and ill health) two of the families who used her services were no longer able to afford her. Andrea tried hard to replace this business by finding new families, but due to the economic downturn this was difficult. Eventually, it became financially impossible to continue.

Andrea was nervous about her working future, but she knew that she was very skilled as her changing careers and paths had ensured that she was a lifelong learner who had adapted and improved on her skills, attitude and qualities.

In the past two years Andrea has returned to the industry of training, this time helping and assisting those suffering with mental health issues to secure jobs in the retail sector. She uses her skills efficiently and is rewarded financially and with high levels of motivation and positive job satisfaction.

Activity: Andrea's lifelong learning experience

Read Andrea's case study. It outlines the importance of lifelong learning and how many people have micro careers as well as many changes in their career path.

1. What does this case study tell us about lifelong learning?
2. What did Andrea do when her career in the jeweller's came to an end?
3. How did she adapt what she had learned working in retail to being able to train retail employees?
4. Why did Andrea stop being a childminder?
5. Do you think gaining qualifications has helped Andrea to get employment? Explain your answer.
6. What has Andrea learned about her personal potential through lifelong learning?
7. What has Andrea learned about her professional potential from the process of lifelong learning?

UNIT 3 EMPLOYABILITY

How do employers assess candidates' suitability for jobs?

When employers are looking for new employees, or to promote current employees, they are involved in recruitment and selection. Employers want to select the perfect person for the job. Depending on the job they might be looking for someone with the following qualities and attitudes:

Presentable	Perceptive
Efficient	Enthusiastic
Reliable	Resourceful
Full of energy	Stable
Educated	Organised
Careful	Negotiator
Tactful	

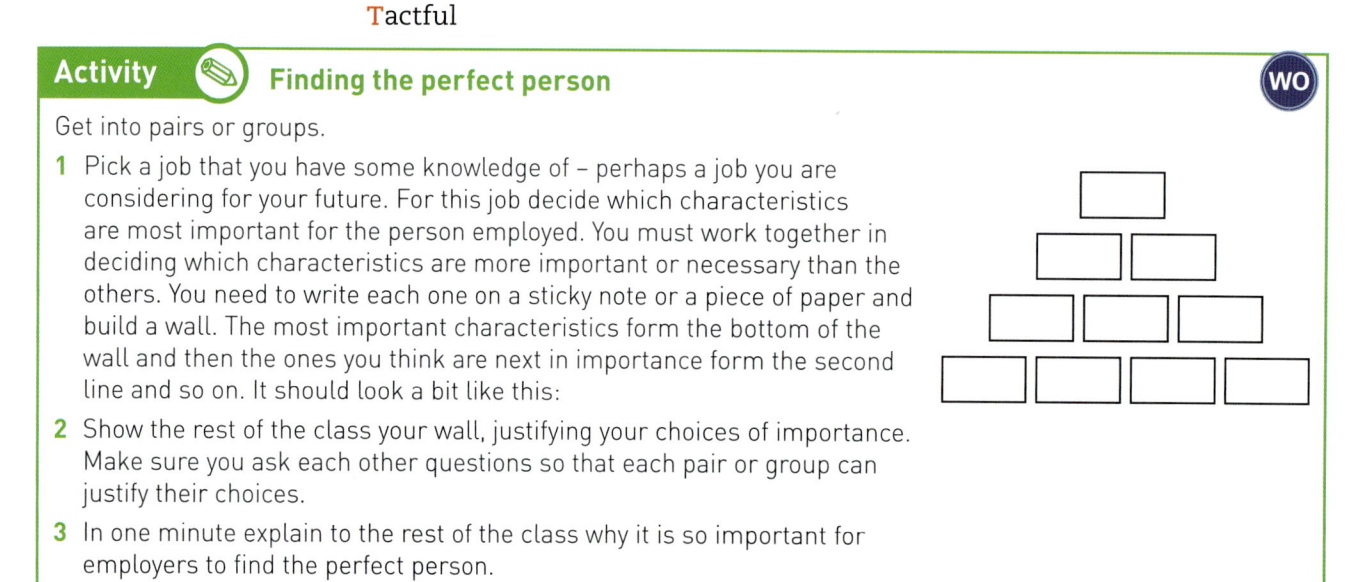

Activity — Finding the perfect person

Get into pairs or groups.

1. Pick a job that you have some knowledge of – perhaps a job you are considering for your future. For this job decide which characteristics are most important for the person employed. You must work together in deciding which characteristics are more important or necessary than the others. You need to write each one on a sticky note or a piece of paper and build a wall. The most important characteristics form the bottom of the wall and then the ones you think are next in importance form the second line and so on. It should look a bit like this:

2. Show the rest of the class your wall, justifying your choices of importance. Make sure you ask each other questions so that each pair or group can justify their choices.

3. In one minute explain to the rest of the class why it is so important for employers to find the perfect person.

Filling a job vacancy

Employers have to recruit people in order to fill their jobs. If a job is empty it is called a job vacancy. The process by which a vacancy is filled is shown in the flowchart below.

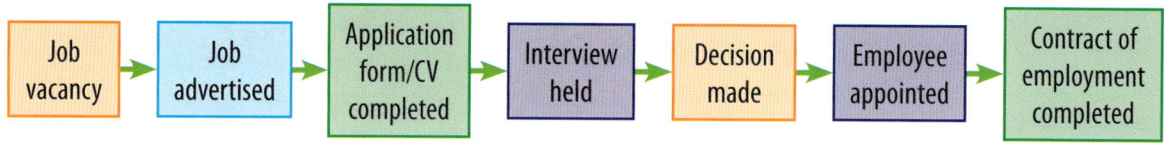

Job vacancy → Job advertised → Application form/CV completed → Interview held → Decision made → Employee appointed → Contract of employment completed

▲ Filling a job vacancy

Employers have to advertise vacancies so that people can find out about the availability of jobs. Jobs can be advertised in newspapers, job centres, through recruitment agencies and on the internet. Can you think of any more places?

The job advert usually tells you about the job and outlines the key competencies, qualities and experience the employer is looking for. Nowadays it often directs you to a website where more information can be found about the vacancy such as a job description and job specification. You can see an example of a job advertisement on the next page.

Job advertisement

Sports Shop For All is currently recruiting part-time team members. We are looking for very special individuals who have the following skills and qualities to offer:

- A good standard of literacy (reading, writing, talking and listening)
- A good standard of numeracy (working with numbers, problem solving)
- A good standard in ICT (using technology)
- Commitment (sticks with things)
- Loyalty (keeps his/her word)
- Flexibility (willing to change)

Successful applicants will join a vibrant and fun team where they will be expected to deal with all aspects associated with a busy retail environment.

Application forms and more information are available from www.SportsShopForAll.co.uk or by writing to:
Sports Shop For All • 54 Arcade Road • Belfast • BT1

We are an equal opportunities employer

▲ An example of a job advertisement

Job description

A job description sets out the duties of a particular job. A job description for the Sports Shop For All position might look like this:

Title: Part-time sales assistant

Duties: Operate till, restock, display stock and assist customers

Responsible to: Supervisor and manager on duty

Job specification

A job specification sets out the qualities, skills and desirable features that the company is looking for from a potential employee. A job specification for the Sports Shop For All job might look like this:

	Essential	Desirable
Qualifications		GCSE Maths and English or equivalent
Skills	Good literacy and numeracy and ICT skills	
Experience		Retail Working with the public
Qualities	Loyal Flexible Committed Responsible	Sense of accountability

Activity

Job descriptions and job specifications

1. Explain why you think a business would invest time and money drawing up job descriptions and job specifications for the recruitment process.
2. Give three reasons why a job description and job specification could help a potential employee in the recruitment process.

167

Application forms

A job advert also tells you how to apply for the job. This will usually either be through filling in an application form or by sending a Curriculum Vitae (CV) with a covering letter.

The employer would expect the person applying to demonstrate in their application how they meet some or all of the requirements set out in the job description and specification.

An application form will usually ask you to fill in the following details:

- **personal details** – name, address, email address, date of birth, nationality
- **educational history** – including examination results, schools/universities attended, professional qualifications
- **previous employment history** – names of employers, positions held, main achievements, pay, reasons for leaving
- **suitability and reasons for applying for the job** – a chance for applicants to 'sell themselves'
- **names of referees** – often a recent employer or people who know the applicant well (but not family or friends).

Increasingly businesses ask applicants to complete and submit applications online and usually contact them about the success or otherwise of their application by email.

What is a CV?

A CV is a document setting out your details in a clear, brief and interesting manner. As well as showing your previous qualifications and experience, it should show the employer that the skills and qualities you have match the job you are applying for. It can be used instead of or with an application form to get an interview, depending on what the employer asks for.

Remember: your CV should be modified according to the job you are applying for.

What should be included on a young person's CV?

A CV should not exceed two sides of A4 paper and should be structured to include the following details:

- **Personal details** – name, address, telephone number, email address and any other details you wish to include.
- **Education, qualifications and training** – list your exam passes and mention any courses/training you have done. Remember that accurate dates are very important.
- **Work experience**
  - Include any work experience you had while at school: part-time and full-time work. Put these in order starting with the most recent job you had.
  - Say where the job was, give the job title and say briefly what you did.
  - If you had any gaps, for example because of unemployment or bringing up a family, include them.
- If you have done any voluntary work add this here.
- Highlight the experience you have had already and be positive!
- **Skills** – this lets the employer see what you have learned from past experiences and what you can bring to the new job; for example, can you speak another language? Have you got a driving licence?
- **Interests/hobbies** – this area can say a lot about the type of person you are. Try to include interests which are relevant to the job you are applying for.
- **Referees** – always ask a person's permission to use his/her name as a referee. You usually need to supply two names, preferably including one who has known you in a work setting. Give their job titles and full addresses and telephone numbers.

What is a covering letter?

A covering letter may be included along with a CV. It should encourage the employer to want to know more about the person applying for the job by making them stand out from the rest. The following guidelines should be followed:

- Keep the letter to one A4 page.
- Put your address, telephone and email details at the top right-hand corner and remember to include the date.

- Include the reference number from the job advertisement if there is one.
- If you have a contact name write 'Dear Mr Jones' and end with 'Yours sincerely'; if you do not have a contact name then write 'Dear Sir/Madam' and end with 'Yours faithfully'.
- State what the vacancy is and how you heard about it, for example, 'With reference to your advertisement in the *Belfast Telegraph* on 2 May for …'
- Explain why you want the job and why you think you are suitable for it.
- Include what you are currently doing and how this is relevant to the job you are applying for.
- Sign your name clearly.

Do not forget to enclose your CV with the letter or to attach it if sending it by email.

How is email used in recruitment?

Email is now used for sending and receiving application forms as well as accepting CVs and letters. It is also used in conjunction with, or alongside, phone calls and traditional posted letters to set up interviews and reject applications both pre- and post-interview.

How are telephones used in recruitment?

Telephones are used in recruitment to:
- have an informal chat to see if an application would be appropriate
- set up the initial interview
- carry out an interview when the interviewee cannot attend in person – usually if the job is in another country (video conferencing can also be used for this)
- offer the person the job.

Activity

Good and bad CVs

1. The website www.kent.ac.uk/careers/cv/goodbadCV.htm gives examples of good and bad CV techniques. In pairs, use the website to create a poster called 'The DOs and DON'Ts of CVs'. The poster should be displayed to encourage people to write effective and worthwhile CVs.
2. Complete a CV and covering letter for the Sports Shop For All job and email it to your teacher.

How can applicants successfully prepare for an interview?

Once an employer has received all the applications, they need to be read and sorted out to decide whom to interview. When analysing applications, they are often sorted into three categories:

- **Those to reject:** applicants may be rejected because they do not meet the requirements set out in the job specification, for example they have the wrong qualifications or insufficient experience or they may have shown poor literacy skills in their application.
- **Those to place on a shortlist:** the shortlist often comprises between three and ten of the best applicants who are asked to interview.
- **Those to place on a longlist:** a business will not normally reject all other candidates immediately but keep some on a longlist in case those on the shortlist drop out or do not appear suitable during interview.

Interviewing is the most common form of selection as it is fairly cheap to do. It gives employers the opportunity to meet the applicant face to face and get much more information about what the person is like and how suitable they are for the job. Examples of information that can only be learned from interview and not from a CV or application form are:

- conversational ability – how well an individual can relate to people and different settings
- the natural enthusiasm or manner of the person applying for the job
- how the applicant reacts under pressure
- being able to ask questions about details missing from the CV or application form.

At interview the **interview panel** will usually have a list of questions and sometimes have a scoring sheet where they score the applicant's answers according to what they think are the correct answers to the questions.

As part of the interview process employers sometimes ask the applicant to make a presentation and/or complete a test. These tests could either be a generic **personality assessment** or a more specific competency assessment to see if they are compatible with the requirements of the job. A presentation can allow the applicant to demonstrate their knowledge and communication skills.

UNIT 3 EMPLOYABILITY

Preparing for an Interview

In order to be fully prepared for an interview it is vital that you do the following:

Research the job and employer

Prepare responses to potential questions

Provide examples of your experience and skills in your answers

Participate in a mock interview.

More information on these vital steps is included below.

Interview techniques

An interview is a great opportunity for a potential employee to show that they are the best person for the job and in order to do this the person being interviewed (the interviewee) should remember to research the job and the employer and use personal experience to highlight their suitability for the job.

You could research the job and employer by talking to current employees of the business (if you know any) or by using the internet. Things to research might include:

- range of stock carried by the business
- different types of responsibilities within the business
- bestsellers
- busy periods of business
- types of customers that use the business.

Your research should help you to understand the workings of the business and give you some valuable information that you may be able to use in an interview either through answering a question or by asking a question.

Top tips for interview and presentation preparation

- Find out about the business and the employer – what does the business do?
  - Is it big/small?
  - Is it a new/old business?
  - Try to get an understanding of the business.
- Think about yourself – what skills are you good at?
  - What qualities make you special?
  - What qualities and skills make you employable?
  - What about you would impress an employer?
- Find out where the interview is being held – plan your journey. How long will it take?
  - How will you get there? Try to arrive ten minutes before the interview is due to begin to compose yourself.
- Think about what you will wear – does the clothing give off the right signals?
  - Does your clothing show that you are respectable?
  - Are the clothes neat, tidy and fresh?
- Organise your record of achievement – is everything in order?
  - Is it up to date?
  - Is it clean and not scruffy?
- Have a practice interview – what sort of questions will the interviewer ask?
  - How will you answer them?
  - What questions could you ask the interviewer?
- Practise your presentation – make sure any electrical equipment is operating properly, have a back-up USB with your presentation/notes.

At the interview/presentation

- Try not to be too nervous – be pleasant to the receptionist, the interviewer(s) and anyone else you meet. You want to give the right impression – SMILE!
- Behave in an appealing way – sit up straight, be polite, be positive, listen carefully, speak clearly, make eye contact.
- Answer the questions as best you can – use personal experience to explain a point, show interest, be keen.
- Ask a question(s) related to the job/business, show your knowledge.
- Keep your presentation to the time limit – have a good closing statement that sums everything up

Activity — Interview tips

1 Using the information above and your own ideas, design a leaflet that gives advice and guidance to people attending interviews and/or presentations.

Section 2 Preparing for employment: recruitment and selection

Case study: Possible candidates for the Sports Shop For All job

Janet

Janet is 17 years of age. She really wants a part-time job while studying in Year 13. She has a grade C in both English and Maths at GCSE.

She has changed her post-sixteen course choice three times since returning to school. She has been part of the school's football team, choir and drama group but she has only stayed in each for a few weeks.

She spends quite a bit of time on the computer as she has lots of friends on her social networking site. She uses the computer at least twice a day and she always uses her mobile phone to text and update her status profile on her social networking site.

She really wants the job in the sports shop because she wants to get retail experience so she can get a job in a larger shop that does not just sell sports clothes. She can also get all of her friends a discount!

She only wants to work on Saturday mornings as she likes hanging out with her friends on Saturday afternoons.

Joshua

Joshua is 16 years of age. He really wants a part-time job in a sports shop as he loves every kind of sport and he enjoys working with the public. He is willing to work as much as he can as long as it does not interfere with his studies for his GCSEs. He wants to do well at school and he would like to study sport management at university.

He is very involved in clubs and societies at school. He plays in school sports teams and he coaches younger children. He stays behind one day a week in school to help local primary schoolchildren and the junior children in his school with their homework. He helps them to read and demonstrates how to use Moviemaker and PowerPoint on the computer.

Success at interview

Joshua from the case study above was offered a job in Sports Shop For All after a successful interview. Before this happened the company checked out his references to investigate his character further. Once the company was satisfied with Joshua's history, character and abilities, they then offered him the job by sending him a letter in the post (letter of agreement). This could also have been sent via email, or some companies telephone and then send out a letter of agreement. Joshua decided to accept the job and he then signed his contract of employment and began his training.

Some people may still want clarification from their prospective employers on salaries, holidays and career progression before they sign their contract and it is after the letter of agreement is received that they will negotiate these issues with their potential employers.

Activity

Sports Shop For All applicants

1. Study the information above. Who do you think will be the successful candidate for the job? Justify your answer.

171

UNIT 3

EMPLOYABILITY

Section 3 Rights and responsibilities of employers and employees

Key content:
- the employment contract and terms and conditions of employment
- employee and employer responsibilities
- codes of conduct in the workplace
- developing positive working relationships, including respectful interactions and managing conflict
- the causes and consequences of employees' work-related stress
- ways of dealing with work-related stress
- the role and impact of trade unions and their impact in the workplace
- the impact on employers and employees of not meeting their responsibilities

This section examines the workplace – the relationship between employer and employee set out in the contract of employment and the consequences when both sides uphold, or fail to uphold, their individual responsibilities. The importance of a code of conduct so that employees know what to expect, is also outlined.

Working environments can be very positive places if successful working relationships are maintained. This topic examines how this can be achieved. When problems exist in a workplace they can take the form of employee stress, and the causes and consequences of this are also explored as well as ways to deal with the problem.

Finally, the role of trade unions and their impact in the workplace is also examined.

What is a contract of employment?

A contract of employment is an agreement between an employer and their employee, outlining the employment relationship. Employment contracts do not need to be in writing to be legally valid, but there are benefits to having a written contract, such as, it outlines what would happen if either the employer or employee wanted to end the working relationship. A written contract also gives both the employer and employee certain guidelines in the working relationship. A working relationship begins at the acceptance of the contract of employment by the employee.

Most employees are legally entitled to a 'written statement of particulars', stating the main terms and conditions of employment, within two calendar months of starting work. This should include details such as the rate of pay, holidays and working hours. An existing contract of employment can be amended only with the agreement of both parties.

Activity

The importance of the contract of employment

1. Search YouTube at www.youtube.com for the clip 'Is a verbal job offer legal?' produced by ACAS (Advisory, Conciliation and Arbitration Service).
   a. State what the acceptance of a job offer means for an employee.
   b. State what is meant by the term 'conditional offer'.
2. Explain, in no more than 20 words, why a contract of employment is important for employees and employers.
3. In pairs, discuss whether you think a contract of employment needs to be written. Give reasons for your answer.

Section 3 Rights and responsibilities of employers and employees

What are employee and employer responsibilities?

In a working relationship and as part of the contract of employment, both employers and employees have responsibilities to themselves and to each other. A responsibility is something we have to be aware of and live up to if we are to be successful in employment both as employees and as employers.

Employers' responsibilities

Every employer has a responsibility to the workforce to ensure all employees are:

- paid for the work they do
- safe in work
- given opportunity for promotion
- entitled to holidays
- protected from discrimination
- shown consideration for personal matters.

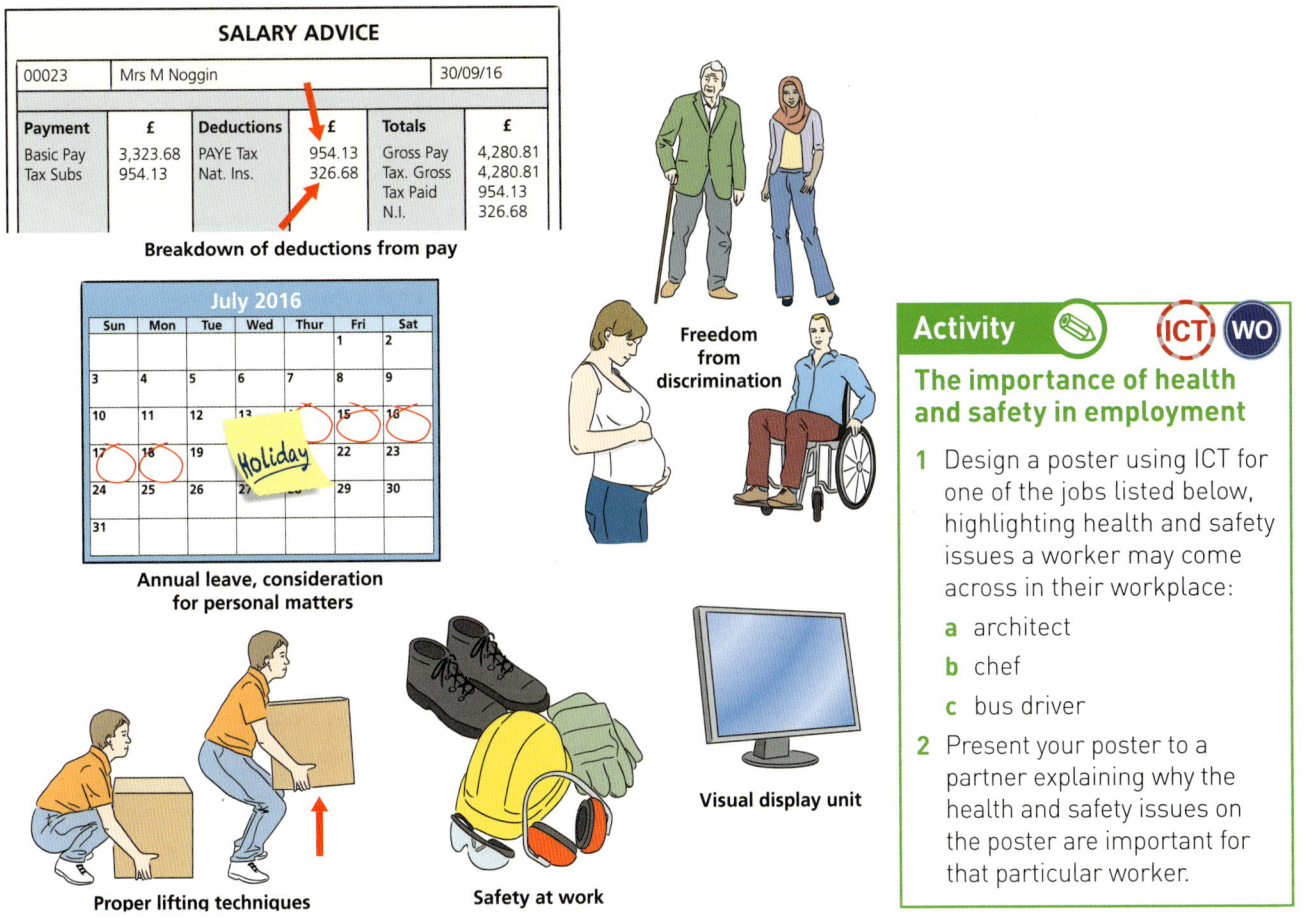

Breakdown of deductions from pay

Annual leave, consideration for personal matters

Freedom from discrimination

Proper lifting techniques

Safety at work

Visual display unit

▲ Employers' responsibilities to employees

Activity

The importance of health and safety in employment

1. Design a poster using ICT for one of the jobs listed below, highlighting health and safety issues a worker may come across in their workplace:
   a architect
   b chef
   c bus driver
2. Present your poster to a partner explaining why the health and safety issues on the poster are important for that particular worker.

The real Living Wage

As part of their responsibility to pay employees, employers must also consider the rates of payment. For example, they should consider whether the use of zero hour contracts is fair and appropriate and whether staff are entitled to the minimum wage or the real Living Wage.

SOURCE A National Living Wage and the National Minimum Wage hourly rates from 1 October 2016. The rates are re-calculated every year and announced in November. The current rates can be found at livingwage.org.uk.

Year	25 and over	21 to 24	18 to 20	Under 18	Apprentice
October 2016 (current rate)	£7.20	£6.95	£5.55	£4.00	£3.40

175

UNIT 3 EMPLOYABILITY

Source B Article on the living wage from www.livingwage.org.uk

What is the living wage?

- The real Living Wage is independently-calculated each year based on what employees and their families need to live.
- The current UK Living Wage is £8.45 an hour.
- The current London Living Wage is £9.75 an hour.
- Employers choose to pay the real Living Wage on a voluntary basis.
- The rates apply to all workers over 18, recognising that young people face the same living costs as everyone else.
- The real Living Wage that meets the cost of living enjoys cross-party support, with public backing from successive London Mayors and MPs across the four nations of the UK.
- Paying a wage that is enough to live on is good for business, good for the individual and good for society.
- The Living Wage Employer Mark and Service Provider Recognition Scheme provide an ethical badge for responsible pay.

What are the benefits?

Good for business

By paying the real Living Wage employers are voluntarily taking a stand to ensure their employees can earn a wage that is enough to live on. That basic fairness is at the heart of what our campaign is trying to achieve and why great businesses and organisations choose to go further than the government minimum. Many employers also report wider business benefits as a result of investments in staff pay.

An independent study found that more than 80 per cent of London Living Wage employers believe that implementing the real Living Wage had enhanced the quality of the work of their staff. Two-thirds of employers reported a significant impact on recruitment and retention within their organisation, while absenteeism had fallen by 25 per cent on average. Seventy per cent of employers felt that the Living Wage had increased consumer awareness of their organisation's commitment to be an ethical employer.

Good for individuals

For people who are paid the real Living Wage it means the difference between just getting the government minimum and earning enough to afford the things you need to live, like a decent meal, a warm home and a birthday treat for your children.

Full-time employees earning the real Living Wage earn £45 a week more than those on the government minimum, and £95 a week in London.

Many employees also report improved job satisfaction. An independent study found that 75 per cent of employees reported increases in job quality as a result of receiving the Living Wage. Fifty per cent of employees felt that the Living Wage had made them more willing to implement changes in their working practices; enabled them to require fewer concessions to effect change; and made them more likely to adopt changes more quickly.

Good for Society

Low pay makes it difficult for employees to find time for community and family life. The causes of poverty are complex and in order to improve lives there should be a package of solutions across policy areas. The Living Wage can be part of the solution.

How is it different from the government's 'national living wage'?

In April 2016 the government introduced a higher minimum wage rate for all staff over 25 years of age inspired by the Living Wage campaign – even calling it the 'national living wage'.

However, the government's 'national living wage' is not calculated according to what employees and their families need to live.

The real Living Wage rates are higher because they are independently-calculated, based on what people need to get by. That's why we encourage all employers that can afford to do so to ensure their employees earn a wage that meets the costs of living, not just the government minimum.

Activity — The real Living Wage

Working in small groups, use Source B to design a presentation about the real Living Wage.

You could use the following as headings for your presentation:

- What is the Living Wage?
- Why is the Living Wage good?
- Why is it important to know about wages?

Employees' responsibilities

Every employee has responsibilities to their employer as laid out in the contract of employment. These are likely to be:

- Excellent attendance and punctuality – be at work every day and on time.
- Appropriate behaviour – be respectful and ready and willing to work at all times.
- Work efficiently – complete the tasks required using a high level of skill and commitment.
- Manage time – look for help and support when required.
- Be loyal and committed.
- Be honest.
- Make sure deadlines are met to the best of an individual's ability.
- Have a positive attitude and desire to work efficiently.

What happens if employees and employers fail to meet their responsibilities?

The consequences of not meeting these responsibilities impact on both employers and on employees. Employees may feel uncomfortable or unhappy in the workplace if their colleagues are not meeting their responsibilities. This is because the work environment may become uncomfortable as targets are not being met and this could impact on the levels of motivation and productivity. For employers, this means that the workplace is not as efficient as it could be and it could impact negatively on profit or targets.

Employees failure to meet responsibilities

If employees fail to meet any of their responsibilities they may be in breach of their contract of employment and they can be disciplined. Disciplinary action will depend on the seriousness of the breach in responsibility. The action is usually broken down into:

- verbal warning
- written warning (an employee may receive more than one, depending on the employer's policy)
- dismissal.

A less serious breach, such as being late for work on a few occasions, may result in an employer giving a verbal warning to the employee. A more serious breach, such as missing an important deadline, may result in a written warning being presented to the employee. A very serious breach, such as stealing or receiving a few written warnings, may result in the employee being dismissed.

Activity — Employees failing to meet their responsibilities

Divide into pairs and devise a role-play situation that demonstrates disciplinary action between an employer and an employee. The degree and nature of the situation is to be decided by you and your partner. Act out your role play for the class.

Examples of situations:
- an employee has arrived late for work three times in a month
- allegations of an employee stealing.

UNIT 3 EMPLOYABILITY

> **Activity** — Meeting and failing to meet responsibilities
>
> 1 Place a seat in the middle of the classroom. This is called the hot seat. Three people in the class are asked to take on the following roles for the hot seat:
>   - an employee who meets all their responsibilities
>   - an employee who often fails to meet their responsibilities
>   - the employer of the two employees.
>
> a The three people in the hot seat should be given time to think about their character as they are going to be asked questions by the rest of the class.
>
> b Everyone else in the class should think of one question each to ask the three people who will be in the hot seat. Possible questions include:
>   - What are your responsibilities to your employer?
>   - What is your favourite type of reward and why is this?
>   - Why do you think you should be rewarded for your work?
>   - Do you think all employees should be rewarded? Why?
>   - What rights do you have as an employee?
>   - What rights do your employees have?
>   - When would you discipline an employee?
>   - How would you discipline an employee?
>
> c When asking the questions to the people in the hot seat, vary the questions so that the three 'characters' can give different answers.
>
> d Once you have finished the hot seat activity write down what you have learned from it. Share your thoughts with the class.

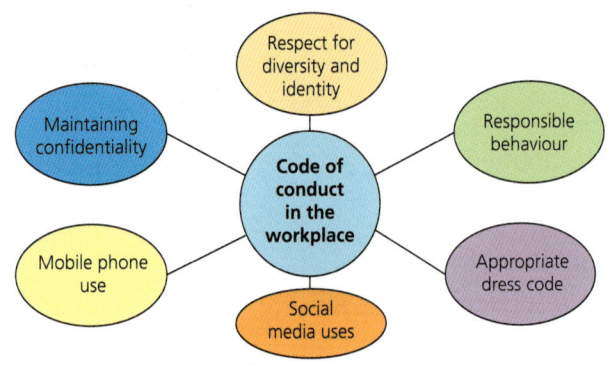

▲ A code of conduct in the workplace

What is a code of conduct in the workplace for all stakeholders?

Stakeholders are people who have an interest in a workplace and they all must be aware of the importance of a code of conduct. This is a set of rules that indicate the proper way to behave and act in the workplace for both employers and employees. It gives all stakeholders a clear framework of expectations of behaviour. The diagram on the left shows the information contained within a code of conduct that is usually written and adheres to a business' equal opportunity policy:

Respect for diversity and identity

This means that all stakeholders must show regard and consideration for all individuals by treating everyone equally and with dignity. In the areas of diversity and identity the following aspects of individuality should be honoured:

- race
- age
- religion
- gender
- sexual orientation
- levels of mobility.

All stakeholders are expected to behave in a respectful way towards one other and refrain from any kind of discriminatory behaviour, harassment or victimisation. This atmosphere of respect and dignity must be applied to all aspects of the workplace environment, including interpersonal relations between employees.

Responsible behaviour

All stakeholders must be responsible in how they communicate within the workplace and in many instances outside of the workplace too. Verbal communication should be calm, respectful and non-judgemental. Shouting or using an aggressive tone in speech would be considered a breach of the code of conduct as it is not considered to be responsible behaviour – it can make the person being shouted at feel uncomfortable and intimidated.

The same applies for written communication, especially the use of emails. This is a form of communication that is widely used in workplaces and it should be used in a respectful way. It is important to get the tone of the email correct in order to avoid any offence to the reader. Emails should be clear and concise in their message and they need to be professional in their content. The use of capital letters should be avoided as this can be interpreted as the sender shouting at the reader of the email.

Activity

Communicating professionally

Read the email below and answer the questions that follow.

> I am not pleased with how you conducted the meeting earlier. You didn't address everything that was on the agenda. You let that old woman take over and she is STUPID AND JUST LIKES THE SOUND OF HER OWN VOICE. You need to sort this out ASAP. If you don't fix this I will make your working life a misery. You are being well paid and you need to start earning your money. The monthly review meetings are coming up and I am taking yours, just remember that.
>
> The Manager

1. List three things that are wrong with this email.
2. How would you feel if you received this email?
3. Rewrite the email in a responsible way that follows a typical code of conduct.

Appropriate dress code

▲ In many professions a dress code is stipulated in the code of conduct

Again the appropriate dress code for the working environment is usually laid out clearly in the code of conduct for all stakeholders. This part will identify what clothing is acceptable to wear in the workplace and whether items of jewellery, emblems, piercings or visible tattoos are accepted. It will usually include guidelines on smart/casual dress, business dress and whether 'dress down' days in the workplace are permitted.

Some workplaces require stakeholders (usually employees) to wear a uniform; some businesses will supply this, while others will indicate what items of clothing employees are expected to wear in the workplace.

Social media use

▲ A code of conduct usually stipulates the allowed social media usage

Social media use during working hours is usually forbidden in a working environment, as this is viewed as a leisure or personal activity that should be done outside of working hours. What individuals post or share on social media even in personal time can also be included in a workplace code of conduct. It is considered to be unprofessional, and in some cases a breach of the code of conduct, if employees use social media to express negative opinions about their workplace or colleagues. Stakeholders may be actively encouraged not to engage in any social media activity where the workplace can be viewed in a poor way. It has also been known for employers to 'screen' (look at) either current or potential employees' social media profiles while investigating circumstances of poor behaviour or to decide on the suitability of potential employees.

Mobile phone use

▲ Often businesses provide employees with mobile phones for work purposes

Many workplaces now require stakeholders to use mobile phones for work purposes (in many cases, the workplace supplies a mobile phone for work). However, stakeholders are normally discouraged from using their mobile phones during working times if it is not for professional use. This means that mobile phone use is discouraged at meetings, when dealing with customers and when engaged in 'work duties', unless the duty requires the use of an employee's mobile phone to send/check emails or take/make a work-related phone call or text message.

Maintaining confidentiality

All stakeholders are expected to treat any information they acquire through their workplace in the strictest of confidence. Information about work should not be shared or discussed with anyone unless they need to have access to the information. This includes what is discussed at meetings, through emails or in dealings with customers. The code of conduct is very clear that confidentiality is to be maintained at all times.

Activity — Social media and the workplace (PS)

Look at the social media posts below. Decide which are appropriate and which are not, by putting a cross or a tick in the table. Justify your choice as to whether they breach a typical code of conduct.

Social media post	✗ / ✓	Justification of choice
Such a busy day in work; it will be an early night tonight!		
Customers are nothing but moaners and complainers; I wish they would all go away!		
I just told my manager that he is stupid … like if you agree!		
Ten days until my holiday leave ☺		

How can positive working relationships be developed?

By having and following a code of conduct working relationships can be positive and respectful. If the code of conduct is not followed then this can lead to conflict. Negativity and conflict can be avoided, assisted and/or diffused in the workplace by some of the following strategies.

Participating in staff training

Staff training is used to improve the performance or knowledge of employees in the workplace. The training is usually designed specifically for individual workplaces or businesses.

Training in the workplace is usually carried out by existing colleagues or by specialist training providers, although some people also carry out independent study in order to become more skilled in their job.

New employees usually go through **induction** training when they first start a job. This training helps them to:

- learn about the duties of the job
- meet new colleagues
- see the layout of the building
- learn about the aims and policies of the business.

Many organisations offer opportunities for training throughout the year for all employees. Training is usually divided into two categories: **on-the-job training** and **off-the-job training**.

On-the-job training

This is training that happens while someone is working. It usually takes place when a new employee is watching an established employee perform a task (**job shadowing**), such as operating a machine or dealing with a customer. What form this takes will depend on the type of job.

Off-the-job training

This is training that takes place outside the normal working environment. This may be at a training agency or local college, although some larger businesses also have their own training centres or employ training providers to come into the workplace. Off-the-job training can take the form of training courses that last a day or more, or self-study. Quite often it is completed online. The training can be used to develop more general skills and knowledge that can be used in a variety of situations, for example, management skills or health and safety procedures.

Activity — Training decisions

1. Below are some advantages of on-the-job and off-the-job training. Sort them out by copying and completing the table below.

On-the-job training	Off-the-job training

   a Cheaper to carry out
   b Learn from specialists in that area of work who can provide more in-depth understanding
   c Can more easily deal with groups of workers at the same time
   d Training is very relevant and practical, dealing with the day-to-day requirements of the job
   e Workers are not taken away from jobs so they can still be productive
   f Employees respond better when taken away from the pressures of the working environment
   g Employees who are new to a job role become productive as quickly as possible
   h Workers may be able to obtain qualifications or certificates

2. What do you think are the disadvantages of on-the-job and off-the-job training?
3. How do you think training could build positive working relationships?

UNIT 3 EMPLOYABILITY

Following equality employment legislation

Laws have been designed to help develop and maintain positive working relationships as well as helping to manage conflict. Some of the laws that have been passed in Northern Ireland are outlined below.

Law	Employees' Rights	Employers' Responsibilities
Equal Pay Act (NI) 1970	Men and women must be paid the same amount if they are doing a job of 'equal value' (same skills, same level of knowledge and same demands), in both part-time and full-time work.	Must ensure that all employees are paid equally if they are doing jobs of 'equal value'.
Sex Discrimination (NI) Order 1976	Men and women must have equal treatment and opportunity in the workplace. This includes areas such as: • recruitment • promotion • job conditions and pay.	Must ensure that no one is discriminated against because of their gender.
Race Relations (NI) Order (2003)	People of all races, colours, nationalities and ethnic origins must be treated equally in the areas of recruitment, employment and training.	Must ensure that no one is discriminated against because of their race.
Disability Discrimination Act 1995	Able-bodied, disabled and some people with mental impairments (depending on the nature of the mental impairment) must be given the same opportunities in recruitment and employment.	Must ensure that no one with a disability is discriminated against and employers must make reasonable adjustments to accommodate those employees who are disabled.

▲ Legislation passed on employee and employer rights and responsibilities

As well as contracts of employment and codes of conduct, this legislation assists in keeping working relationships positive because both employers and employees have work-based boundaries to adhere to.

Workplace policies

The design and following of workplace policies also help employers and employees understand how to maintain positive relationships. This is because policies are designed within the business and to suit the needs of the employment practices. Examples of policies include health and safety, acceptable behaviour, child protection (when working with children), safeguarding, confidentiality and respecting diversity. In many workplaces the code of conduct is complemented by these policies.

> Use the following link to show guidelines for writing a child protection/safeguarding policy:
>
> www.nspcc.org.uk/preventing-abuse/safeguarding/writing-a-safeguarding-policy
>
> There is an example of a safeguarding policy that gives guidelines and instructions on the procedures that should be followed when communicating with or about children. It will lay out step-by-step actions that should be followed in various circumstances where children may be considered at risk. It will also specify that all employees who have direct contact must be police-checked by Access NI to ensure they have no previous criminal convictions that may leave children in their care vulnerable to not being protected properly.

Activity

Legislation and positive working relationships

Divide into four groups. Each group should choose a piece of legislation from the table above and, using the information in the table and your own internet research, design a presentation for your class answering the question:

'How can the piece of legislation help to maintain positive working relationships and minimise conflict in the workplace?'

Sharing good practice

Another way of maintaining and encouraging positive working relationships is to encourage an atmosphere where good practice is shared between employees so that ideas and suggestions about how best to perform tasks and jobs can be suggested and shared. It is an opportunity for colleagues to learn from each other and to pass on tips and/or knowledge that will help to improve the business. Teachers often share good practice by exchanging teaching resources and strategies with each other. This can involve observing each other teach or passing on resources that have led to successful teaching and learning.

Promoting a positive working atmosphere

A positive working relationship is evident when staff morale and motivation is high, when there is evidence of open communication and a sense of a strong team is apparent. A positive working atmosphere can be achieved when there is the correct balance and use of workplace policies, a code of conduct and employment legislation, and a culture of sharing good practice is encouraged.

I know about our policies.

I understand and respect the code of conduct for the company I work for.

I can ask for support from and give support to my colleagues.

I am protected by employment legislation.

▲ Examples of a positive working environment

What are the causes and consequences of work-related stress among employees?

Stress is when a person experiences mental tension and worry that can at times result in anxiety. In the working environment it is important that levels of stress are managed properly so that stress does not negatively impact on individuals.

Causes of work-related stress

There are many reasons that can lead to work-related stress for employees:

- ▶ **Management:** stress can be brought about when employees do not feel sufficiently supported by their employers or managers. If employees do not feel they can ask for advice or support when they come across a work-related problem then they can begin to feel as though they are working in isolation.
- ▶ **Workload:** stress can also come about when the demand placed on the employee is too much for the employee to handle. This could be because the employee is expected to work too many hours or to reach unrealistic targets. It can also be because an employee does not have the correct skill set to perform the job or task. This can lead to the employee feeling unable to do their job and it can result in costly mistakes being made.
- ▶ **Working relationships:** work-related stress can also be brought on by poor working relationships. This could be because the employee does not feel that they can approach their manager or because the employee feels uncomfortable in a team or there is conflict between colleagues.
- ▶ **Periods of change:** stress can also be heightened during particular periods, for example, when a business moves premises, when there is a possibility of job cuts, or when a change in employer takes place. If these changes are not managed properly this can result in high levels of stress because employees will feel insecure and unsure of what is expected from them.

UNIT 3 EMPLOYABILITY

Consequences of work-related stress

There are many consequences of work-related stress. They can be categorised into emotional and physical symptoms.

Emotional symptoms

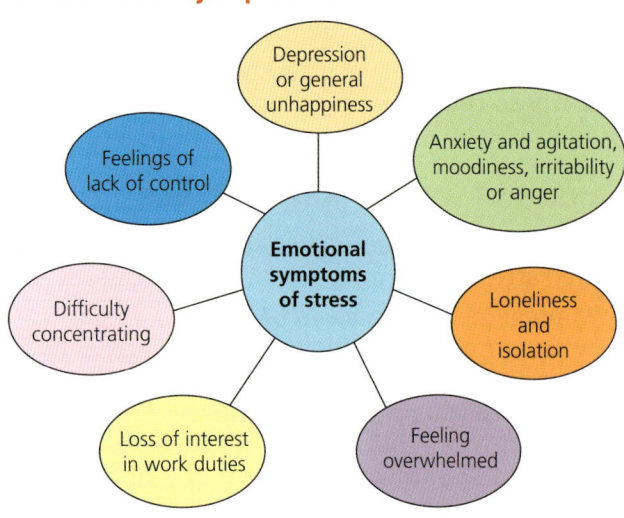

Emotional symptoms of stress:
- Depression or general unhappiness
- Anxiety and agitation, moodiness, irritability or anger
- Feelings of lack of control
- Difficulty concentrating
- Loneliness and isolation
- Loss of interest in work duties
- Feeling overwhelmed

▲ Emotional symptoms of stress

These symptoms usually result in changes in an individual's attitude and behaviour as well as their motivation and energy.

Physical symptoms

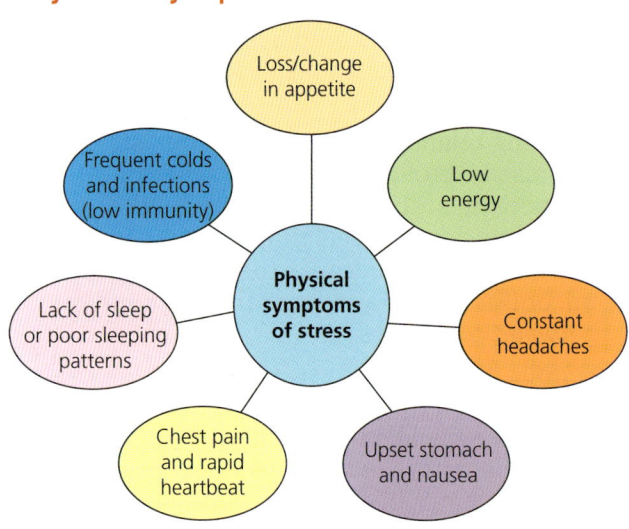

Physical symptoms of stress:
- Loss/change in appetite
- Low energy
- Frequent colds and infections (low immunity)
- Lack of sleep or poor sleeping patterns
- Constant headaches
- Chest pain and rapid heartbeat
- Upset stomach and nausea

▲ Physical symptoms of stress

There are numerous physical symptoms and how stress affects individuals varies. However, all or some of these symptoms can result in changing employee behaviour, such as higher levels of sickness, lower work rates or disinterest in tasks – none of which will be good for the employer or employee.

What are the ways of dealing with work-related stress?

There are many different ways to deal with work-related stress. The method(s) used will depend on the individual and their personal circumstances.

- **Plan and organise:** make lists of jobs that have to be completed and try to finish one job before starting another. Do not accept jobs that you know you cannot complete. Plan your tasks and make sure you have all of the required skills, knowledge and resources needed to complete the tasks.
- **Talk with employer:** tell your employer if you are feeling overwhelmed at work. If you feel you do not have the correct skill set to complete the tasks asked of you, ask for additional training. Share your thoughts and feelings with a colleague or friend. Social contact is very important both personally and professionally.
- **Seek advice from outside agencies:** make an appointment to see your doctor. Tell the doctor how you are feeling, how long you have felt this way and if you know why you are feeling stressed. Investigate the possibility of relaxation therapies such as reflexology or massages.
- **Seek counselling:** this can be organised through your GP or you can make an appointment to see a counsellor privately. Organisations such as The Samaritans offer telephone services to people who are feeling stressed.
- **Absence from work:** take some time off from the workplace to reassess your working position or to rebuild your emotional and physical strength.
- **Exercise and diet:** eat well, avoid foods and drinks that are high in sugar and saturated fats. Avoid alcohol and nicotine. Take time to be active, walk when possible. Join a gym or an exercise class. When moving focus on your body and the good you are doing yourself.
- **Sleep:** try to improve the quality of your sleep by keeping to a consistent bedtime routine that avoids stimulating activities such as checking emails.
- **Relax:** learn to relax. Find out what helps you to relax and wind down. Spend time doing these things.

Many believe that to avoid work-related stress, you need to ensure you have a healthy work/life balance. This means getting the correct balance between energies spent in work and leisure pursuits.

SOURCE A Article from www.nhs.uk

According to the Health and Safety Executive (HSE), in 2014/15, 440,000 people in the UK reported work-related stress at a level they believed was making them ill. That's 40 per cent of all work-related illness. Psychological problems, including stress, anxiety and depression, are behind one in five visits to a GP.

Some pressure at work can be motivating, but when it becomes excessive it can eventually lead to work-related stress. Stress is 'the adverse reaction people have to excessive pressures and demands placed on them', according to the HSE.

Stress symptoms include a pounding heart or palpitations, a dry mouth, headaches, odd aches and pains and loss of appetite for food and sex.

What causes work stress?

The main reasons given for work stress include work pressure, lack of support from managers and work-related violence and bullying. The way you deal with stress can lead to unhealthy behaviours, such as smoking and drinking too much, which might increase your risk of heart disease.

How to manage work stress

Good stress management in the workplace is critical to your overall health. Life coach Suzy Greaves says one of the key skills to managing workplace stress is knowing how to say no.

'I'm constantly challenging clients who say they have no choice but to overwork,' she says. 'I coach people to become empowered and believe they have a choice.'

She explains that saying yes can win you brownie points in the short term, but if you take on too much and fail to deliver, it can be a disastrous long-term strategy. 'Have confidence in your "no" when you think it's the right decision, even though it may not be the most popular one,' she says. 'In the long term, your ability to say no will be one of your most valuable attributes.'

Learn to speak out

Greaves says you can prevent exhaustion by knowing how much work you can take on. By taking on too much, you could end up doing nothing well. Calculate how long you'll need to deal with your current workload so that you can see if you have any extra capacity.

'If you're extremely busy and your boss asks you to do more, you can say no. Outline your reasons in a specific, measurable way, but always offer a solution.'

Spot the signs of work stress

Learn to recognise the physical effects of stress and do something about it before it makes you really ill. Beware of work stress spilling over into other areas of your life. Whatever the source of your stress, speak to your manager or someone in your organisation that you feel comfortable talking to. Or get outside help.

Employers have a duty to ensure the health, safety and welfare of their employees. This comes under the Health and Safety at Work Act 1974. They're also required to conduct risk assessments for work-related stress. If the problem is not work-related, they may be able to support you in some way or help to take some pressure off you at work while you resolve the stress in your personal life.

Who else can help with work stress?

The HSE supports anyone who is responsible for tackling work-related stress in an organisation. That might be the person who has responsibility for human resources, a health and safety officer, trade union representatives or line managers.

The HSE believes good management practices can help reduce work-related stress. It offers a management standards approach to help employers take sensible and practical steps to minimise stress in the workplace. Your GP can also help. Doctors aren't experts in employment law, but they can help you analyse the situation and refer you to more specialised help if necessary.

(www.nhs.uk/Conditions/stress-anxiety-depression/Pages/workplace-stress.aspx)

Activity — Beat stress at work

Go to www.nhs.uk/Conditions/stress-anxiety-depression/Pages/workplace-stress.aspx and watch the video. Use the video and Source A to complete the following:

1 Imagine you are a workplace health and safety officer and you have been asked to write a 200-word report to inform employees about the signs and symptoms of work-related stress and give advice on how to deal with work-related stress.

UNIT 3 EMPLOYABILITY

What is the role and impact of trade unions in the workplace?

A trade union is an organisation that looks after the interests of employees. A trade union's main concern is to make sure that all employees are receiving their rights and that employers are meeting their responsibilities to staff. They do this by:

- giving advice and information to members about things relating to their employment (holiday pay, sick pay, etc.)
- defending employees' rights and resolving conflict
- negotiating pay and working conditions.

Many employees are a member of a particular trade union. Their choice of trade union will depend on their job, as there are different trade unions for different types of jobs. Some examples are shown in the box below.

> The **NASUWT** is a teacher's union which represents teachers in England, Northern Ireland and Wales.
>
> **UNITE** is Britain's biggest union with 2 million members in every type of workplace such as the transportation, manufacturing and aviation industries.
>
> **UCATT** is a trade union specialising in the construction industry with 125,000 members spread throughout England, Wales, Scotland and Northern Ireland.
>
> **UNISON** is Britain and Europe's biggest public sector union with more than 1.3 million members. It represents people working in the public services (hospital staff, civil servants, etc.).

Trade Unions have many impacts on the workplace, such as:

Protecting employees' rights

This can involve negotiating rates of payment, working conditions; ensuring employees receive their full entitlement for holidays, maternity and paternity leave and pay. If an employee is sick or unable to work for a period of time a trade union will be able to assist the employee in making sure the correct workplace procedure is followed. This may involve filling out forms or speaking to members of management or human resources department.

Promoting positive working relationships

At times there may be situations where there are areas of dispute between employees and employers. Perhaps about working conditions, contracts of employment or rates of pay. A trade union can assist in clear communication between the two groups. The trade union will be able to negotiate with management on behalf of its members. This means that workers have one voice that is able to put forward their grievances or suggestions. A trade union will seek to establish positive working relationships where employees feel consulted and recognised for their efforts in the workplace.

Providing benefits to trade union members

Members of trade unions do not have to speak to management alone if they have a problem within the workplace. A trade union will have vast knowledge and expertise in the area of contracts of employment and workplace rights and members can seek advice and guidance from their trade union.

Promoting health, safety and well being

One of the main role of the trade union is to ensure the employer complies with the health and safety legislation and regulations. The trade union can investigate complaints, possible hazards, and workplace accidents. It can conduct regular health and safety inspections of the work place and assess risks.

A trade union will also try to ensure that its members are respected and valued and that there are opportunities for training and development, career progression and career security.

Drawbacks of being in a trade union

There can be some drawbacks to being part of a trade union for employees. Some of these are as follows:

- You have to pay to be a member and if you never need to use the services then this can be seen as a waste of money.
- If you are part of a trade union and the majority of members decide to take industrial action (strike, go slow, etc.), then you have to follow the industrial action too even if you do not want to – all actions are taken as a united group.
- Some employers do not encourage the membership of trade unions and so some employees will decide not to join one.

Section 3 Rights and responsibilities of employers and employees

Employers and trade unions

Some employers encourage their employees to join a trade union while others do not. This is because there are both advantages and disadvantages to the employer if employees are in a trade union. What are they?

- **Advantages to employers of employees being trade union members**
  - Can deal with the shop steward (union representative) rather than a number of different employees
  - Just need to distribute information to the trade union which then passes it on to their members

- **Disadvantages to employers of employees being trade union members**
  - Can encourage members to go against the company's wishes
  - Trade unions can force employers to increase wage rates and improve other terms and conditions
  - Industrial action from the whole staff can result in profit losses for the company

▲ Advantages and disadvantages to employers of employee trade union membership

Activity — Trade union membership (PS)

1. Copy the diagram above showing the advantages and disadvantages of trade union memberships, and in small groups discuss other advantages and disadvantages from the employer's point of view. Add your suggestions to the diagram.

Activity — To join or not to join

Joe is employed as a paramedic and he is thinking about joining a trade union.

1. Find out which trade union he could join by asking a paramedic or searching the internet (try typing 'paramedic union in Northern Ireland' into a search engine).
2. List the reasons he should join the trade union.
3. List the reasons he should not join the trade union.
4. What would you do if you were Joe? Justify your answer.

UNIT 3 EMPLOYABILITY

Section 4 Social responsibility of businesses

Key content
- The ways that businesses can demonstrate social responsibility:
  - Addressing environmental issues
  - Supporting the local community, for example, sponsoring local teams and projects, scholarship programmes, voucher schemes, work experience placements
  - Encouraging the use of local products
- The benefits to businesses of being socially responsible:
  - Publicity
  - Improved sales
  - Better community relations
  - Attracting potential employees

This section looks at the areas in which social responsibility is shown by businesses. It looks at this by exploring how businesses address factors such as **environmental issues** and their role in the local community. The ways in which businesses encourage the use and distribution of local products in order to encourage local economic growth is also examined, and finally the benefits that businesses can reap from being socially responsible are outlined.

How do businesses demonstrate social responsibility?

The term 'social responsibility' in relation to business means that a business examines its decisions and growth in the light of the environment it operates in, both at a local and global scale. Many businesses have adopted a **Corporate Social Responsibility (CSR)** policy. This covers areas such as monitoring the impact the business has on the well-being of the local and global environment, consumers, employees and other stakeholders (people who have an interest in the business). Social responsibility is an expectation that businesses will try to benefit society. It is an important part of any business as a good approach to social responsibility can attract and keep existing employees. A positive approach to social responsibility can enhance a business' reputation and this can increase employees' self-esteem.

Many large businesses pour resources into developing and monitoring a CSR policy. For many businesses the CSR is built into their mission statement, and thus positioned at the centre of their business. Often a CSR is based around **sustainability** and assisting the local community as well as reducing the business' **carbon footprint**.

▲ A carbon footprint from www.insolergy.com

188

Addressing environmental issues

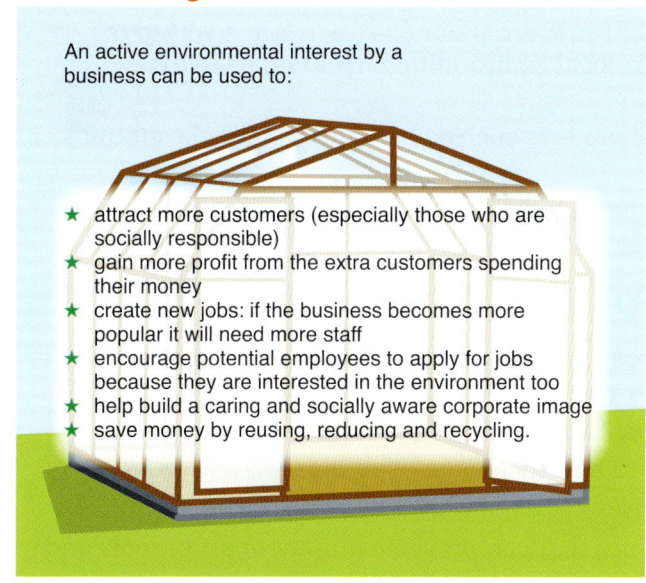

An active environmental interest by a business can be used to:

★ attract more customers (especially those who are socially responsible)
★ gain more profit from the extra customers spending their money
★ create new jobs: if the business becomes more popular it will need more staff
★ encourage potential employees to apply for jobs because they are interested in the environment too
★ help build a caring and socially aware corporate image
★ save money by reusing, reducing and recycling.

▲ Benefits for a business of an active environmental interest

There are many environmental issues that businesses need to be aware of if they are to be socially responsible; some of these are outlined below.

Reducing waste

Businesses can reduce waste: through creating less packaging; by using email instead of paper; by using both sides of the paper when printing documents; by using fewer toxic cleaning products; by turning off lights and computers when they are not needed; by closing doors (conserving energy).

Reusing

Businesses can reuse: by buying refurbished furniture and equipment; by refilling ink cartridges; by not using plastic cups for drinks; by using scrap paper for telephone messages.

Recycling

Businesses can recycle: by always using recycled products; by making sure the products sold can be recycled; by setting up recycling points and recycling paper, cardboard, plastic, broken machinery and computers; by having appropriate and well-labelled bin facilities for paper, plastic, cardboard and food waste; by encouraging employees to use the facilities and rewarding them for doing so.

Mitigating (reducing) greenhouse gas emissions

The three main greenhouse gases are carbon dioxide, methane and nitrous oxide. Carbon dioxide comes from burning fossil fuels such as oil and coal; methane comes from rotting vegetation and landfills; nitrous oxide comes from fertilisers, burning fuels and industrial production. It is believed by many scientists that greenhouse gases have contributed to **global warming** which causes climate change. They think that, in order to slow down or halt climate change, governments, businesses and individuals need to reduce the amount of greenhouse gases produced.

Business can reduce greenhouse gas emissions by:

▶ purchasing **energy efficient** appliances
▶ using renewable energy sources such as wind turbines
▶ reducing electricity and heating demands by, for example, switching everything off at the weekend
▶ buying goods that will last a long time
▶ using trains or buses rather than cars when attending meetings, and planning trips more carefully
▶ recycling and throwing away less rubbish which fills landfills.

Activity

Being socially responsible

1 What do you think are the three most important issues (from those outlined above) for the following businesses to consider in being more socially responsible? Explain your choices:
   • a busy supermarket
   • a solicitor's office
   • a large taxi company.

2 a In groups, discuss the effects of being socially responsible on business. Your discussion should include the following:
   • What does it mean to be socially responsible?
   • How can businesses be socially responsible?
   • The effects of being socially responsible for the business and society.

   b After your group discussion, on your own summarise the main points your group made.

Supporting local communities

Many businesses throughout Northern Ireland are actively involved in helping and supporting their local communities. This can be in many forms, including:

- financially assisting local projects such as helping to build playgrounds or sports facilities
- providing mentors for schools to help students with career decisions
- sponsoring local or school teams by providing kits and/or equipment
- funding scholarship programmes for university undergraduates and graduates
- providing work experience placements for school and university students and people seeking employment who need work experience
- donating or raising money for a variety of charities
- employees volunteering to help local organisations
- supporting local enterprises
- setting up voucher schemes that can provide equipment for schools and/or youth clubs
- allowing local charities to collect donations on business premises (for example, bag packs in supermarkets).

Activity: Ulster Bank and the community

- http://digital.ulsterbank.co.uk/content/dam/Ulster/documents/group/Community-leaflet-sustainability-2016-UBGROUPDF0229.pdf
- http://digital.ulsterbank.co.uk/content/dam/Ulster/documents/group/community-in-numbers-our-2015-impact-UBGROUPDF0251.pdf

Using the PDFs from the websites above, study the information from Ulster Bank about how they are striving to be socially responsible in local communities and answer the following questions:

1. What is the 'Community Cashback' programme designed to do?
2. What does the 'Give a Day' programme encourage Ulster Bank employees to do?
3. How do you think the 'Give a Day' programme helps to attract and maintain employees for Ulster Bank?
4. What is the partnership with the Prince's Trust designed to do?
5. Using the bullet point list above, decide and explain how many of the activities Ulster Bank are doing help support local communities.
6. How do you think Ulster Bank is being socially responsible?

Encouraging the use and distribution of local products

As we have seen, Northern Ireland operates in a global environment and many of the businesses we use and depend on for employment are based in other countries. However, many of these companies buy products from Northern Ireland so that they can use them or resell them to us, the customers. This means that global companies are being socially responsible as they are helping the Northern Ireland economy to grow and be sustainable.

Case study: Northern Ireland produce

The big three supermarkets in Northern Ireland, Tesco, ASDA and Sainsbury's, all sell products that are from Northern Ireland. Some of the Northern Irish products are sold throughout the UK and Ireland and others are also sold abroad. This has played a part in the 8.3 per cent increase in the turnover of the Northern Ireland food sector in 2015 to a healthy £3.7 billion.

- ASDA has invested over £60 million in the 'island of Ireland' products from 2010, so that 20 per cent of all food in the Northern Irish stores is sourced from Northern Ireland and Republic of Ireland companies.
- Sainsbury's has sold around £250 million worth of products from Northern Ireland and approximately £40 million of this total is sold in Northern Irish stores.
- Tesco has increased the value of Northern Irish products to £522 million from £50 million in 1996 and there were at least 100 local lines introduced in the last year.

It is believed to make very good business sense to source products locally because customers from Northern Ireland like locally sourced products and there is a large demand for products such as Tayto Crisps and Club Orange soft drinks. Customers also like to know that their bread, vegetables and fresh meat have not had to travel very far so are as fresh as possible.

All of ASDA's meat, produce and dairy comes from local businesses. It also has a small number of local suppliers, such as a popcorn supplier from Glengormley and a sandwich supplier in Newtownards. As well as this, Mash Direct, a home-cooked meal producer, now have lines sold in all ASDA stores across the UK.

Sainsbury's also uses local suppliers to meet customer demands. All of the fresh beef and lamb is sourced in Northern Ireland and a large proportion of its fresh pork, milk, eggs and dairy are also sourced locally. Northern Ireland-based Fivemiletown Creamery also supplies some of Sainsbury's own-brand products.

Tesco believes that using local suppliers helps to keep customers happy as there is a demand for local food at competitive prices. Tesco sell milk from Dale Farm, meat from Foyle meats and eggs from Skea eggs. This ensures the quality is high and enables Tesco to act in a responsible way by helping to grow the Northern Irish economy.

▲ ASDA sources goods from local businesses

All of the supermarkets know that Northern Irish customers want to support their local suppliers and economy and they want to be able to trace their food origins back to a local farm or producer. There is some evidence to suggest that local customers are willing to pay a little more if there is a guarantee that the food they buy is locally sourced or produced.

This is supported by the increase in demand for local food products from smaller, independent shops and markets. There has been a sharp increase in farmers' markets throughout Northern Ireland. These are markets that operate once or twice a week in different locations throughout Northern Ireland. The vast majority of the products sold are local products from local farms or businesses. One of the largest of these markets is St George's Market in Belfast.

> **Activity — Sourcing local products**
>
> 1 Read the case study and, in small groups, discuss the following:
>   - Why is local produce important to Northern Irish customers?
>   - How do local businesses benefit from the situation outlined in the case study?
>   - How do local communities benefit from the situation outlined in the case study?
>   - How does the above information show social responsibility?
>   - Why is this important for social responsibility?
> 2 After discussion, complete the following question on your own:
>   'Justify why selling locally produced and sourced products demonstrates social responsibility.'

What are the benefits social responsibility offers to businesses?

In a modern world that is increasingly concerned with how businesses operate and the impact of these operations locally and globally, there are multiple benefits available to businesses that are socially responsible. These benefits include the following:

- **Good publicity:** businesses can improve their reputation and image by being socially responsible. It is important that businesses publicise their social responsibility to customers, suppliers, employees and potential employees, as positive stories will help to build a good image of the business.
- **Improved sales:** socially responsible businesses can increase their sales by targeting customers who appreciate social responsibility. This can help build long-term value to the business as customers may feel more comfortable purchasing products or services from a company that is socially responsible.
- **Saving money on energy:** saving money on paper, electricity and energy efficient sources of production and heating can be cost effective. Savings in this area mean the money can be used to create more sales or to reinvest in the business.
- **Building customer loyalty:** customers who appreciate socially responsible business operations are likely to keep using these businesses. They may be more likely to leave positive comments on social media sites and tell their friends and family about the good attitude of the business to social responsibility.
- **Building better community relations:** local communities may feel that businesses who are socially responsible have an interest in the well-being of their community. Local communities are therefore more likely to spend money and support businesses that are seen to be contributing to the well-being of the community.
- **Attracting potential employees:** those seeking employment or who are looking to change employment may be attracted by a business which is socially responsible. The potential employee may have job offers from more than one business and a good attitude and actions towards social responsibility may mean the employee will be drawn towards the business. This means that the socially responsible business obtains the skills and knowledge of the employee. It also means that the beliefs of the employee and the business are in sync when it comes to social responsibility, leading to a better working relationship.

Some people argue that social responsibility is just another way that businesses try to promote themselves and that high profits are more important than being socially responsible. Many businesses' social responsibility is therefore measured by the actions and changes they implement rather than the policies they write on paper or publish on their websites.

> **Activity** — **Benefits of social responsibility** (ICT)
>
> 1 Using the following websites, copy and complete the table below:
>   - www.boots-uk.com/Corporate_Social_Responsibility
>   - www.diageo.com/en-ie/csr/Pages/CSR-in-Ireland.aspx
>   - www.yankeecandle.com/about-us/sustainability-commitment
>   - www.costa.co.uk/responsibility
>   - www.moypark.com/en/news/corporate-social-responsibility-at-moy-park
>   - www.mcdonalds.co.uk/ukhome/whatmakesmcdonalds/questions/running-the-business/csr/what-is-mcdonalds-corporate-social-responsibility-policy.html
>
> | Business | Examples of social responsibility | Benefits to the community | Benefits to the business |
> |---|---|---|---|
> | Boots | | | |
> | Diageo | | | |
> | Yankee Candle | | | |
> | Costa Coffee | | | |
> | Moypark | | | |
> | McDonald's | | | |
> | Add a company of your choice to research | | | |

EMPLOYABILITY

Unit 3 — Section 5 Exploring self-employment

Key content

- The importance of an entrepreneur carrying out research on the following before starting up a business:
  - Researching the need for a product or service
  - Funding options for the business
  - Providing the product or service
  - Marketing and promoting the product
  - Placement of the product
- The advantages and disadvantages of being self-employed, for example opportunities and risks
- The support provided by government and non-government agencies for new and developing businesses

This section looks at the area of entrepreneurship and enterprise using two case studies of people who have established their own businesses in Northern Ireland. It examines the steps that can be taken in order to create your own business, including researching the market for the product or service, how to fund the business and how the product or service can be provided. The need to understand the process of marketing is investigated and the importance of placement in regard to the success of the business is also examined.

The nature of self-employment is also outlined with emphasis on the advantages and disadvantages and finally the support available to individuals hoping to start their own business.

Why is it important for an entrepreneur to carry out research before starting a business?

An entrepreneur is the name given to a person who has the will and desire to work for him/herself and set up a business with all the risk that that entails. Entrepreneurs have an idea or a vision and turn it into an actual business, sometimes with help from various support agencies.

Famous entrepreneurs include:

- Steve Jobs – founder of Apple Computers
- Bill Gates – founder of Microsoft
- Mark Zuckerberg – founder of Facebook
- James Dyson – founder of Dyson products
- Coco Chanel – founder of Chanel
- Oprah Winfrey – founder of Harpo Productions
- Stelios Haji-Ioannou – founder of EasyJet
- Cher Wang – founder of HTC phone company
- Sara Blakely – founder of Spanx undergarments
- Levi Roots – founder of Reggae Reggae Sauce (see case study).

▲ Do you know any entrepreneurs? What do they do?

Section 5 Exploring self-employment

What does it take to be an entrepreneur?

PLANNING
- Think through ideas, look at both the risks and rewards of the idea.
- Think about future problems that might arise and decide how they can be dealt with.
- Be prepared for changes and problems to arise and have plans to solve them.
- Allow time and thought for creativity.
- Research as much as possible.
- Be willing to try different things.

LEADERSHIP
- Be willing to take risks and lead by example.
- Be able to manage time, people and investors.
- Use persuasion to encourage people to do what you want.
- Make good decisions even under pressure.
- Use all the information available to make judgements.
- Remain focused even when feeling confused.
- Show commitment and dedication.
- Be able to multi-task (do more than one thing).
- Be confident about ideas.
- Be willing to make sacrifices.

DECISION MAKING
- Trust in the decisions taken.
- Be able to make decisions alone.
- Know when a bad decision has been made and try to fix it.
- Be ready to make quick decisions, sometimes relying on 'gut feeling'.
- Always be responsible for your decisions.

CONNECT IDEAS
- Realise that all decisions will have knock-on effects.
- Understand the possible outcomes of decisions.
- Be able to see everything – 'The Big Picture'.
- Realise when something is not working.
- Do not be afraid to stop or change something if it is not working.

Case study: Levi Roots

Levi Roots is a singer turned entrepreneur who featured on BBC2's *Dragons' Den* in 2006. His Reggae Reggae Sauce product was born from his grandmother's recipe and Levi's desire to be an entrepreneur.

Levi had been selling his cooking sauce at Notting Hill Carnival in London, but he needed investment to expand and grow his business idea. With the investment of £50,000 and the expertise of fellow entrepreneurs from the *Dragons' Den*, Levi was able to expand and grow his business.

Within a year the Reggae Reggae Sauce brand was born and available in Sainsbury's to a mass market. The Levi Roots range has continued to grow with Caribbean Cooking Sauces, ready meals, soft drinks, desserts and more. In late 2015 Levi opened his first Caribbean-inspired restaurant and has had six cookbooks published.

Levi has embraced the concept of self-employment and made employment possible for many others.

UNIT 3 EMPLOYABILITY

Activity — Levi Roots

1. Using the diagram above and the example of Levi Roots, copy and complete the following table using other entrepreneurs you may know of, to show some of the skills involved in being an entrepreneur:

Entrepreneur	Planning	Leadership	Decision making	Connect ideas
Levi Roots	Thought about the risks involved in accepting the £50,000 investment.	Led a team to ensure the Reggae Reggae Sauce was available to Sainsbury's customers initially.	Decided on how the brand would be expanded and developed.	Connected the ideas of the different products to create an established brand.

Read the following case studies on two people who set up their own businesses. You will refer to these case studies throughout this section.

Case study

Pop Notch (formerly 'It's So Popcorn')

Declan McBride, a butcher by trade, has taken the bull by the horns and opted for an altogether different career manufacturing popcorn under the brand of 'Pop Notch!'. Taking part in Invest Northern Ireland's Regional Start Initiative, Declan consolidated his idea and developed a business plan which was to be his launch pad to success.

Declan started in August 2013 manufacturing luxury popcorn from his home in Straw, Draperstown, but recently Declan set up premises in an industrial park in Maghera. He is now producing 2,000 bags per week of flavoured popcorn, which is sold through distributors to high-profile retailers such as ASDA, SPAR and Applegreen.

'Starting a manufacturing business during the economic downturn was daunting,' explains Declan, 'but having developed a successful business when times are tough, I would encourage others to take the plunge and follow their dream. Invest Northern Ireland's Regional Start Initiative really helped me to focus on developing my product range, how to identify and segment my customers and how to effectively market to them.'

From Cheese and Bacon, Chilli Coriander and Coconut and Lime to sweet temptations such as Double Butter and Chocolate and Marshmallow, Pop Notch has a flavour to tickle every taste bud. And according to proprietor Declan, a range of new and innovative popcorn products are on the way!

(www.popnotch.co.uk)

Case study

Home Hopes

After working for others in the retail sector for years, Jenny O'Hara decided she too wanted to be her own boss. By combining her passion for household furnishing and trinkets and her own retail knowledge she decided to open 'Home Hopes' in the busy shopping place of Newry.

'I have always had an interest in home furnishings and design and I knew there was a potential market to sell household trinkets and items to. I always had friends when visiting my own home asking me where I had bought home accessories that were dotted around my home.'

'I knew it was vitally important to have the correct pieces of stock and to ensure that new pieces were added to the collection often, and to ensure that I displayed new stock prominently. This would encourage customers to revisit the shop to find out what was "new in". I utilised the large window at the front of the shop to encourage passing and existing trade to buy in the shop.'

Jenny looked for help and advice from the Go For It programme to make sure she would be successful. She says 'The support I received enabled me to bring the idea of "Home Hopes" into reality and into an actual business. I had a personal advisor assigned to help me with all aspects of running a business.'

Thanks to her help from the Regional Start Up Initiative, Jenny is looking forward to growing her business in the years ahead.

Steps for setting up a business

Entrepreneurs will usually start their business venture with a new idea or they will adapt an idea that already exists and try to improve it. In order to start a business, entrepreneurs have to work through the following steps:

1. Researching the need for a product or service
2. Funding options for the business
3. Providing the product or service
4. Marketing and promoting the product
5. Placement of the product.

Both Declan and Jenny from the case studies on page 196 went through the process outlined above before launching their businesses. To be able to do this successfully they may have needed some help and support as they had to research, design and market the product or service. This is why many entrepreneurs go to specialist agencies for advice and support. Part of this process is designing a business plan.

Researching the need for a product or service

All entrepreneurs must conduct market research to ensure their product or service is a success. There are two different types of market research that are carried out: primary research and secondary research.

- **Primary research** is new information that is gathered specifically for the entrepreneur. It can be gathered through questionnaires, interviews and focus groups. Declan McBride from Pop Notch may have gathered primary research about the popcorn flavours people prefer, how much people would pay for popcorn and how often people buy popcorn.
- **Secondary research** is information that is already available from sources such as census data, business databases, competitors' information and internet searches. Declan McBride may have found out information about the popcorn industry such as where popcorn is sold, the age group of popcorn eaters, how it is made and what equipment it takes to produce popcorn.

Both types of research have advantages and disadvantages:

Advantages	Disadvantages
Primary research	
Reliable	Costly
Up to date	Time consuming
Relevant	Complicated to gather
Secondary research	
Easy to access	May be outdated
Inexpensive	Not exactly suitable for purpose

Funding options for the business

A business is funded by different sources of finance in order to start it up. Successful entrepreneurs usually use a combination of available sources of finance to fund their business venture so that the financial risk is spread. They try to be flexible in their approach to investors and with the terms of payback. Some of the sources of finance include:

- personal savings
- sale of an asset (house, car)
- overdraft (short-term loan from a bank)
- bank loan
- credit cards
- investors (people who put money into the business for a share of the profits or company)
- redundancy payment
- government assistance (see table on page 203 on government support).

Activity — Financial support

1. Give an advantage and a disadvantage for each of the options for funding listed above.
2. How do you think Declan funded Pop Notch (see page 196)? Explain your thoughts.
3. How do you think Jenny funded Home Hopes (see page 196)? Explain your thoughts.

Providing the product or service

In order for a business to be a success the entrepreneur must make sure that the product or service they are offering is in demand and the raw materials are readily available to provide the product or service.

> **Case study**
>
> ### Pop Notch – providing the product
>
> In order for Pop Notch to be successful Declan has to make sure that he is able to produce enough popcorn to meet the demand from his customers. Pop Notch cook large kernels of corn and then flavour them at the Pop Notch factory in Draperstown. The following videos demonstrate the process of producing popcorn:
>
> - 'How popcorn is made': www.youtube.com/watch?v=704tA5z7XjY
> - 'Popcorn production line: www.youtube.com/watch?v=kgfaSqKQwjg
>
> As these videos show, in order for Pop Notch to make and sell their popcorn, they must have the raw materials – the kernels and the flavourings – as well as suitable production facilities to be able to meet the demand placed on the business. As the business grows Pop Notch will need to ensure that they have sufficient raw materials as well as production and packaging facilities that will be efficient enough to meet growing demand.

Pop Notch are now supplying large supermarkets like Tesco and Sainsbury's as well as cinemas and other wholesale suppliers. This means that they have had to enlarge and improve the production process that they use. When an enterprise has huge demand they need to invest in **mass production**.

Mass production (also known as flow production) is the name given to the method of producing goods in large quantities at a low cost per unit. Mass-produced goods are standardised by means of precision-manufactured, interchangeable parts.

> This video, entitled 'Methods of Production', shows the three types of production: www.youtube.com/watch?v=CLPFG5QCx0g

Mass production can be used in the production of items such as cars, toothpaste, chocolate and popcorn. Advantages of mass production are as follows:

- Each employee becomes very skilled at one particular task and can work faster.
- Detailed and lengthy training is avoided, saving money for the employer.
- Employees do not have to move between tasks and jobs, saving time for the employer.
- Increased supply of products hopefully leads to more sales and in turn higher profits.
- Tools and machinery are used only when needed and by employees who know how to operate them, making sure the tools and machinery are well looked after.
- Only the tools and machinery needed for the mass production process have to be bought and maintained.

> **Activity**
>
> **Mass production**
>
> 1. List three disadvantages of mass production.
> 2. Evaluate whether a company like Pop Notch (see case study on page 196) should use mass production techniques to grow their company.

Marketing and promoting the product or service

In order to make a business successful the product or service that is offered for sale must be marketed to ensure there is a continued demand. The process of marketing is designed to ensure that the right product or service is offered at the right price in the right place using the right promotional activities. It involves selling, promoting, branding, costing and locating production and selling efficiently and effectively to ensure growth and to beat the competition.

The process of marketing is commonly broken down into the 'four Ps', to help entrepreneurs understand the process of successful marketing:

- PRODUCT: designed to meet customer needs.
- PLACEMENT: deciding where to sell so that it is accessible to all.
- PRICE: to attract customers, but still make profit for the business.
- PROMOTION: to inform/persuade customers in the best way possible.

These four ingredients are combined to ensure that **marketing objectives** are achieved. Emphasis will shift from one 'P' to another, depending on the marketing objective at the time, but all four Ps are essential for success.

Product

The product ingredient of marketing is about the level of quality, the name, the packaging and the branding of the product or service.

Case study
The Pop Notch product

Pop Notch was originally called 'It's So Popcorn', but the business decided to change the name of the company and product as part of a rebranding process so that they could get their product right. To enhance their product they also developed different flavours.

Placement of a product

The place ingredient of the marketing mix is about getting the goods to the place where they are going to sell most successfully. This means that manufacturers must study carefully where to sell their products as well as how to get them, in good condition, to that place. To do this, the business must consider:

- the most appropriate sales outlets for the product
- the most appropriate channel of distribution to use
- the most appropriate method of transport for the product.

Price

Once a business has decided on its product and place the price will need to be set. It is important that the business gets the price right as it directly influences profits by creating revenue.

The price set can also help the business to differentiate its product or service from others on the market, i.e.:

- high price might mean better quality
- low price might mean lower quality or perhaps better value.

It is also important that the price set is consistent with everything else in the marketing mix. For example, a high-priced product needs to be well made, sold in the appropriate stores and have a promotional campaign that makes customers feel justified for paying more.

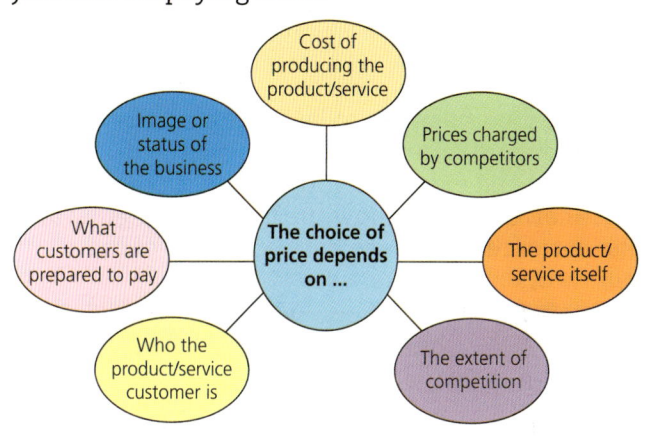

The choice of price depends on...
- Cost of producing the product/service
- Prices charged by competitors
- The product/service itself
- The extent of competition
- Who the product/service customer is
- What customers are prepared to pay
- Image or status of the business

▲ How the price for a product or service is decided upon

Promotion

The promotion ingredient is concerned with how the customer is found and persuaded to buy the product or service. It involves promotional activities such as public relations, advertising, sponsorship and sales promotions (buy-one-get-one-free, loyalty cards and free products with purchases).

Advertising campaigns are now more reliant on customers and potential customers engaging with the campaign through social media platforms. This can take the form of 'sharing' information, using hashtags, watching videos and commenting on videos and information.

> Increasingly businesses are using social media to promote their products and services, as this video, '10 of the best social media campaigns of 2015', outlines: www.youtube.com/watch?v=Xxr7whDfCdg.

The beauty company Dove had a promotional campaign called 'Dove Choose Beautiful'. The campaign was designed to promote the Dove range by encouraging women to associate beauty with Dove products.

The campaign involved an advertisement that invited women to enter through a door marked 'average' or 'beautiful'. The doors were placed in locations across the globe and then Dove encouraged customers and potential customers to share stories or comments on being beautiful via social media. This was done using social media accounts, writing on blogs or using hashtags associated with the campaign.

UNIT 3 EMPLOYABILITY

More about the 'Dove Choose Beautiful' campaign can be discovered here: www.dove.com/uk/stories/campaigns/choose-beautiful.html.

In order for a business to be successful the marketing mix must be correctly planned, designed and executed. If the balance of the 'four Ps' is correct it will allow the business to grow and the entrepreneur to see benefits for all of their hard work and efforts.

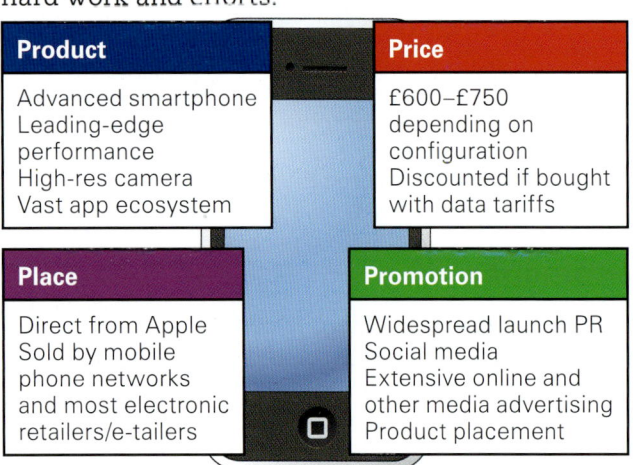

Product
- Advanced smartphone
- Leading-edge performance
- High-res camera
- Vast app ecosystem

Price
- £600–£750 depending on configuration
- Discounted if bought with data tariffs

Place
- Direct from Apple
- Sold by mobile phone networks and most electronic retailers/e-tailers

Promotion
- Widespread launch PR
- Social media
- Extensive online and other media advertising
- Product placement

▲ The marketing mix for an iPhone 7

An effective marketing mix:
- meets customer needs
- achieves marketing objectives
- is balanced and consistent
- makes the product/service appear better than the competition.

The marketing mix for each business will be different and it will change over time. For most businesses, one or two ingredients of the mix will be seen as more important than the others, as shown below:

Most important ingredient	Example of business
Product	Tailor-made dresses or suits Luxury vehicles
Placement	Sandwich shops Fuel garages with convenience stores
Price	Low-cost hotels Low-cost supermarkets
Promotion	Soft drink providers Toothpaste companies

Activity

Marketing a product/service

1. Copy and complete the following table to show the importance of each of the 'four Ps' to different businesses:

Product/service	Most important of the 'four Ps'	Justification of decision
Washing powder	Promotion	Highly competitive market – heavily advertised, discounted offers
Coffee shop		
Low-cost airline		
Bespoke furniture		

2. Look back at the information on Pop Notch and Home Hopes (see page 196). In groups of four, pick one of the businesses or another one of your choice and explain how it could use 'the four Ps' to market its product.

3. Design a presentation for your class entitled: 'How to market a product/service'.

What are the advantages and disadvantages of being self-employed?

'Self-employed' is the term used to describe people who work for themselves. They are their own boss. They are often both the employer and employee. People become self-employed to set up and build a business and make their own money – they are often known as entrepreneurs. Others are self-employed because that is the nature of their work, but they are not necessarily entrepreneurs, such as self-employed taxi drivers, supply teachers and freelance journalists.

The advantages and opportunities of self-employment

The main advantages of being self-employed can be broken down into financial and non-financial as shown on page 201.

Section 5 Exploring self-employment

The benefits of being self-employed

Financial benefits

Profits: any money made in the business is profit for the owner of the business. A very successful entrepreneur can make large profits which can enable a good lifestyle and can also be used to expand the business or to invest in other businesses. Controlling the profits can be a good motivating factor to work hard.

Growing value of the business: if a business develops then employees can be hired and eventually an entrepreneur could sell their business and use the profits to work in other areas.

Non-financial benefits

Satisfaction: being directly in control of profits and working hard to get good customer feedback can be hugely satisfying.

Control: when you are self-employed you are in control of all of the decision making and the direction of the company. This responsibility can be hugely motivating.

Flexibility: being self-employed means being in charge of your own time. You can dictate how much time you spend working and when you work. The flexibility of self-employment can be particularly appealing to people who are juggling work with family life.

The disadvantages of being self-employed

Financial disadvantages

Irregular income: there is usually no guarantee of a weekly or monthly amount in wages; instead the income will depend on the amount of work completed.

No holiday pay: if a self-employed person is not working then they will not be paid.

No pension: unless a self-employed person sets up a private pension scheme they will have no pension at retirement.

Non-financial disadvantages

Working long hours: someone who is self-employed may have to work hours outside of the 'normal' working day in order to meet the demands of the job.

Staying motivated: it can be difficult to have the energy, enthusiasm and drive needed for self-employment all of the time.

Lack of social interaction: many self-employed people work from home so they will miss out on the social interaction of working in a team environment in an office.

Impact on work/life balance: the working day and environment may invade the home environment and time.

UNIT 3 EMPLOYABILITY

The risks of self-employment

A risk can either go well or fail. When a business risk fails the entrepreneur may lose money, have to pay back money borrowed, have difficulty finding a job and have low self-esteem because of the failure.

Business failures are quite common and it is often difficult to know if a business will be successful or not. Some reasons businesses fail include:

- there is lots of competition
- poor cash flow (money in the business)
- an underestimation of the time and effort needed to be self-employed
- not enough customer demand
- poor economic climate
- poor market research
- the business growing too quickly and a resulting failure to manage the growth.

Activity — Self-employment pros and cons

Using the case studies on page 196, or another example of someone who is self-employed, copy and complete the following tables. Some of the information you will need to infer from what you have read.

Advantages of self-employment	Pop Notch	Home Hopes
Profits		
Growing value of the business		
Satisfaction		
Control		
Flexibility		

Disadvantages of self-employment	Pop Notch	Home Hopes
Competition		
Money to reinvest		
Time and effort needed		
Not enough customer demand		
Poor economic climate		
Poor market research		
No management of growth		
Irregular income/no holiday pay/no pension		
Staying motivated		
Lack of social interaction		
Impact on work/life balance		

What support is provided for new and developing businesses?

Many people who are self-employed or who want to become self-employed get a lot of support from their family and friends. This can be financial support and/or emotional support. However, other specialist support is usually needed if a self-employment venture is to be successful; this can only be provided by designated agencies that specialise in offering advice and assistance to self-employed people.

Agencies that provide support to the self-employed

There are many different designated agencies that can help support self-employed people. Some of the agencies are run by the government and some are NGOs.

The agencies you need to know about are:

- Northern Ireland direct government services
- Department for the Economy
- The Prince's Trust
- Invest Northern Ireland (Invest NI)
- NI Business Info
- Enterprise Northern Ireland.

Each one of these agencies can be useful for self-employed people. The table below tells you more about each one of them.

Agency	Role	Support provided	How?	Examples of assistance	Websites
Northern Ireland direct government services	Help people to get new skills and provide guidance to those who want to be self-employed	Advice and guidance and tips on becoming self-employed	Information on the website and hyperlinks to direct you to further information	Information about benefits and drawbacks of being self-employed	www.nidirect.gov.uk Education, learning and skills > Careers > Plan your career > Looking for a new career
Department for the Economy	Helps to deliver government policy on areas such as tourism, economy and enterprise	Advice and information on particular sectors that a self-employed person might be interested in	Guidance on areas around: • economic policy • employment rights • consumer affairs • tourism	A place to go if you need any information on areas listed on the left	www.economy-ni.gov.uk
Invest NI	Gives advice and guidance to new and existing businesses on starting up or growing domestically or internationally. Attracts new business to NI	Through the Go for It programme advice on developing business plans and accessing funding	Meetings, workshops and training seminars (on IT, marketing, design, accounting, etc.) Mentoring support from experts	Personal business advisers Training and work shops One-to-one mentoring Networking opportunities Online support Developing business plans and ideas Grants International trade fairs	www.investni.com/

UNIT 3 EMPLOYABILITY

Agency	Role	Support provided	How?	Examples of assistance	Websites
NI Business Info	Advice on business planning, forming a business, running a business and growing a business	Comprehensive questions and answers to consider for new business start-ups	Information on the website as well as information about where to find additional support	Lots of questions and answers and links to other support offered	www.nibusinessinfo.co.uk
The Prince's Trust	Helps young people aged 18–30 who are unemployed to start up in business	Advice on: • employment options that are available • business training • business planning • funding • guidance from a mentor	Downloadable guides with help in the following areas: • Business planning • Finding premises • Sales and marketing • Managing finances • Legalities • Taxation • Business behaviour	24-hour helpline Virtual office space Online accounting system Web designing Money grants Town and country marketing opportunities to sell products or services Networking opportunities	www.princes-trust.org.uk
Enterprise Northern Ireland	Represents the local Enterprise Agencies in NI. Helps local entrepreneurs to grow and develop their businesses	Supports the interests of local Enterprise Agencies with government and private companies Provides a network of assistance to help with start-up, research and professional development	Guidance on grants and initiatives available to small businesses Professional advice from experienced business people Advice on programmes available to help businesses and entrepreneurs grow and develop	Help with finding financial assistance in a particular area Help with finding business accommodation Help with new technologies Help when using programmes such as Go for It (Invest NI)	www.enterpriseni.com

Activity — Supporting businesses

1 Match the business needs a–d below with the correct agency (in the table above) that could help.

　a A local shopkeeper who wants to expand his premises but is unsure about applying for planning permission.

　b An unemployed 20-year-old who has a great idea for a business.

　c A furniture manufacturer who wants to start exporting his products to the USA and Europe.

　d An unemployed person wanting to retrain and get qualifications in order to be able to set up in business.

UNIT 3

EMPLOYABILITY

Section 6 Personal career management

Key content
- Career planning as a lifelong learning process involving the following:
  - reviewing and evaluating learning, progress and achievements
  - goal setting
  - target setting (specific, measurable, achievable, realistic and time-constrained [SMART] targets)
  - taking action
- The personal skills, qualities and attitudes required for a chosen career
- Developing decision-making strategies and the benefits of making informed career choices
- External influences and their impact on young people's attitudes to education, training and employment

This section looks at the importance of career planning and why it is so essential to consider individual skills, qualities and attitudes when investigating and deciding on career choices. It examines how to develop decision-making strategies that can help make informed career choices and looks at external influences that can impact on these decisions.

How can career planning become a lifelong learning process?

Career planning is an ongoing process that can help with lifelong learning and development. It is the continuous process of:
- thinking about your interests, values, skills and preferences
- exploring the life, work and learning options available to you
- ensuring that your work fits with your personal circumstances
- continuously developing, learning and adapting plans to help you manage the changes in your life and the world of work.

As you have yet to begin a working career you are in a very privileged position, as you can take the time now to think, plan and design a career path that will work for you. You can adapt and change the plan as often as you wish and you may find that your career path adapts as your life matures and changes.

Career planning in four steps

Career planning can be carried out in an organised way using the following four steps:

1. Review and evaluate learning, progress and achievements
2. Set goals
3. Set targets
4. Take action

Step 1: Review and evaluate learning

This step allows you to think about where you are now in terms of learning and skills, where you want to be and how you are going to get there.

205

UNIT 3 EMPLOYABILITY

Evaluate your current skills and experience. Use this as a basis for planning so that you can monitor and review your progress at different stages in your plan.

Activity: Review and evaluate

1. In groups of four ask yourself the following questions. Possible answers are in colour.
   a. Where am I now?
   At school/Studying for my GCSEs/Part of a youth club/Involved in sports
   b. Where do I want to be?
   Working and earning a wage/Studying further to get more qualifications
   c. What do I like to do?
   Play sports/Spend time with friends/Use social media
   d. What are my strengths?
   Good communication skills/Organised/Able to solve problems and work with others
   e. What is important to me?
   My friends and family/Being successful/Being in control of my future

2. In your groups share your answers and discuss the following statement: 'It is important to know yourself when career planning because…'

At the end of Step 1 you may have a clearer idea of your preferred work or learning goal and your individual preferences. You can use this information about yourself as your personal 'wish list' against which you can compare all the information you gather in Step 2: Setting goals. Your personal preferences are very useful for helping you choose your best option at this point in time, which you can do in Step 3: Target setting.

Step 2: Setting goals

This step is about exploring the occupations and learning areas that interest you. Once you have some idea of your occupational preferences you can research the specific skills and qualifications required for those occupations.

Activity: Researching occupations

1. Explore occupations that interest you and ask yourself how your skills and interests match up with these occupations. Use the following table and websites to help you.
   - www.nidirect.gov.uk/information-and-services/careers/plan-your-career
   - www.careeronestop.org/Videos/CareerandClusterVideos/career-and-cluster-videos.aspx
   - www.careerwise.mnscu.edu/careers/careervideos.html

Occupation	Skills/interests needed	Do I have the required skills/interests?

2. Now answer the questions below and hopefully you will have a list of preferred occupations or learning options that you can use to build your career profile.
   a. Where are the gaps in my skills and knowledge?
   b. How can I go about acquiring these skills or qualifications for these occupations?
   c. What skills do I need?
   d. Where is the work?

Step 3: Target setting

As part of your career profile it is a good idea to have career goals/targets. If targets are to be successful they should be SMART:

- **S**pecific – about the career path
- **M**easurable – know when the goal has been met
- **A**ttainable – possible to achieve
- **R**elevant – to your own individual circumstances
- **T**ime related – within a set time period.

Look back at Andrea's case study in Section 2 (page 165). When she was considering the career of childminding she set herself the following SMART targets:

- To gain qualifications and accreditation in childminding within 12 months.
- To have an established childminding service within 24 months.
- To grow the number of children being cared for within the first six months of operation.

These SMART targets allowed Andrea to remain focused and gave her a clear path to follow so that she could bring her career 'wish list' to a reality. Andrea used her targets to become a childminder. However, as discussed in the case study she then had to reassess her career choices. This meant that she had to develop a new career plan and devise new SMART targets to ensure she was successfully employed.

Activity

SMART targets

1. List three SMART targets that Andrea may have used to gain employment in the training industry after her childminding career.
2. Evaluate the importance of setting and following SMART targets for a successful career path.
3. What were the benefits to Andrea of having a career plan?
4. Were there any disadvantages?

Making decisions

Making informed decisions can be difficult but it will be easier if you have plenty of reliable information and you take advice from positive influences. The best decisions are the ones you make for yourself by knowing what it is you want, the best way of getting what you want and then by weighing up the advantages and disadvantages of the decision. This step involves comparing your options, narrowing down your choices and thinking about what suits you best at this point in time. Ask yourself the following questions:

- What are my best work/training options?
- How do they match with my skills, interests and values?
- How do they fit with the current employment patterns?
- How do they fit with my current situation and responsibilities?
- What are the advantages and disadvantages of each option?
- What will help and what will hinder me?
- What can I do about any obstacles?

At the end of this step you will have narrowed down your options and have more of an idea of what you need to do next to help you achieve your goals.

Activity

Career options

1. Using the following website, register yourself and take the quiz that follows. It may help you to think about other career options that may be suitable for you:

   www.prospects.ac.uk

2. Pick three of the career options that have been suggested for you (or pick three career options that interest you) and use the bullet points listed above to design a career profile for yourself. Your career profile may look like the one below and can form the basis of your career goals.

> **Career profile**
>
> Name:
>
> Possible occupation:
>
> What skills/qualities/qualifications/attitudes do I need for this occupation?
>
> Where can I get the skills/qualifications for this occupation?
>
> What are the job prospects for this occupation in the future?
>
> What is going to help and hinder me to get this occupation?
>
> What can I do to help myself achieve my career goal?
>
> What are the different ways of being successful in this occupation?

UNIT 3 EMPLOYABILITY

Step 4: Taking action

Here you plan the steps you need to take to put your plan into action. Use all you have learnt about your skills, interests and values, together with the information you have gathered about your chosen occupations, to develop your career plan.

Begin by asking yourself the following questions:

▶ What actions/steps will help me achieve my work, training and career goals?
▶ Where can I get help?
▶ Who will support me?

At the end of this step you will have:

▶ a plan to help you explore your options further (for example, work experience, new skills, additional qualifications or more research); or
▶ a plan which sets out the steps to help you achieve your next learning or work goal.

As you grow and mature, the step that suits you best in the four-step plan may change. Decide which step is relevant for you right now and start from there.

Career planning is especially important in a global job market where employment patterns are changing continuously because it is important to follow a career path that will have job opportunities.

Activity — Important terms (PS)

The following terms are very important when thinking about career planning. Use the internet and the Glossary (see page 215) to write your own definitions of each term and explain their importance in career planning.

Term	Definition	Importance
Flexibility		
Upskilling		
Retraining		
Evaluating		
Monitoring		

What are the personal skills, qualities and attitudes required for a chosen career?

Look back at Section 2 (page 158) and remind yourself of the skills, qualities and attitudes that employers are looking for. Also look at the skills, qualities and attitudes discussed in Section 5 for entrepreneurs (page 194).

Activity — Skills, qualities and attitudes for careers (PS)

1 Write out a table like the one below, and fill it out to show the skills, qualities and attitudes needed for the following careers: doctor, entrepreneur, plumber, retail assistant, zookeeper, farmer, bank official, mechanical engineer, food scientist, computer game programmer. Add your career choice if it hasn't been covered.

Careers	Skills	Qualities	Attitudes
Doctor			
Entrepreneur			

2 Can you notice any similarities in the skills, qualities and attitudes required for different careers?
3 Do you possess the skills, qualities and attitudes needed for your occupation in the career path you previously designed?
4 If you do not have the required skills, qualities and attitudes for your career choice, what should you do? Choose from the following options and explain your choice:

  a Look at other career choices.
  b Investigate how to get the required skills, attitudes and qualities.
  c Do nothing.

5 Design a presentation to deliver to your class about your career path. Include the following:

- your career choice
- the skills, qualities, qualifications and attitudes needed for your career choice
- evidence to show that you have the skills, qualities, qualifications and attitudes needed for your career choice
- how you plan to fill any gaps you have for the skills, qualities, qualifications and attitudes needed for your career choice
- SMART targets to help you in your career path
- how you could overcome barriers that may hinder you in your career choice
- the different routes/paths that you could take to be successful in your career choice.

How can decision-making strategies be developed to make informed career choices?

Decision-making strategies are the processes used to select a logical choice from the available options. When trying to make a good career decision, a person must weigh the positives and negatives of each option, and consider all the alternatives. For decision making to be most effective you must be able to forecast the outcome of each option as well and, based on all this research, determine which option is the best for you. Some of the following sources of information and people are willing to help you with your decision making.

Careers advice: careers officers might be available in your school. Arrange an appointment with the service. They will be able to give you information and advice on all different types of careers.

Friends and family: these people know you well and they can be great at giving you ideas that you may wish to investigate for career opportunities.

Support and guidance with career decisions

Government agencies: the Northern Ireland direct website (www.nidirect.gov.uk) offers a range of information about different careers and how you can plan to be successful in a chosen job.

Media reports: look out in the media for new career opportunities, where new jobs are being created and in what areas. This can indicate the likely demand for particular jobs and careers in your area or in other areas.

Teachers: teachers are a great place to start, not just your careers teacher but also subject teachers. They will know what careers are accessible with their subject and what your strengths are.

▲ Areas of support for career decisions

In order to make good decisions about your career you need to know yourself very well. Understand what you are good at, what you enjoy and where the job opportunities are to allow you to follow a career path. As we saw in the case of Andrea (page 165), many people move between careers as they grow and mature and as employment patterns change.

What is the impact of making informed choices on future career pathways?

It is important that career choices are influenced in a positive way as this positive influence will help make informed choices. An informed choice is a choice that is made after reviewing all of the information, advice and guidance that is available. The four-step planning process along with SMART targets and advice from reliable support and positive influences can help with making informed choices.

Consider skills, qualities and attitudes	Concentrate on securing a suitable job
Assess strengths and limitations	Have SMART career targets
Research all career interests	Obstacles are learning opportunities
Engage with positive influences	Investigation and questioning help make informed choices
Encourage an open mind	Careful planning can lead to employment success
Review changing skills, qualities and attitudes	Essential to make good career decisions
	Success is very possible

UNIT 3 EMPLOYABILITY

Activity — Informed choices

Read the case study below on Marguerite's career path and answer the following questions:

1 What advice would you give to the 16-year-old Marguerite?
2 How do you think informed choices could have helped Marguerite with her career plan?
3 Evaluate the route that Marguerite took to reach the level of manager.

Case study — Marguerite's career path

Marguerite is 30 years of age with two children at primary school. She has always enjoyed learning and was a good student during her school career. At 16, Marguerite was awarded a good GCSE profile that enabled her to access an A-Level route. She chose to study A-Levels in Biology, Sociology and History.

She already enjoyed Biology and History and as Sociology was a new subject to her she felt she would enjoy the challenge. She did not have a specific career plan as she had never really discussed her career options or been self-evaluative in her approach to making decisions.

Six months into her A-Level course Marguerite was approached by the manager of the high street retail outlet that she worked for part time. The manager explained to her that they valued her skills and attitude to work and would like to offer her more hours in the retail outlet. Marguerite was very flattered and decided to accept the manager's offer as she was not happy in her A-Level choices and she was attracted by the increase in money and independence the extended hours would offer her.

For the next three years Marguerite worked in the retail outlet. However, she began to feel bored and unchallenged as there were no promotion prospects in the retail outlet and Marguerite realised that it was not a workplace where she felt fulfilled or motivated.

At the age of 19, Marguerite began working in a care home as a support worker for the elderly and she quickly realised that this type of work environment was much more suited to her skills and abilities. For the next four years Marguerite developed her skills by taking all the workplace opportunities for training and upskilling offered to her. She was especially interested and challenged by training in skills for working with vulnerable adults. By 23 Marguerite had her first child and moved to work at a supported living project for vulnerable adults.

In the past seven years Marguerite has had another child and has gained qualifications that have enabled her to apply and be successfully appointed as the registered manager of the supported living project. She manages 15 staff (support workers) and is responsible for the welfare and safeguarding of ten vulnerable adults who all live on site. She is responsible for the care plans, the frequent inspections, the wages and maintenance of the building, to name some of her many duties.

The above case study shows how informed choices and lack of informed choices can impact on an individual's working life. Marguerite has continued to be a lifelong learner. Her lack of self-awareness, research and investigation as a young person limited her choices. However, as she became more self-reflective and evaluative about her skills and attitudes she was able to find a career path that suited her. She has developed decision-making strategies that will help her to make informed choices for her future career pathways.

What external influences are there and what is their impact on young people's attitudes to education, training and employment?

All of us, no matter what age, are influenced by others. We need to know and recognise how these influences can impact on us and on our attitudes to education, training and employment. External influences that can impact on attitudes can be grouped into the following:

- **Significant adults:** family members, friends, neighbours
- **School:** teachers, classroom assistants, coaches, fellow students
- **Media:** films, TV series, magazines, social media
- **Role models:** TV stars, film stars, sports stars, musicians.

Section 6 Personal career management

These groups/people can have a huge influence on how young people feel about, relate to or do not relate to education, training and employment.

Education, training and employment describes a lifelong process by which a person can secure a good standard of living and reach their individual potential. A young person who is not involved in education, training or employment is referred to as a NEET (Not in Education, Employment or Training). According to the Office of National Statistics (ONS), in August 2016 there were 843,000 young people (aged 16–24) who were categorised as NEETs. This is approximately 11.7 per cent of the 16–24 year-olds in the UK.

Many of these young people categorised as NEETs may have had little or no opportunities to access positive and fulfilling education, training and employment. This could be because they have been influenced by negative external influences, such as 'friends' who do not encourage good decisions, and celebrities who engage in activities that are damaging to health and well-being.

Those who are categorised as NEETs are more likely to be disadvantaged and have poorer health and are less likely to have secure employment at the age of 30 and older.

Activity — External influences and their impact

1 In groups discuss and decide whether the information contained in each speech bubble has a positive or a negative impact on young people's attitudes to education, training and employment. Justify each of your choices to those in your group.

Significant adult soundbites

- Listen to your teachers and complete all of your work to the best of your ability. It will help you get a successful career.
- A job is a hassle, it takes up too much time and you end up giving most of the wages to the government.
- Just leave your revision for tomorrow and come out with us to the cinema, the exam isn't for weeks!

School soundbites

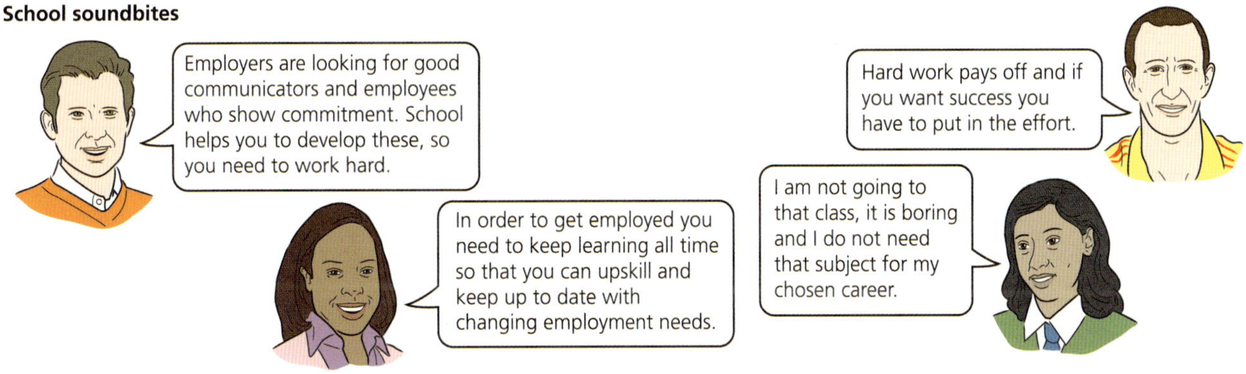

- Employers are looking for good communicators and employees who show commitment. School helps you to develop these, so you need to work hard.
- Hard work pays off and if you want success you have to put in the effort.
- In order to get employed you need to keep learning all time so that you can upskill and keep up to date with changing employment needs.
- I am not going to that class, it is boring and I do not need that subject for my chosen career.

2 In your groups copy and complete the following table to show how external influences can impact on young people's attitudes to education, training and employment.

External influence	Positive influence	Justification	Negative influence	Justification
Films				
TV series				
Magazine				
Social media				
Other type of media				

Exam focus

CCEA GCSE Learning for Life and Work Examination Papers

The GCSE in Learning for Life and Work consists of three externally assessed 1 hour examination papers. Each paper is marked out of 60 (worth 20% of total marks for the course). The examination papers have a similar structure and use the same types of questions. Each examination paper includes questions which ask you to:

- Write down … (1 mark)
- Name … (1 mark)
- Explain … (2 marks)
- Describe … (2 marks)
- Analyse … (6 marks)
- Discuss … (6 marks)
- Evaluate … (10 marks)

increasing level of demand

The level of demand of the questions increases from the 1 mark questions to the 6 and 10 mark questions.

In preparation for CCEA GCSE Learning for Life and Work examinations and answering questions you should:

- be familiar and know the type of question in the examination paper and the type of expected response
- practise past paper questions
- create your own questions and mark schemes
- carefully read the question, think about what it is asking:
  - What length of response is expected?
  - What level of detail is required in your answer?
- always leave time before the end of the examination to read over and check answers.

Command words

Write Down/Name

Questions that begin with 'write down' and 'name' are assessing what you know and can recall or remember. They are worth 1 mark and require only a short response, usually a few words, phrase or sentence.

Explain/Describe

'Explain' or 'describe' questions are assessing what you know and can apply in your response. These questions require more information than a 1 mark question but can still be well answered in usually at least two clearly written sentences. To gain 2 marks you need to:

- give more than a statement
- demonstrate your understanding of the issue in a clearly written explanation or description.

Activity

1. Choose a section from the specification and use this book and your notes to create three questions for each of these question types:
   - 'write down' questions (1 mark for each question)
   - 'name' questions (1 mark for each question)
   - 'explain' questions (2 marks for each question)
   - 'describe' questions (2 marks for each question).
2. Write down two or three points (assessment criteria) that you will use to assess the answers to your questions.
3. Give your questions to a partner to answer, and answer the questions that your partner has written.
4. Once you have both answered all the questions, use your assessment criteria to mark your partner's responses.
5. Discuss your answers, and what marks you gave them.

Analyse

This question is based on a source which contains a short extract of information related to a topic or issue covered in the Learning for Life and Work units. It is more demanding than the 1 and 2 mark questions because it requires you to use higher order thinking skills. It is intended to assess your ability to read, assess and interpret information for meaning (6 marks). To gain the full 6 marks you need to:

- demonstrate excellent knowledge and understanding of the topic/issue and apply this accurately to the question

- select at least three key points from the source and interpret what they mean
- use your own words and do not copy large pieces of information from the source
- demonstrate highly competent QWC.

Discuss

This question is intended to assess your ability to recall and apply your knowledge and understanding about a topic or issue and to consider information from different perspectives and present a reasoned argument. The question may require you to consider the pros and cons of a particular statement (6 marks). To gain the full 6 marks you need to:

- demonstrate excellent knowledge and understanding of the topic/issue and apply this accurately to the question
- discuss at least three relevant key points in detail
- demonstrate highly competent quality of communication (QWC).

Evaluate

This question is intended to assess your ability to recall and apply your knowledge and understanding about a topic or issue and to assess or weigh up relevant factors and present a reasoned justification for the points made in your evaluation. You should also provide a conclusion (10 marks). To gain the full 10 marks you need to:

- demonstrate excellent knowledge and understanding of the topic/issue and apply this accurately to the question
- identify and comment on at least four relevant points
- draw a detailed conclusion
- demonstrate highly competent quality of communication (QWC).

Quality of Communication (QWC)

The quality of communication is assessed in questions 5a, 5b and 6 in each unit. The quality of communication is a measure of how well students write their responses. There is not a separate mark for this. The quality of communication is assessed with other assessment criteria. The teacher/examiner makes a judgement about the level of your response (see table 1) and gives a mark based on your overall response.

A **Level 3 Highly Competent** response should use the most appropriate form and style of writing and be well organised and structured. Throughout the response there should be a consistent and accurate use of spelling, punctuation, grammar and vocabulary related to the topic. The meaning of the response should be clear.

Assessing responses

When marking your examining paper responses to questions 5a, 5b and 6, examiners judge them against assessment criteria to be at one of three Levels and award marks as shown in table 1.

Table 1: Questions, Levels and Marks

Levels	Level of response	Question 5a and 5b Marks	Question 6 Marks
Level 1	Basic response	1-2	1-4
Level 2	Competent response	3-4	5-8
Level 3	Highly competent response	5-6	9-10

EXAM FOCUS

Practice questions

This section provides some **analyse**, **discuss** and **evaluate** questions for Local and Global Citizenship, Personal Development and Employability.

Local and global citizenship

SOURCE A The Good Friday/Belfast Agreement

The Good Friday/Belfast Agreement was signed in 1998. It led to the establishment of devolved government, the creation of the Northern Ireland Human Rights Commission and Equality Commission, the reform of policing and decommissioning of weapons. It also gives citizens the right to self-determination and to hold dual British and Irish citizenship.

According to a 2016 report paramilitarism remains a problem in Northern Ireland. The issues around dealing with the past are unresolved. Many people are living in segregated social housing while only 7% of children attend integrated schools. In 2015/16 the PSNI recorded just over 1,350 sectarian incidents.

Source based on Northern Ireland Peace Monitoring Report Number 4, 2016.

Activity

Read the information carefully in Source A to answer question 1.

1. Using the information in Source A **analyse** the impact of the Good Friday/Belfast Agreement in promoting peace in Northern Ireland (6 marks)
2. Human rights are a feature of a democratic society. **Discuss** the importance of human rights. (6 marks)
3. Sectarianism contributes to conflict in many countries around the world. **Evaluate** the role of the local community in dealing with sectarianism. (10 marks)

Personal Development

SOURCE B Teenage parents

The teenage years are a time when most young people are developing their independence, enjoying socialising and making decisions about education, careers and other life choices.

For some teenage couples the arrival of a baby can impact on these experiences. Often pregnancy is unplanned. It can change their lifestyle, relationship and affect their health and emotional well-being. They may face financial difficulties. It is expensive to raise a baby.

Activity

Read the information carefully in Source B to answer question 1.

1. Using the information from Source B **analyse** the impact on a young teenage couple of having a baby. (6 marks)
2. People need to be able to manage their money and make good financial decisions. **Discuss** the benefits of budgeting for a young person. (6 marks)
3. The age between 10 and 25 is a crucial period for young people. Their lifestyle choices will have consequences in adulthood. **Evaluate** the impact of lifestyle on a young person's health and well-being. (10 marks)

Employability

SOURCE C Business and Social Responsibility

A business can benefit from being socially responsible. Some of the ways a business can be socially responsible include, waste recycling, supporting the local community, local events or clubs and by promoting local products and creating employee volunteer schemes.

A business may benefit from being socially responsible as it promotes a good public image. They may attract more customers. Some initiatives may save it money and increase employee motivation.

Activity

Read the information carefully in Source C to answer question 1.

1. Using the information in Source C **analyse** the benefits to a business of being social responsible (6 marks)
2. Globalisation has resulted in access to world markets for trade. **Discuss** the impact of globalisation on businesses. (6 marks)
3. Many employees are members of a trade union. They can play an important role in building good employee/employer relations. **Evaluate** the impact of trade unions on employee/employer relations. (10 marks)

Glossary

addiction when the body becomes reliant on a substance to function normally

adaptable being able to adjust to new conditions or circumstances

AIDS a syndrome caused by the HIV virus. It is when a person's immune system is too weak to fight off many infections, and develops when the HIV infection is very advanced

amnesia a partial or total loss of memory

amnesty an official pardon for people who have been convicted of political offences

anxiety a feeling of nervousness, worry or unease about something

anti-spyware software used to detect and remove unwanted spyware

anti-virus software used to detect and destroy computer viruses

apathy a lack of interest or concern

apartheid a political and social system in South Africa while it was under white minority rule. It was used from 1948 to 1994. This was stricter than the racial segregation that had existed for many years in South Africa

APR Annual Percentage Rate – the percentage of interest charged per year on money borrowed

autocratic relating to a ruler who has absolute power

balanced diet a healthy diet

bankruptcy a legal status taken on by someone who cannot pay their debts

biased unfairly prejudiced against something or someone

bigotry intolerance towards those who hold different opinions from oneself

binge drinking drinking a lot of alcohol in a short period of time in order to get drunk

budget a summary of income and expenditure

budgeting the process of forecasting incomes against expenditure in order to plan financially

bullying unwanted, intimidating and often aggressive behaviour which could physically or emotionally affect a person

buy versus rent a consumer decision whereby a consumer makes a decision to buy a property or rent it

carbon footprint the amount of carbon dioxide released into the atmosphere due to the activities of an individual, organisation or community

card skimming when credit card information is stolen and used for criminal activity

career planning an ongoing process to help manage learning and developing in the pursuit or survival of a career

carer someone who cares for a friend or family member who struggles to look after themselves

cashback website a type of reward website that pays its members a percentage of money earned when they purchase goods and services with its affiliate links

cash versus credit a shopping decision based on whether a person should use their own cash or credit from a lender

changing employment patterns the jobs that need to be filled change due to the needs and wants of economies

channel of distribution the process by which a product or service reaches a customer

cholesterol a fat chemical made by cells in the body

Citizens Advice Bureau a network of charities throughout the UK that give free, confidential advice and information to help people with money, legal and consumer problems

Cognitive Behavioural Therapy (CBT) a talking therapy that can help you manage your problems by changing the way you think and behave

competitive job market when there are lots of people skilled and qualified for jobs resulting in high levels of competition for jobs

commission a sum of money, typically a set percentage of the value involved, paid to a seller when something is bought

confidentiality keeping information private and restricted from people who do not have any legitimate reason to know the information

conflict a serious disagreement or argument that results in bad feeling

consumer someone who buys goods and services to use personally

contactless payments a fast, easy and secure way to pay, for purchases costing £30 and under. It involves touching debit/credit cards, key fobs or smartphones onto a terminal

contract of employment a document which contains terms and conditions of employment

convenience food processed food, prepared for ease of consumption, e.g. microwaveable meals

crash dieting a weight-loss strategy which is usually adopted on a short-term basis with the aim of achieving very rapid results

credit the term used to describe obtaining goods or services without paying for them in full immediately but instead paying for them over an agreed term

creditor someone that gives loans or credits

credit card a card that allows the owner to purchase goods or services on credit

credit rating an evaluation of how risky it is to lend money to a person or organisation

credit reference agency a company that collects information relating to the credit ratings of individuals and makes it available to banks and finance companies

criminals a person who has committed a crime

GLOSSARY

Corporate Social Responsibility (CSR) a business approach that contributes to sustainable development by delivering economic, social and environmental benefits for all stakeholders

current account non-interest-bearing bank account which allows the accountholder to withdraw without notice

Curriculum Vitae (CV) provides a summary of an individual's personal details, qualifications, skills and work experience

debit card when used, debit cards take money directly out of the user's current account

debt money that is owed

deficiency a lack or a shortage of a particular nutrient the body needs

dementia a brain disease that gradually affects a person's ability to think and remember

depression a mental health condition whereby a person experiences a low mood and aversion to activity

design to make a plan to show the workings and functions of an object

digital content content that exists as digital data

disadvantaged a person or an area that is faced with unfavourable circumstances, especially in regard to social or financial opportunities

discrimination to treat someone unfairly because of the group they belong to

displaced force (someone) to leave their home, typically because of war, persecution, or natural disaster

disposable income the amount of money a person has left after paying expenses

diverse a community containing people or groups with differences between them

economic growth an increase in the amount of goods and services per head of the population over a period of time

ecotherapy nature-based programmes and courses aimed to improve mental health

efficient to be working well in a competent way that does not waste time or money

emotions a state of consciousness in which feelings such as joy, sorrow, fear or hate are experienced

employment patterns the types of jobs people are employed in at a certain point in time

empowered a feeling of strength and control due to confidence in a job

endorphins natural chemicals released from the brain

energy efficient when the amount of energy used to produce products or services is reduced

environmental issues problems with the world's systems (air, water, soil, etc.) that have developed due to human mistreatment

evaluate to assess the worth or weight of a skill or situation

eviction the removal of a tenant by a landlord

exclusion the act of leaving out, rejecting or refusing to consider

expenditure money spent

exploitation treating people unfairly in order to benefit yourself

fast food mass-produced food that is prepared quickly

fatigue chronic tiredness

Financial Conduct Authority an organisation that regulates the financial services industry in the UK. Its role includes protecting consumers and keeping the industry stable

Financial Services and Markets Act 2000 created the Financial Services Authority (FSA) as a regulator for insurance, investment business and banking, and the Financial Ombudsman Service to resolve disputes as a free alternative to the courts

firewall a network security system designed to prevent unauthorised access to or from a network

flashing displaying areas of the body, usually concealed by clothing or underwear

flexibility ability to change and adapt easily due to changing circumstances

Foetal Alcohol Syndrome a condition that can occur in a person whose mother drank alcohol during pregnancy. Problems may include an abnormal appearance, short height, low body weight, small head size, poor co-ordination, low intelligence, behaviour problems and problems with hearing or seeing

fraudster a person who deliberately deceives someone else for their own personal gain

genocide the killing of a large group of people, especially those of a particular nation or ethnic group

gig economy working in temporary jobs or having different part-time jobs with various employers

global economy the international exchange of money, goods and ideas across countries' geographical boundaries

global village the world considered as a single community linked by telecommunications

global warming a gradual increase in the overall temperature of the earth's atmosphere due to pollution and an increase in carbon dioxide levels

globalisation the movement of goods, people and ideas around the world

go slow a type of industrial action where work productivity is deliberately slowed or delayed

goodwill a positive feeling that is generated through strong relationships

grooming when someone builds an emotional connection with a person in order to exploit them

hepatitis B an infectious disease caused by the hepatitis B virus that primarily affects the liver

hepatitis C an infectious disease caused by the hepatitis C virus that primarily affects the liver

HIV stands for Human Immunodeficiency Virus. It weakens a person's immune system by destroying important cells that fight disease and infection

identity fraud/theft the deliberate use of someone's identity to commit a financial crime

income the amount of money earned

Glossary

induction the process of introducing an individual to a new place or organisation

infibulation the practice of excising the clitoris and labia of a girl or woman and stitching together the edges of the vulva to prevent sexual intercourse

insurance excesses the amount of money that must be paid out of a person's own pocket before an insurance company will pay out

interest rates an interest rate, or rate of interest, is the amount of interest due per period, as a proportion (usually percentage) of the amount lent, deposited or borrowed

internet banking availing of banking services on the world wide web, for example, checking a balance or transferring money

interpersonal relations a connection or relationship between two or more people

interview panel a number of people put together to interview potential employees

ISA Investment Savings Accounts – accounts in which people are not taxed on the interest they receive

jeopardy danger of loss, harm or failure

job description a written account of an employee's duties and responsibilities

job satisfaction a feeling of fulfilment or enjoyment from a job

job shadowing when an employee follows, watches and learns from an established employee in a particular job role so that he/she can understand what the job involves and the skills required

job specification a written account of the qualities, skills, qualifications and attitudes required for a particular job

junk food cheap food containing high levels of calories with little nutritional content

lifelong learning the process of continuing to develop skills, knowledge, attitudes and expertise throughout life

loan sharks illegal and unauthorised people or organisations that lend money, usually with very high interest rates

malware abbreviation for malicious software

manipulation to manage or influence someone in an unfair way

marginalisation treatment of a person, group or concept as insignificant

market to advertise and or promote a product or service

marketing objectives goals set by a business when promoting and advertising products and services to be met within a set time period

market research gathering information about consumers' needs and preferences

mass production the manufacture of large quantities of usually standardised products, quite often using an assembly line process

media the media is a communication outlet and can refer to such mediums as newspapers, TV, radio, billboards and the internet

merchandising to promote goods and/or services through placement of availability or by introducing items associated with the original product or service

method of transport the type of vehicle used to move products from production to sales outlet or customer

monitoring observing and checking the progress of a skill or situation

motivation the reasons for acting or behaving in a certain way

multicultural a society that is made up of a range of different cultural identities

multinational companies companies that have locations and or assets in at least one country other than their home country. A central base known as headquarters will usually make corporate decisions

multi-skilled having a range of skills that can be utilised

Nationalist one of the two largest cultural/political groups living in Northern Ireland. Most Nationalists are from the Catholic community and wish to be politically linked to the Republic of Ireland

net income the amount of money after expenses such as tax have been accounted for

obesity a medical condition whereby excessive fat has accumulated in the body

obsessive behaviour a mental condition where people feel the need to check things repeatedly, perform certain routines repeatedly, or have certain thoughts repeatedly

occupations the various types of employment roles

Ofcom a regulatory body for broadcasting, telecommunications and postal industries

off-the-job training training that takes place outside of the work environment

on-the-job training training that takes place in the work environment

overspending spending more money than is planned in the budget

payday loans an amount of money lent at a high interest rate which is repaid when the borrower receives their next wage

personality assessment a professionally designed test designed to find out about personality traits and characteristics

personal loan credit given to a person for personal reasons, e.g. to go on holiday

phishing emails emails trying to encourage the recipient to divulge their financial details

physical disability a limitation on a person's physical function

postnatal depression a type of depression that many parents experience after having a baby. It is a common problem

post-traumatic stress an anxiety disorder caused by very stressful, frightening or distressing events

GLOSSARY

Pre-Contract Information a document that must be given to a customer containing all the terms and conditions, before a contract is signed

prejudice having inaccurate or irrational opinions about others and making judgements (pre-judging) about an individual or group without reason

primary research new research that is carried out for a specific purpose, sometimes through questionnaires or interviews

profits the difference between what it costs to make and produce a product or service and the amount of money the product or service is sold for

promiscuity when someone has casual sexual relations regularly with different partners

promotion to be rewarded with higher payment or responsibilities in the workplace/to encourage the sales of a product or service through advertising or publicity

quality versus price a shopping behaviour whereby a customer is torn between shopping for the quality of a product or by price

racism prejudice, discrimination or antagonism directed against someone of a different race. It is based on the belief that one race is superior to another. This can also be because of ethnic origin, skin colour and language

referendum a general vote by the electorate on a single political question which has been referred to them for a direct decision

reflection thought and consideration about completed tasks

refugee a person who has been forced to leave their country in order to escape war, persecution or natural disaster

rehabilitation a process that assists a person with recovery

responsibilities being accountable and taking ownership of actions and expectations

repossessed when the mortgage provider takes back ownership of a property due to non payment of the mortgage

responsibilities duties that have to be completed because there is accountability and or expectation

restricted advisers can only give advice based on a limited amount of products and cannot advise based on the whole market

revenue the income of a business usually generated by sales of products or services

ringworm a contagious skin infection caused by a fungus. Usually red and circular

sales outlets locations where product/services are sold

scabies a contagious skin infection which itches intensely. It is caused by tiny mites which burrow into the skin

scenario a possible situation or circumstance

secondary research existing research that has been gathered, also known as desk research

security software software that can be installed on a computer to protect content from viruses and malware

sectarianism intolerance of other religious groups, which can lead to prejudice, discrimination and violence between religious groups

segregation setting something apart from others. It can be the separation of humans into ethnic, racial or religious groups in life

self-concept how we think of ourselves physically, emotionally and morally and how we perceive others to see us

self-confidence a person's ability to trust themselves in terms of their abilities, qualities and judgements

self-esteem a term used to describe a person's feelings of self-worth or personal value

self-evaluation awareness of progress, development and learning in order to inform level or progress and areas for improvement

self-help using one's own efforts and resources to achieve something

septicaemia a serious condition where bacteria enter the blood stream

shoulder surfing direct observation over someone's shoulder

single parent a parent who raises a child on their own

SMART targets specific, measurable, achievable, realistic and time-constrained targets that are used for focus and pinpointing goals

social responsibility an obligation to work for the benefit of society as a whole

social stigma the disapproval or discontentment of someone as they are perceived as being different from the rest of society

solvents usually legal products that were never intended to be used for the purpose of getting high. They are not drugs; they are poisons that can be found in many typical household products, such as glue

spam electronic junk mail

spending leaks unconscious spending which causes money 'leaking' from a person's bank account

stakeholder any individual or group, either internal or external, that has an interest in a business

STDs/STIs (Sexually Transmitted Diseases/Infections) diseases/infections that are passed on through sexual contact

step-parent a parent who has children that are not genetically related to them and may be from a spouse's previous relationship

stock control ensuring appropriate amounts of stock are maintained to ensure customer demand is met without delay while keeping costs to a minimum

strike the withdrawal of work due to poor industrial relations

sustainability being maintained or continued for a long period of time

talking therapies a method of treating psychological disorders or emotional difficulties that involves talking to a therapist or counsellor, in either individual or group sessions

targets set goals or objectives that will be met

tariffs a published list of charges or prices

teenage parent a person who becomes a parent between the ages of 13 and 19

training the skills and knowledge needed to complete a job effectively

Unionist one of the two largest cultural/political groups living in Northern Ireland. Most Unionists are from the Protestant community and believe in maintaining strong cultural/political ties between Northern Ireland and Great Britain

unsolicited emails unwanted emails sent to you without your consent

upskilling developing and learning additional and/or new skills

well-being a word that describes when a person is feeling healthy. It includes feeling physically, socially and emotionally healthy

withdrawal symptoms potentially life-threatening symptoms which can occur after an addict stops taking alcohol or drugs. Symptoms can include fever, chills, shakes, nausea and hallucinations

work-life balance getting the correct amount of time spent on job activities and time spent with family, friends and enjoying leisure activities

Index

abuse
    emotional/physical 109–10, 111, 116–17
    sexual 110, 112, 113–14, 117
    strategies against 112–16
accommodation 20, 22–3, 68, 140–1
active citizenship 59–63
addictions 93 4, 109
Africa
    conflict resolution in 29, 31
    NGOs in 65
    violence in 12, 15
agriculture 153
agri-food 156
alcohol 79–81, 92
    see also addictions
animal rights 66
anxiety and stress 88, 90–1, 183–5
attitudes, positive 76–8
Belfast Agreement 53–5
Belfast Conflict Resolution Consortium 29
bereavement 98
bias 17, 132–3
Bosnia 12
boycotts 31
budgeting 128–31
bullying 109, 115–16
business
    setting up in 194–204
    and social responsibility 188–93
business and financial services 156
care, children in 120, 124
career goals/targets 206–7
career planning 205–11
    see also employment
carers, children as 120
cash versus credit 139–40
change, and personal development 97–9
children
    and care 120, 124
    child labour 37–8
    and democracy 60–3
    development of 126–7
    mortality 66
    rights of 36–9
    and social responsibility 46

civil society 30, 51–2, 63, 64–8
code of conduct 178–80
communication technology see media
community
    active citizenship in 61
    and business 190
    and immigration 20, 23
    and inclusion 25
comparison websites 141–3
confidentiality 180
conflict 26–33
    global 29
    local 27
    national 28–30
    and NGOs 67
    resolution of 29–33
consumer choices 61, 138–43
consumer rights/protection 144–6
contactless payment 134
counselling 65, 104–5, 113, 184
creative and digital media 156
cultural identity
    expressions of 9–10, 11, 12
    influences on 9
    and marginalisation 20
decision-making 61–2, 209
democracy 58–63
depression 91–3
developing countries, and NGOs 66
diet 70–4, 77–8, 184
direct action 64
discrimination 14–15, 23, 25–6
diversity 55, 178
    and inclusion 7–33
drugs and drug taking 84–7, 94, 107
economy, and immigration 19–20, 150–1
    see also globalisation, and employment
education
    and curriculum 50
    and democracy 60–1
    and health/well-being 97, 107, 114, 116
    and inclusion 23, 24–5
    and poverty 66
emails, scam/phishing 136–7
emotional/social development 126–7

emotions 88, 90–3, 95
    and change 97–9
    dealing with 96–7
    and parenting 122
employment
    business/self-employment 188–204
    career planning 205–11
    changes in 155–7
    discrimination 25–6
    Northern Ireland 147–57
    preparing for 158–73
    and rights/responsibilities 174–87
    unemployment 20, 47, 98
energy efficiency 189, 192
engineering 156
entrepreneurs 194–204
environmental issues 66, 188–9
Equal Pay Act (1970) 25
equality/inequality 14, 25, 47–52, 55, 181–2
ethical consumerism 61, 62
exercise 74–8, 184
fair trade 61
fast food 71
Female Genital Mutilation (FGM) 113–14
festivals 9, 11
finance 128–46
    advice on 131–3, 144–6
    and business 197, 199, 201
    and parenting 122–3
food 70–4, 77–8, 184
    lack of 66
    manufacturing 156, 191
foster care 120, 124
fraud and identity theft 109, 134–7
freedom of expression 40
freedom of movement 41
fundraising 61, 64, 68
gender identity 102–3
genocide 12
gig economy 148
global citizenship 61–2
global conflicts 12
global warming 189
globalisation, and employment 147–57
Good Friday Agreement 53–5
government

Index

devolution of 54
and education 50
and employment legislation 181–2
on immigration 22
on inclusion 24
and media 50
self-employment, support for 203
and social responsibility/equality 44, 49
see also Northern Ireland
health 41, 65, 66, 69–94, 126
healthcare, and immigration 20, 23
homelessness 68
housing
    buying versus renting 140–1
    and immigration 20, 22–3
human rights 34–42
    children's 36–9
    and democracy 58, 59
    and government 49–51
    and NGOs 67
    Northern Ireland 55
    and society 39–42
Human Rights Act (1998) (UK) 35
hygiene 88
identity theft and fraud 109, 134–7
illness, serious 98
immigration 10, 17–23, 150
inclusion 7–33, 59
income *see* wages
inequality *see* equality/inequality
informed choices, careers 209–10
intellectual development 127
international courts 31
international mediation 31
interviews 169–73
investment scams 136–7
Iraq 36
Ireland, Republic of 53
job applications and interviews 168–73
job descriptions/specifications 166–7
justice system, and immigration 21
    see also social justice
languages 23, 55
legislation *see* government
life events, and personal development 97–9
lifelong learning 161–5
    see also career planning
Living Wage 175–6
malnutrition 66

market research 197
marketing, business 198–200
maternity rights 26
media
    and government 50
    ownership 45
    rights/responsibilities and 40, 45
    social media 40, 45, 109, 179–80
mediation 31–2
migration 10, 17–23, 150
mobile phones 180
moral development 127
multiculturalism 10–11
Murdoch, Rupert 45
Muslims, burka bans 42
national security 40
natural disasters 65
neglect 110–11
Non-Governmental Organisations (NGOs) 30, 51–2, 64–8, 203–4
Northern Ireland
    changing industries/careers 155–7
    commissions for equality/human rights 50–1
    conflict in 12, 27
    conflict resolution 29
    diversity in 10, 11
    globalisation/work in 147–57, 190–1
    government 23, 24, 50–1, 53–7, 203
    immigration 18
Northern Ireland Act (1998) 23, 24, 50
Northern Ireland Assembly 54, 55–6
Northern Ireland Executive 56–7
Northern Ireland Human Rights Commission 51
online banking 135
parents/parenting
    impacts of 122–3
    older/younger 121, 122, 125
    opportunities and challenges 123–5
    role of 126–7
    same-sex 124
    single or step- 120, 124, 125
peacekeeping 32–3
physical development 126
policing 16, 21, 57, 113
poverty 66, 89
prejudice 13, 14–15
Prince's Trust 204
privacy, right to 40
production, business 198, 199

prostitution 113
protest, right to 40, 65
public agencies 44–5, 203–4
public health 41
public sector jobs 148, 154
racism 12, 16–17
rape 112
recycling 189
relationships
    families and friends 100–1, 209, 210
    positive working 180–3
    sexual 101
    unhealthy 104–5
religious festivals 9
renewable energies and recycling 156
research
    and business 194, 197
    financial 131–3
    and NGOs 65, 66
risk-taking 106–8, 202
sanctions 31
scams 136–7
schools *see* education
Scotland, devolution 54
sectarianism 12, 15–16
security/law enforcement, and immigration 21
segregation 12, 20, 29
self-concept 95, 97
self-employment 194–204
self-evaluation 212–13
sexual assault 112
    see also abuse
sexual exploitation 39, 109, 112
sexual orientation 102–3
sexual relationships 101
shopping 61, 136, 138–43
skills shortages 150, 154
sleep 92, 184
smoking 81–3
    see also addictions
social development 127
social equality/inequality 14, 25, 47–52, 181–2
social justice 47, 48, 49–51
social media 40, 45, 109, 179–80
social responsibility 43–6, 188–93
social security 20, 66
social strategies, against abuse 114–16
soldiers, child 38–9
stakeholders 178–9, 180

INDEX

stress and anxiety 88, 90–1, 183–5
surveys, on immigration 21–2
Syria 28, 30
talking therapies *see* counselling
technologies, new, and work 151–3, 155
terrorism 40
tourism 11
trade unions 186–7
trafficking 114
training, staff 161–5, 180–1
unemployment 20, 47, 98

United Nations Convention on the Rights of the Child (UNCRC) 36–7
United Nations (UN)
    in conflict resolution 32–3
    formation of 34
    Youth Delegate Programme 62
Universal Declaration of Human Rights (UDHR) 34–5
volunteering 61, 68
wages 89, 175–6, 201
Wales, devolution 54

war *see* conflict
wealth distribution 47
welfare/social security 20, 66
working relationships 180–3
work/life balance 89, 201
workplaces, and inclusion 25–6
work-related stress 183–5
young people
    and democracy 60–3
    and social responsibility 46
    see also children

Acknowledgements

The Publishers would like to thank the following for permission to reproduce copyright material:

Text acknowledgements

p.16 'Racism is rife in English football with over 350 incidents from the Premier League to grassroots since 2012, investigation reveals' published in The Daily Mail © Press Association 2015; p.26 'Maternity leave discrimination: A working mother's story of losing her job – and how she got over it' © Telegraph Media Group Limited 2013; p.42 'Burka bans: the countries where Muslim women can't wear veils' © Telegraph Media Group Limited 2016; p.46 'UK welfare fiasco: The 100,000 addicts and obese who get benefit bonanza' © www.express.co.uk/N&S Syndication 2016; p.49 'Premier League clubs face legal threat unless disabled access is improved' © Guardian News & Media Ltd 2017; p.59 'Bulgaria seen as most corrupt in EU' © euobserver 2016; p.78 'Our attitude to food and fitness is fixed at ten years old' © MailOnline 2011; p.83 'Ban e-cigarettes in bars and restaurants, leading doctors say' © Telegraph Media Group Limited 2016; p.103 'Homophobic hate victim James Hall speaks out after attack in Belfast' reproduced courtesy of Belfast Telegraph; p.111 'NSPCC helpline flooded by abuse and neglect calls in past year' © Belfast Live 2016; p.121 Mirror 'Mum who gave birth aged 62 pictured smiling as she leaves hospital carrying her one-week old daughter' © Gerard Couzens 2016; p.137 'Money returned to internet banking scam pensioner Michael McCartan' reproduced courtesy of Belfast Telegraph; p.143 'Car insurance: the pros and cons of using comparison sites' © Telegraph Media Group Limited 2011; p.149 'Changes of career the driving force behind job creation in Northern Ireland' reproduced courtesy of Belfast Telegraph; p.176 'What is the Living Wage?' © Living Wage 2016; p.185 'Beat stress at work' © www.nhs.uk article last reviewed for accuracy 2014; pp.196l, 198 & 199 Pop Notch case study reproduced courtesy of Pop Notch.

Photo credits

p.8 (tl) szefei, (cl) dziewul, (br) Charnsit Ramyarupa / 123RF.com; p.8 (tr) Stephen Barnes, (bl) Michael Diggin / Alamy Stock Photo; p.10 romanslavik.com / Fotolia.com; p.11 © Photograph by Justin Kernoghan; p.22 Christopher Furlong / Getty Images; p.27 (t) Ian Pilbeam / Alamy Stock Photo, (b) JLBvdWOLF / Alamy Stock Photo; p.30 Paul Faith / PA Archive / PA Photos; p.33 Bullen Chol / Anadolu Agency / Getty Images; p.38 BestForBest / Shutterstock.com; p.39 (t) NABIL HASSAN / AFP / Getty Images, (b) Eakachai Leesin / Shutterstock.com; p.40 Alex MacNaughton Photography Limited / REX / Shutterstock.com; p.43 snowwhiteimages / 123RF.com; p.44 (t) fotoluminate, (c) sam74100, (b) mkirnt / 123RF.com; p.46 Chris Ratcliffe / Bloomberg / Getty Images; p.49 MCERLANE PAUL MCERLANE/ PA Archive / PA Photos; p.51 Equality Commission for Northern Ireland; p.53 (t) Good Friday Agreement (Public Domain); p.55 (b) logo of the Northern Ireland Assembly; (b) Dan Chung / AFP / Getty Images; p.55 (t) Hoberman Collection / Alamy Stock Photo; p.57 logo of the Police Ombudsman for Northern Ireland; p.60 MBI / Alamy Stock Photo; p.61 Digital Vision / Getty Images; p.63 Echo / Getty Images; p.65 (t) Xinhua / Alamy Stock Photo, (b) Tommy E Trenchard / Alamy Stock Photo; p.67 Reuters / Alamy Stock Photo; p.70 Public Health England in association with the Welsh Government, Food Standards Scotland and the Food Standards Agency in Northern Ireland. Crown Copyright. https://www.nationalarchives.gov.uk/doc/open-government-licence/version/3/; p.76 (tl) http://www.nhs.uk/Change4Life. The Department of Health / http://www.nationalarchives.gov.uk/doc/open-government-licence/version/3/, (tr) https://www.gov.uk/government/publications/uk-physical-activity-guidelines - Department of Health: Obesity and Healthy Eating, 11 July 2011, (b) AFP Stringer / Getty Images; p.77 FatCamera / Getty Images; p.78 (l) bikeriderlondon / Shutterstock.com, (r) Sergey Novikov; p.81 Jan Andersen / 123RF.com; p.87 (l) Zoonar GmbH, (r) dolgachov; p.91 Ben Gingell / Alamy Stock Photo; p.93 Sergey Novikov / 123RF.com; p.96 Wavebreak Media Ltd / 123RF.com; p.101 MBI / Alamy Stock Photo; p.110 Gennady Kireev / 123RF.com; p.111 (l) Marcel de Grijs / 123RF.com, (r) Apatcha Muenaksorn; p.116 childline logo used with permission of the NSPCC, EACH logo used with permission of Educational Action Challenging Homophobia (EACH), bullybusters logo used with permission of Local Solutions; Stonewall logo used with permission of www.stonewall.org.uk, BullyingUK logo used with permission of Bullying UK – Family Lives; p.119 Juriah Mosin / Fotolia.com; p.121 (t) Wavebreak Media Ltd / 123RF.com, (b) Eliseo Trigo / Epa/ REX/Shutterstock; p.129 PhotoDisc / Getty Images; p. 131 Juice Images / Alamy Stock Photo; p.134 (t) Ratmaner, (b) Rusian Grigoriev / 123RF.com; p. 135 (l) Andrey Popov, (c) Wavebreak Media Ltd, (r) Semmickphoto / 123RF.com; p.137 'Money returned to internet banking scam pensioner Michael McCartan' reproduced courtesy of Belfast Telegraph; p.138 Iswan Nawi / 123RF.com; p.139 Daniel Acker / Bloomberg / Getty Images; p.140 Kevin Eaves / Fotolia.com; p.144 (l) Zerbor , (r) Turhan Yalcin / 123RF.com; p.145 the Money Advice logo granted with permission moneyadviceservice.org.uk; p.151 Blablo101 / Shutterstock.com; p.152 (t) Roger Viollet / REX / Shutterstock.com, (b) Wavebreak Media Ltd / 123RF.com; p.153 (tl) Andriy Popov, (bl) Dmytro Sidelnikov, (tr) Iakov Filimonov / 123RF.com, (cr) Historical / Getty Images, (br) Maurice Branger / Roger Viollet /REX /Shutterstock; p.157 Department for the Economy https://www.economy-ni.gov.uk/sites/default/files/publications/del/Skills-in-Demand.pdf; p.161 (l) Misha, (r) ManicBlu / Fotolia.com; p.164 (tl) claudiodivizia, (cl) Chutchawarn Samwang, (bl) Matthew Howard, (cr) Aleksanderdn 123RF.com, (tr) Lordanis / Shutterstock.com, (br) Hugh Threlfall / Alamy Stock Photo; p.165 Kurhan / 123RF.com; p.173 (bl) Design Pics Inc / Alamy Stock Photo, (tr) Pressmaster / Fotolia.com; p.179 (tl) Leung Cho Pan, (b) Freddy Cahyono / 123RF.com, (tr) Chris Mansfield / Getty Images; p.180 Ammentorp / 123RF.com; p.183 (t) Baranq, (b) Dmitriy Shironosov; p.187 Lopolo / Shutterstock.com; p.188 Luciano Lozano / Alamy Stock Photo; p.191 © ASDA 2017; p.195 Levi Roots use with permission; p.196 & p.199 Pop Notch case study reproduced courtesy of Pop Notch; p.201 (l) PhotoDisc / Getty Images, (r) claudiobaba / iStockphoto